American M[c
Physicians dedicated t[

A Compliance Guide for Health Care Professionals

Carolyn P. Hartley, MLA, CHP
Edward D. Jones III

Foreword by Louis W. Sullivan, MD

HIPAA Plain and Simple
A Compliance Guide for Health Care Professionals

Internet address: www.ama-assn.org

Additional copies of this book may be ordered by calling 800 621-8335 or from the secure AMA Press Web site at www.amapress.org. Refer to product number OP320703.

ISBN 1-57947-419-5

Library of Congress Cataloging-in-Publication Data

Hartley, Carolyn P.
    HIPAA plain and simple : a compliance guide for healthcare professionals / Carolyn Hartley, Ed Jones.
        p. ; cm.
Includes index.
    ISBN 1-57947-419-5 (alk. paper)
1. Medicine—Practice—United States. 2. United States. Health Insurance Portability and Accountability Act of 1996.
    [DNLM: 1. United States. Health Insurance Portability and Accountability Act of 1996. 2. Medical Records Systems, Computerized—United States. 3. Confidentiality—United States. 4. Practice Management, Medical—organization & administration—United States. WX 173 H332h 2004] I. Jones, Ed (Edward Douglass) II. Title.
    R728.H3628 2004
    610'.68—dc21
                            2003010099

BP02:04-P-033:5/04

To my brother, Jim, whose determination is my inspiration; and to my daughters, Kristen and Laurie, who light my world every day. —cph

To my wife Ann, who has lived HIPAA vicariously through me for years, and to my two granddaughters, Caitlyn (10 years) and Keegan (9 years), and my new grandson, Nathaniel (7 months), who I hope will be enjoying the benefits of HIPAA Administrative Simplification when they are my age. —edj

Foreword

It gives me great pleasure to write the foreword for *HIPAA Plain and Simple: A Compliance Guide for Health Care Professionals*. During my tenure as Secretary of the US Department of Health and Human Services (HHS) from 1989 to 1993, I recognized that the federal government had to address the problem of rapidly rising healthcare costs.

In 1991, I asked leaders in the healthcare industry, from business and government, to come together in a collaborative effort to examine ways to lower administrative costs, particularly those associated with paper transactions, and to ascertain how electronic technology could help. This collaborative effort was the genesis of the Workgroup for Electronic Data Interchange (WEDI). The work of WEDI in the early 1990s provided the framework for the Administrative Simplification provisions that were enacted as part of the Health Insurance Portability and Accountability Act of 1996 (HIPAA). WEDI was one of four organizations to serve as advisors to the Secretary of HHS on HIPAA implementation issues. Those regulations are the subject of *HIPAA Plain and Simple*.

To facilitate its advisory role, WEDI created the Strategic National Implementation Process (SNIP) initiative in 2000 as a forum for healthcare industry participants to collaborate on addressing and resolving business and technical issues associated with implementing the HIPAA Administrative Simplification standards. Many of these standards and implementation specifications are detailed and complex.

Fortunately, the authors of *HIPAA Plain and Simple* have taken these details and complexities and turned them into understandable explanations of actions healthcare providers, particularly physician practices, must take to become "HIPAA compliant." As you read through the chapters on HIPAA Administrative Simplification transactions, privacy, and security rules, I think that you will find the following sections (with examples) particularly useful:

- What is it?
- How to do it
- Critical points

As you move toward HIPAA compliance, I would like you to keep in mind the original objectives of Administrative Simplification, which were to:

- attain more efficient and effective healthcare system exchange of administrative and financial information using electronic transaction standards;
- realize increased protection of such information and patients' medical records; and
- reduce costs of healthcare transactions.

I am as certain today as I was in 1991 that in the years ahead the healthcare industry in the United States will realize these objectives. Further, with a more efficient and less costly administrative structure, the healthcare industry can devote more of its resources to improving the quality of healthcare delivered.

Access to healthcare and improving the quality of healthcare are significant focal points of my career as a physician, as US Secretary of Health and Human Services, and as founding dean and president of Morehouse School of Medicine (MSM) in Atlanta, Georgia. The mission of MSM, an historically black institution, is to recruit and train minority and other students as physicians, biomedical scientists, and public health professionals committed to the healthcare needs of the underserved in our society. Enhancing that mission is MSM's new National Center for Primary Care (NCPC), directed by Dr David Satcher, the former Surgeon General of the US Public Health Service. The Center's focus will be on "improving healthcare and healthcare access for low-income, minority, and other underserved populations using a number of strategies—research, health policy alternatives, cost-effective programs, professional training, and supporting collaborative efforts."

For clinical staff, like those at MSM, *HIPAA Plain and Simple* presents a set of understandable explanations, tools, examples, and references that will help healthcare providers become compliant with HIPAA Administrative Simplification standards. Many underserved provider communities will gain by having access to the information presented in the book, including references to additional sources of information that can be accessed through the Internet.

HIPAA compliance opens up new possibilities for improving access to and delivery of quality healthcare in all medical practices. The electronic standards and accompanying privacy and security mandates discussed in *HIPAA Plain and Simple* are the beginning of the electronic revolution in healthcare. Electronic methods of communicating data, including email, facilitate collaboration. This opens new ways for patients to communicate with medical staff and physicians. It also supports an easier way for physicians, specialty organizations, and academic medical centers to communicate with each other and with remote healthcare facilities. The development of electronic medical records will provide greater access to healthcare resources and the delivery of quality healthcare to all of our citizens.

Those are goals that we all strive for as we go into the future.

I recommend *HIPAA Plain and Simple* and wish for you successful compliance with HIPAA Administrative Simplification standards.

Louis W. Sullivan, MD
President Emeritus, Morehouse School of Medicine
Former Secretary, US Department of Health and Human Services

Preface

The Health Insurance Portability and Accountability Act of 1996 (HIPAA), like most new laws, has been fraught with eleventh-hour updates, and billion-dollar budgets for updates, with lobbyists and lawyers debating their interpretations of the law—a prequel, if you will, to a future thriller in the courts. Add to that a flurry of passionate cases made for and against HIPAA—"normal anxiety," the federal government calls it—when a new law is passed.

In this book, what we refer to as HIPAA is a very small portion of the Health Insurance Portability and Accountability Act of 1996, Public Law 104-191. That small portion, fourteen pages, then known as Subtitle F—Administrative Simplification—has developed into HIPAA's privacy, security, and transactions and code sets rules.

These three rules have an enormous impact on our nation's healthcare system.

- They cover a broad range of the estimated 30 billion healthcare transactions made each year in the United States.
- They impact a large percentage of the more than $1.4 trillion in annual healthcare expenditures in the United States.[1]
- They require compliance by millions of healthcare stakeholders, including hospitals, physicians, dentists, and pharmacists; insurers and self-funded payers; employers; health plans; clearinghouses; and vendors associated with providers, health plans, and clearinghouses.
- They require some changes in systems and business processes. Y2K, on the other hand, focused only on systems.

Physicians and their office staff aren't new to regulations, and most of them knew HIPAA was coming. Those who have been around the regulatory block knew to wait for the dust to settle. April 14, 2003, the Privacy Rule compliance date, came with the appropriate amount of expected hype, yet the sun came up on April 15, 2003, and you filed your tax forms. Then, on April 16, 2003, you began to test your transaction and code sets in exchange for the one-year compliance date extension. (About half of physi-

---

1. Katharine Levit, et al. "Trends in U.S. Health Care Spending, 2001," *Health Affairs*, v. 22, n. 1, January/February 2003, p. 155.

cians' offices filed for an extension so they could have until October 16, 2003, to comply with the transactions and code sets.) In spite of these federal mandates, patients still came into the office seeking relief, and office staff implemented HIPAA as best they could.

As you move forward, you should keep HIPAA's goals in mind. The next few months and years won't be an easy time for us in health care, but the results may well be worth applause:

- Increased efficiency and effectiveness of the US healthcare system by exchanging administrative and financial data electronically.

- Enhanced security (protection) and privacy (confidentiality) of patient-identifiable information.

- Decreased US healthcare system transaction costs.

We have a lot of work to do to attain those goals.

We have been working with HIPAA since 1995 while the legislation was still being drafted. The more we get into HIPAA, the bigger it gets. But one thing remains unchanged—medical office staff are a resilient resource for physicians. Mention HIPAA and staff members are likely to roll their eyes and say a few choice words under their breath, but one way or another, they'll learn the law and do their best to implement it for the sake of patients and the physician.

HIPAA Plain and Simple could have been one of the first books on the HIPAA market, but it wouldn't have been widely used. Too many people believed HIPAA was complicated—it is—and also believed they needed a big book to understand a big law—they do. Carolyn was team leader in creating two of those big books, the *Field Guide to HIPAA Implementation* (AMA Press, 2002) and *HIPAA Policies and Procedures Desk Reference* (AMA Press, 2003). A special thanks to you if you purchased and read those guides. We hope they gave you a road map to implementing HIPAA and in some way simplified the unearthly challenge of developing the required policies and procedures without breaking the practice's bank account. Ed took a leadership role as chair of the Workgroup for Electronic Data Interchange (WEDI), an organization whose mission is to facilitate efficient and cost-effective information exchange and management in the healthcare industry and, as specified in the HIPAA legislation, advise the secretary of the Department of Health and Human Services on regulatory and implementation issues related to HIPAA Administrative Simplification.[2]

---

2. Much of the work of WEDI in the past several years on HIPAA has been conducted through WEDI's Strategic National Implementation Process (SNIP) initiative, a forum for over 6,000 volunteers from the healthcare industry and government to develop strategies and solutions for achieving a successful implementation of HIPAA Administrative Simplification standards.

But this book is different. *HIPAA Plain and Simple: A Compliance Guide for Health Care Professionals* is designed to uncomplicate "HIPAA heavy."[3] It is not "HIPAA lite" but rather "HIPAA easy to understand." It is your reference tool when the legal dossier seems a little over the top. HIPAA requires a certain level of legal and documentation accuracy, so we didn't substitute a simplified approach for necessary legal advice. The practice's management team should be consulting a health-law attorney to implement HIPAA with or without the plain and simple advice in this book.

This book is for nurses who spend the majority of their time in clinical and personal patient interaction—and are likely to field privacy and security questions for the physician. It's also for the vulnerable receptionist and scheduler—employees frequently confronted by patients with near-impossible questions even as these employees keep the office running smoothly. To the billing and insurance specialists—hats off for staying current with the new transactions and code sets. You may have the greatest appreciation for Administrative Simplification. Office staff may require business associates to read specific chapters, because business associates hold significant responsibility to safeguard patient information.

This book also is designed for people taking on new responsibilities within the medical practice and new employees as they join the practice. Physicians and office managers may use this book as a resource as they integrate complicated HIPAA pieces. You have been on our minds throughout the entire development process.

In writing this book, we spoke with many of our friends, who like you, are in the trenches making HIPAA happen. A prerequisite to being included in this book was that each person interviewed would be willing to take your call or e-mail inquiry if you had a question. You'll find those interviews in sidebars throughout the book, along with contact information.

Each chapter contains "What to do" and "How to do it" directions. The book is chock-full of checklists, charts, quick reference guides, timelines, training plans, and communications plans to make HIPAA easier for you to understand. In each chapter, you'll find "Critical Points," where we highlight the key learning point(s) in that discussion. After you've reviewed the content, you can test your knowledge of HIPAA's Transactions, Privacy, and Security rules. In Appendix B, you'll find 25 questions that have been taken directly from content included in *HIPAA Plain and Simple*. You'll find an answer key at the end of the book.

HIPAA's bottom line is that implementation is focused on relieving a lot of billing headaches and simplifying how the provider gets paid. There are some hurdles we'll need to get over, but the best way is to work on them together.

Finally, with the help of a dynamic team of editors, publisher, and marketers, we fully engaged in the earlier "HIPAA heavy" products so that we

---

3. Downloadable texts of "HIPAA heavy" regulations as published in the *Federal Register* are available via the Internet at aspe.hhs.gov/admnsimp.

could confidently bring you this plain and simple version. We are better authors for knowing the professionals at AMA Press, and we're sure you'll find that they had you in mind when publishing this valuable addition to your compliance library.

Warmest wishes as you continue your HIPAA journey. We hope you'll let us know how you're doing.

Carolyn Hartley
Ed Jones

Acknowledgments

It is our good fortune to have worked with so many of you, our readers, who have helped us frame the plain and simple content of this book. Together, we have wrestled, analyzed, dissected, and reread this complex healthcare law, and together we'll experience the far-reaching benefits that it brings to all of us in this dynamic healthcare community.

The authors want to thank Edward F. Shay, Esq, a partner with the law firm of Post & Schell, P.C., in Philadelphia, Pennsylvania, for his generous contribution of time in reviewing the book from a legal perspective. Ed practices law in the healthcare field with special emphasis on HIPAA compliance, health informatics, managed-care contracting and regulation, and infrastructure issues for risk-assuming entities. He also is a contributing editor for *Briefings on HIPAA and Health Information Security* and a commissioner of the Electronic Healthcare Network Accreditation Commission (EHNAC).

We also want to thank the many individuals and business and government organizations involved in health care that have given countless hours to developing HIPAA Administrative Simplification implementation strategies and solutions. Of particular note are Jim Schuping, executive director of the Workgroup for Electronic Data Interchange (WEDI), his very efficient staff, and the over 6,000 volunteers who participate in WEDI's Strategic National Implementation Process (SNIP) initiative. Their many hours of work in meetings, listservs, audiocasts, and teleconferences is reflected in the many SNIP documents that will be of help to the readers of this book as they implement HIPAA standards. Check them out at www.wedi.org/snip.

We're also grateful to the more than 300 members of the North Carolina Healthcare Information and Communications Alliance (NCHICA) and to the 18 states that hold membership in that organization. We're grateful for the many hours of critical thinking and advice from work groups, transactions, privacy and security implementation strategies, invaluable HIPAA documents, listservs, and conferences. Check them out at www.nchica.org.

A special thanks goes to John Kinney, Marsha Mildred, Shelley Benson, and Katharine Dvorak at AMA Press who put in extra hours getting this book into your hands.

About the Authors

Carolyn Hartley is senior vice president, communications and content development, for Healthcare Training Strategies, LLC, in Raleigh, North Carolina. She writes and publishes products for the American Medical Association (AMA Press) and has co-authored the *Field Guide to HIPAA Implementation* along with Jan Root, PhD, David C. Kibbe, MD, MBA, and Mike Hubbard, JD; the *HIPAA Policies and Procedures Desk Reference* with Mike Hubbard, JD, and Kari Glover, JD; and was the lead creator of Healthcare Training Strategies' flagship product, *The HIPAA Privacy Tool Kit.*

Before joining HTS, Carolyn was a seasoned healthcare journalist, managing editor, and strategic-marketing communications and crisis-communications manager for national public-relations agencies. She also has co-authored and produced twenty-nine nationally distributed books and video training courses, thirteen of which are in health care and health-information management for publishers including Prentice Hall, McGraw-Hill, and Andrews McMeel Universal. Carolyn has held significant appointments as executive producer, *Healthcare Business Review*, vice-president, Center for Advanced Media Studies, and media and publications director for Mayer Hoffman McCann's Professional Resources division, where she worked with Sen. Nancy Landon Kassebaum's staff to educate insurance professionals on HIPAA. Her clients have appeared in proactive and confrontational situations on morning news shows and in hundreds of consumer and trade publications including *Wall Street Journal, New York Times, Forbes, Bloomberg Radio, USA Today, Universal Press Syndicate, Associated Press, Dateline, 60 Minutes, 20/20, The Early Show, The Today Show,* and *Good Morning America.* She holds an undergraduate degree in education and a master of liberal arts degree from Baker University, where she also has been an adjunct professor in the MBA and MLA programs.

Ed Jones is chair of the board of directors of the Workgroup for Electronic Data Interchange (WEDI), a not-for-profit association of more than 200 members, including providers, payers, employers, government organizations, and standards groups. WEDI's mission is to foster successful implementation of Administrative Simplification standards required under the federal Health Insurance Portability and Accountability Act of 1996

(HIPAA) and to further healthcare industry adoption of efficient information-exchange and management tools. He also is a founding commissioner of the Electronic Healthcare Network Accreditation Commission (EHNAC).

Ed lives near Charleston, South Carolina, where he consults on design of healthcare business strategies for companies in financial services, insurance, and computer technology and with health plans and providers on achieving compliance with HIPAA transactions, privacy, and security standards.

Until it was acquired in December 1999, Ed served as senior vice president of The Centris Group, Inc, which comprised seven subsidiary companies with a core focus on underwriting and reinsuring self-funded health plans for US employers. Ed was a member of the CEO's executive operations committee and was responsible for corporate strategic, business, disaster-recovery, and contingency (business-risk) planning; government affairs; European business development; and coordinating design of corporate electronic business strategies.

Before joining Centris in 1993, Ed served as executive vice president and as a member of the board of directors of Medical Review Systems, a firm that he co-founded in 1990, and that was acquired in 1995 by Equifax. Before that, he served as a consultant to the National Research Council of the National Academy of Sciences, the United States Sentencing Commission, and firms in insurance and other industries. He also has held senior positions in the US Department of Justice and the Central Intelligence Agency.

Ed holds degrees in economics from the University of Chicago and Washington University in St. Louis.

Contents

Chapter 3: The Privacy Team   57

Chapter 5: Communicating HIPAA: Inquiring Patients Want to Know   163

Chapter 6: HIPAA Compliance Costs and Return on Investment 183

Appendix A 197

Appendix B 227

Glossary 233

Index 245

HIPAA Overview

In 1991, several distinguished leaders in the healthcare community came to Congress asking for help. At the time, health care as an industry was about 10 years behind in claims-management technology and there didn't seem to be an end to the claims-management problem in sight. The message healthcare leaders gave to Congress was, "You've got to regulate us, because we can't do it ourselves."

Working closely with healthcare associations, vendors, payers, and consultants, Congress drafted and approved the Health Insurance Portability and Accountability Act of 1996 (HIPAA).

Health care's reaction? "You're giving us a law?"

Five years from now, HIPAA regulations will become standard operating practice. But cleaning up the mess we've created will take a focused effort on everyone's part. This chapter offers an overview of that massive cleanup process.

What You Will Learn In This Chapter:

- Why health care needs HIPAA.
- The basics of Administrative Simplification.
- The four sets of standards and their compliance deadlines.
- An overview of the Transactions and Code Sets Rule, the Privacy Rule, the Security Rule, and an overview of National Identifiers.
- Who must comply with HIPAA.
- The benefits of HIPAA to you and your practice.
- Who is enforcing HIPAA.
- Your role in implementing HIPAA.
- A bird's-eye view of risk management.

THE PATHWAY TO HIPAA

Once, health care was simple. Medicine was seen as a "profession, not a business," and patients who could afford to reimburse physicians would pay in cash, farm products, or promissory notes.

While most providers today still view health care as a profession, the business of health care has become enormously elaborate, complex, and haphazard. An insurance clerk might spend 30 minutes on hold to verify coverage for three patients while 10 other patients are backed up in the reception area. An information-technology specialist (often the office manager) uses twenty to thirty software programs to process billing and payment. Reimbursement frequently is incorrect and slow. Reimbursement has become a clogged artery in cash flow, and claim-payment flows have become unpredictable.

An estimated 15 to 30 percent of every healthcare dollar goes to administration for activities like having people review claims, more people to review the people who reviewed the claims, other people to develop and even more people to sell billing software, and a whole lot more people to look at the process to see what's not working. Activities meant to make the claims process easier have become part of health care's administrative black hole.

Then along came managed care, promising to relieve headaches. But instead of relieving pain, it turned claims into encounters, and physicians were limited in the amount of time they could spend with patients. With so many people trying to manage patient care, demands on nurses beyond the scope of health care and treatment multiplied exponentially.

Today, patients watch TV ads or gather information from Internet Web sites suggesting specific treatments. Frequently, these are not insurable treatments, and most often, patients confront their physicians with information from TV or the Internet that is inaccurate or not germane. When physicians try to get back on course with a treatment plan that does not accord with the patients' information from these sources, the physicians' staff (ie, the complaint department) gets an earful from the patients.

Medical malpractice and risk management have turned again into high-dollar concerns for the medical office, yet physicians continue to stand by the principles of their Hippocratic Oath. Most physicians tried not to look at the black hole and instead focused on delivering quality patient care.

To stay in the business of providing such patient care, most physicians have hired practice-management consultants, lawyers, electronic-transcription services, patient-information managers, billing and payment services to manage the business while the staff manages the steady stream of patient inquiries, pains, and expectations. Solutions cured the symptoms but not the problem.

But then a very large group of healthcare and government professionals cried out, "Enough!"

Physician leaders and policy makers within the United States Department of Health and Human Services (HHS), along with concerned executives from the private healthcare sector, started searching for answers to the growing mountain of nonstandardized transaction formats and the increasingly complex and hard-to-manage administrative process. They found an answer in HIPAA.

BASICS OF ADMINISTRATIVE SIMPLIFICATION

In 1991, then-Secretary of HHS, Louis Sullivan, MD, created the Workgroup for Electronic Data Interchange (WEDI) to study what impact replacing paper healthcare transactions would have on containing rising healthcare costs. As a collaboration of government and private industry, WEDI examined the impact of electronic technology in minimizing administrative costs of healthcare transaction and published its findings in a landmark report in 1993. The report indicated that the savings from using electronic technology to process healthcare transactions would be substantial, and it became the foundation of the Administrative Simplification provisions in the Health Insurance Portability and Accountability Act of 1996 that President Clinton signed in August 1996.

The first term in the title of the law, *Portability*, is in place. It guarantees that you can obtain insurance if you change jobs. The second term in the title, *Accountability*, begins to identify who and what should be accountable for specific healthcare activities. One portion of accountability, Administrative Simplification, the subject of this book, is in the process of being put in place and is designed to address some of the messy administrative systems and business issues that we identified above.

The good news is that simplifying messy administrative systems and business issues has been done before in other industries. Health care can learn a lesson from banking, Internet shopping, manufacturing, transportation, retailing, and many other industries. In fact, health care is one of the last industries to start simplifying its messy administrative systems and business issues. The bad news is that health care is the largest industry sector in the US economy, with many types of entities, which makes the task complex.

CRITICAL POINT
Simplifying messy administrative systems and business issues has been done before in other industries. Health care can learn a lesson from them.

Administrative Simplification is of high interest to medical practices because it promises to make the business of health care easier. HIPAA's Administrative Simplification standards for transactions, privacy, and security, the subject of this book, will have significant impact on how your medical office operates for years to come.

Administrative Simplification generally involves the following:

■ Processing specified standard healthcare transactions electronically that are created and transmitted electronically by healthcare providers.

■ Using standard code sets and unique identifiers in that process.

■ Implementing security and privacy standards for transmitting, processing, maintaining, and controlling use and disclosure of patient-identifiable healthcare information.

The overall objectives of HIPAA's Administrative Simplification are to:

■ Improve efficiency and effectiveness of the healthcare system via electronic exchange of administrative and financial information.

■ Protect security and privacy of transmitted and stored administrative and financial information.

■ Reduce high transaction costs in health care, which include, but are not limited to,

  □ Paper-based transaction systems.

  □ Multiple nonstandard healthcare data formats.

  □ Misuse, errors related to, and loss of healthcare records.

Reduced to these objectives, HIPAA Administrative Simplification appears manageable: Simplify transactions so that all entities filing electronic transactions use the same set of codes, data content, and data formats, and keep patient information safe and secure while you're doing it.

But the details of the Transactions, Privacy, and Security Rules are voluminous. The good news is that many of the provisions call for reasonable and appropriate actions on your part, based on the size and complexity of your business. This is known as scalability. Also, most of the specifications are "technologically neutral." That means that you have a choice of inputs (hardware and software systems) as long as you attain the measures of output reflected in the standards.

This book will help you understand how all of these HIPAA provisions affect—and benefit—you. By now, the management staff in your medical practice may already have developed HIPAA policies and procedures, and you may have been trained in those polices and procedures. If you're not there yet, you'll find a list of helpful resources in the appendix of this book and simple step-by-step directions in each chapter that can help you understand and implement HIPAA.

CRITICAL POINT

To be HIPAA compliant, everyone in the medical practice will have to do a few things differently.

Our intent in this book is not only to show you how to be HIPAA compliant but also to explain why compliance is so important. To be HIPAA compliant, everyone in the medical practice will have to do a few things differently. But there's nothing so new in HIPAA that you can't adapt and make it happen. In fact, you probably will find that you already are doing some things that will meet compliance standards. Greater efficiency and cost-effectiveness will be critical as the demand for healthcare resources escalates in the years ahead.

Key Terms

Before you read any further, we're giving you a few key terms that are a part of understanding the HIPAA language. Additional terms are defined in the glossary in the back of this book, but these few will give you a good head start. Legal definitions are available at www.hhs.gov, but these definitions may be easier to understand.

Covered entity: A healthcare provider that chooses to transmit *health* information electronically, a health plan, or a healthcare clearinghouse. A healthcare provider, such as a physician, dentist, long-term-care facility, or hospital, to name a few, that transmits any of four types of medical information electronically—claims or encounter information, eligibility requests, referrals and authorizations, and claim-status inquiries—is required to transmit the information using HIPAA standards.[1] Two important points: A provider has a business choice to make: transmit electronically or on paper; however, the provider must use the HIPAA standards if he uses any of the four transactions above electronically.[2] In contrast, a health plan and a healthcare clearinghouse must be able to receive not only those four transactions but also be able to conduct four others electronically: premium payment, claim payment and remittance advice, enrollment and disenrollment, and coordination of benefits. A covered entity must comply with HIPAA's requirements.

Covered transactions: An electronic exchange of information between two covered-entity business partners using the HIPAA-defined electronic data interchange (EDI) transaction standards for the exchange. A covered transaction would be a physician transmitting an electronic claim to a health plan or sending a referral or authorization electronically to another physician, lab, or hospital. A patient sending an e-mail message to a physician that contains patient-identifiable information would not be a covered transaction because a patient is not a covered entity. As we shall see in Chapter 4, the receipt of that information by the physician invokes security protections that the physician must have in place.

Electronic data interchange (EDI): The computer-to-computer exchange of routine business information using publicly available standards. These standards have been used in the banking, financial, and retail industries for years. The exchange of information is called a *transaction*.

Minimum necessary: HIPAA requires that providers carefully define who has access to personal health information. Your practice has established, and will

---

1. This requirement also pertains to a healthcare clearinghouse working on behalf of a healthcare provider in the role of business associate.

2. While providers may have a choice with respect to how they submit claims, increasingly health plans require electronic submission. As we shall see in the book, there also are incentives for electronic claims submission, including faster turnaround on payment, and disincentives for paper claims submissions, such as no payment for Medicare claims from many providers.

continually evaluate, its policies and procedures on what portions of the patient record are available by front-office staff, utilization managers, billing personnel, and others. Physicians can share the patient's entire medical record with colleagues for treatment purposes. The intent is to discourage anyone from having open access to medical records that contain files of information regarding a person's medical history.

Notice of Privacy Practices (NPP): A legal document developed by the practice and its attorney that states what the practice will do to protect each patient's rights. This NPP is likely to be the cornerstone of your office's privacy policy and it is important that everyone in your practice understand its contents. You'll learn more about the NPP in Chapter 3.

Privacy and security officials: HIPAA requires that the practice appoint one person in your office to oversee the privacy activities and security protections in your practice. The privacy official can delegate responsibility to members of a privacy team if they are trained to fulfill specific responsibilities. Similarly, the security official can delegate responsibility to members of a security team if they are trained to fulfill specific responsibilities. Two important points: First, the privacy and security official(s) can delegate responsibility, but the official(s) alone retains accountability for HIPAA compliance. Second, the privacy and security official may be the same person. In larger practices, you probably will want to have separate privacy and security officials, depending on the workload.

Protected Health Information (PHI): Information that can be used to identify an individual because it contains one or more patient identifiers, such as name, Social Security number, telephone number, zip code, e-mail or web address, and so forth. The Privacy Rule specifies that PHI must be protected whether it is written, spoken, or in electronic form. Health information that has been stripped of its identifiers is "de-identified" and is not considered PHI.

State preemption: HIPAA defers to the laws of the state if that state's laws are more stringent than HIPAA privacy standards.

Treatment, payment, and healthcare operations (TPO): In the Modification to the Privacy Rule, put into force in August 2002, HIPAA gave physicians freedom to continue treating patients, seeking payment, and conducting routine healthcare operations without having to obtain a written consent to conduct business on behalf of the patient. Some states, however, still require signed privacy consents, and many physicians continue to use HIPAA privacy consents whether required or not. A HIPAA Privacy consent is not the same as a Consent to Treat. *Treatment* means that you can provide care, including the coordination or management of health care between healthcare providers, or refer a patient to another provider. *Payment* within HIPAA means that you can disclose personal health information, such as name, address, date of birth, Social Security number, and account number, to obtain reimbursement. *Healthcare operations* refers to a number of activities, from conducting quality assessments and improvement activities and reviewing the competence or qualifications of healthcare professionals, to evaluating a professional's performance. It can also refer to business management and general administrative activities. Healthcare operations is a broad area, so if you must defend an activity within this category, ask the privacy official or your attorney for clarity before proceeding with a task.

FOUR SETS OF STANDARDS

A standard is a requirement, and a rule is a document that includes the standards. Each rule starts out with a Notice of Proposed Rule-Making (NPRM). The sponsoring government entity for HIPAA, the US Department of Health and Human Services, presents the NPRM for public comment and revisions and then publishes a final rule in the *Federal Register.* With few exceptions, the deadline for compliance or implementation is 24 months after the rule's effective date, which may be 30 to 60 days after the publication date.[3] Each of the four sets of standards contains different sets of activities that your practice has either completed or is in the process of completing and revising. (See Table 1.1.)

T A B L E 1.1

HIPAA Timeline

Standards Name	Date of Final Rule Publication	Deadline for Implementation	Comments
Transactions and Code Sets	August 17, 2000	October 16, 2002	If no extension was filed.
		October 16, 2003	If an extension was filed.
		April 16, 2003	Extenders must start testing transactions.
Privacy Rule	Published December 28, 2000, but effective April 14, 2001. Modifications finalized August 14, 2002.	April 14, 2003	HHS continues to release "guidances" that clarify the Privacy Rule. The rule allows for an update only once yearly.
Security Rule	Notice of Proposed Rule Making published on August 12, 1998. Final rule published February 20, 2003.	Effective date, April 21, 2003. Compliance date, April 21, 2005.	April 14, 2003, for security safeguards required by Privacy Rule, even though compliance with Security Rule is two years later.

continued

---

3. The time between publication and effective date generally is a time for public comment or to amend technical errors, or both.

T A B L E   1.1 (continued)

HIPAA Timeline

Standards Name	Date of Final Rule Publication	Deadline for Implementation	Comments
National Identifier Standards	Notice of Proposed Rule Making published in 1998 to create National Provider Identifier. Final rule issued on May 31, 2002, adopting the Employer Identification Number, issued by the Internal Revenue Service as the National Employer Identifier.	Effective date, July 30, 2002. Compliance date, July 30, 2004.	National Provider Identifer Proposed May 7, 1998, with final rule expected in 2003. Proposed National Health Plan Identifier expected in 2003. National Individual Identifier on a "Congressional Hold" regarding regulatory action.

OVERVIEW OF THE FOUR STANDARDS

The following is a summary of each of the major rules included in Administrative Simplification. While each rule is explained in detail in subsequent chapters, you may wish to present these summaries to your management team so that they understand more about what HHS expects from your practice.

Transactions and Code Sets

A *transaction* refers to the transmission of information between two parties to carry out financial or administrative activities. *Code sets* are those data sets that identify diagnoses, treatment procedures, drug codes, equipment codes, and other codes that will be described in Chapter 2. The importance of these codes to the medical office is this: when the diagnostic codes match a complicated set of payer-approved procedure codes, the payers understand how the provider intends to treat the patient, and payers reimburse the provider for services rendered. When cash flows in and out of the office with few interruptions, everyone in the office seems to be happy.

CRITICAL POINT

When cash flows in and out of the office with few interruptions, everyone in the office seems to be happy.

But over the last two decades, a very complicated network of billing and software companies was retained to help physicians collect claims.

Most of the companies used different formats, which sometimes made it difficult for payers to understand the connection between treatment and payment. Also, payers sometimes required information about the treatment or the individual that differed from payer to payer. The result was a proliferation of nonstandard transaction formats and data-content requirements that complicated and slowed the claim-reimbursement process. Each side blamed the other for these complications, but one thing was certain: Everyone was unhappy with the process, including the patient. So the HHS, through HIPAA, said, "Everyone must send or receive transactions using standard formats and data content."

CRITICAL POINT

HHS, through HIPAA, said, "Everyone must send or receive transactions using standard formats and data content."

Achieving agreement on the standard formats for the transactions was a challenge, but the standards process allowed all parties—vendors, payers, providers, clearinghouses, and the government—to come together to make their business cases that would be reflected in the standards. Each of the parties had an opportunity to identify the information that it needed to complete a transaction, and the parties as a group negotiated a common set of data requirements that they would use to transact business. That process is not over because the parties continue to meet to discuss new or revised data requirements and innovations in technologies that may further improve business processing in the healthcare industry. HIPAA provides a *designated standard-maintenance organization* (DSMO) process to handle industry recommended modifications to the standards that may enhance administrative simplification. Considerable resources of time and money from all parties, particularly software vendors, have been spent to get ready for implementation of the transaction and code set standards. The final outcome of the Transactions and Code Sets Rule is that practices will have to ensure that their software vendors can send and receive information using standard data formats and data content. Ultimately, compliance rests with you, the covered entity, not the vendor.

CRITICAL POINT

Your practice must ensure that your software vendors can send and receive information using standard data formats and data content. Compliance rests with you, not the vendor.

What to do:

Begin using standard transactions and code sets by October 16, 2003.

How to do it:

Ask your vendor to test your transactions and code sets between April 16, 2003, and October 16, 2003. The management team in your practice should do the following.

- Talk to your vendors, such as your billing management company, about their compliance activities. Vendors don't have to be HIPAA compliant. You do. But vendors must use standard formats and data content for electronic transmissions.

- Learn about your practice-management system and how you can use it to make the practice more efficient.

- If you have an interest in electronic transactions or billing and coding, ask if there are classes you can take to learn more about this topic.

- Read Chapter 2 on transactions and code sets. And read about organizations that have developed services to help you with transactions and code sets.

- Spend some time on this. The productivity benefits could be substantial and help you improve work flow and workload.

Privacy Standards

HHS recognized that if it required covered entities to use a standard set of formats and data content to transmit files electronically, consumers would expect their medical files to be kept confidential. That's why HHS also developed standards that protect patients' rights, including unauthorized use and disclosure of their health information. The HIPAA Privacy Rule has garnered a considerable amount of attention because the Privacy Rule is nontechnical, mainly administrative policies and procedures, and also because privacy is an important issue to people.

The Privacy Rule requires that you change some of your day-to-day tasks so that information used to identify a patient is protected and that this protected health information (PHI) is secure. This includes PHI that is at rest (storage) or in movement (for example, spoken), as well as PHI in electronic, oral, or written forms. The Privacy Rule also includes safeguard measures to control unauthorized disclosure (access to) and use of PHI. Safeguards include routine activities like locking the doors at night, changing passwords periodically, and keeping computer passwords private—not posted by the computer screen or shared with other staff members.

At HIPAA training sessions, we always ask participants, "How many office managers know their physician's password?" Usually all but one or two raise a hand. In HIPAA security, you cannot exchange passwords, and only the system administrator can know everyone's password. You'll learn more about security in Chapter 4.

CRITICAL POINT
Only the system administrator is allowed to know your password.

The Privacy Rule also grants patients six new rights. Patients can gain access to and have more control over the use and disclosure of their personal health information. This rule also sets obligations for medical practices to respect those rights. Medical practices will be required to answer patient requests, such as, "I'd like a list of all the places you have sent my medical record," or "I don't want the medical records manager to see my medical records because she is a friend of my boss." Many patients may be evaluating the practice not only on the quality of its care and service, but also on the quality of its privacy. These are important customer satisfaction issues. You'll learn much more about patient rights in Chapter 3.

What to do:
You should have met the April 14, 2003, Privacy Rule compliance date. Because privacy must be an integral part of your practice's business, here are some ideas to enhance privacy awareness and compliance efforts.

How to do it:
- Evaluate your policies and procedures. If they aren't working, examine whether you should modify them. If you change them, you must keep records of your old policies for six years after they have been modified.
- Regularly meet with your privacy official who is responsible for implementation of privacy practices and accountable for compliance. It is the privacy official's job to make sure everyone follows the privacy and security policies and procedures.
- Be prepared to answer patient questions. Make sure everyone in the office understands the content of your Notice of Privacy Practices.
- Retrain staff as you encounter new privacy problems or change policies and procedures.
- Assist business associates as they work to safeguard protected health information. Invite them to attend privacy training sessions, and support them if they have questions.
- Develop discussion questions for those undefined procedures that have no clear solution.
- Read Chapter 3 to get a broader understanding of the Privacy Rule, and read about people like you who are solving privacy problems in their practices.

Security Standards

Security and privacy go hand in hand. Security is about controlling access to electronic PHI; privacy is about controlling how electronic, oral, and written PHI is used and disclosed. In 1996 when HIPAA was signed into law, your practice immediately became obligated to build a program that protects the security of personal health information. Tucked inside the Privacy Rule are standards that say you must "safeguard" or protect medical records.

CRITICAL POINT

Security is about controlling access to electronic PHI. Privacy is about controlling how electronic, oral, and written PHI is used and disclosed.

Security refers to your specific efforts to protect health information and prevent unauthorized breaches of privacy that might occur if electronic, oral, or written PHI is lost or destroyed by accident, stolen, or sent to the wrong person by mistake. The final Security Rule was published in the *Federal Register* on February 20, 2003, and includes administrative, physical, and technical safeguards pertaining to electronic PHI that you must have in place no later than April 21, 2005.[4]

The Privacy Rule requires similar safeguards for not only electronic PHI but also oral and written PHI. Furthermore, those safeguards must be in place by April 14, 2003, in order to be in compliance with the Privacy Rule.

We will discuss these safeguards in greater detail in the privacy and security chapters of this book. The following gives examples of the types of safeguards that you must have in place:

■ Physical safeguards: Rooms and storage facilities with locks or other safeguards that control access.

■ Administrative safeguards: Policies and procedures that define who has access to information, user IDs, passwords, and actions taken if violations occur.

■ Technical safeguards: Encryption of electronic data and use of passwords to verify users who have logged into the system.

Security is an ongoing, continual process that is never "done."

When HIPAA's Privacy Rule was enacted, some providers were told that they must spend thousands of dollars to retrofit their offices and pass out beepers rather than call out a patient's name. This was incorrect information. Privacy and security rules are based on the principle of "reasonableness," given the size and complexity of the environment in which the covered entity operates.

As a foundation for developing your practice's policies and procedures, you must conduct risk analyses, determine how you can mitigate those risks, and put the procedures in place. "Your first priority is to develop a way to quantify and evaluate risk. You need to know *what* you are protecting and how much it's worth before you can decide how to protect it."[5] You will find that you likely practice a number of the policies that you will need to have documented and for which you will have to train your workforce.

---

4. The only exception for compliance by this date is small health plans with receipts less than $5 million. These health plans have an additional year to comply, by April 21, 2006.

5. Al Berg, "6 Myths About Security Policies: Leave Your Preconceptions Behind and Write Policies That Work in the Real World," *Information Security,* October 2002, p. 49.

CRITICAL POINT

To implement security, you must conduct risk analyses, determine how you can mitigate those risks, and put procedures in place.

HHS occasionally issues "guidance" in response to questions asked by covered entities that are implementing the standards. The answer format is in plain, understandable language that covered entities such as physician practices can easily put into practice. Even though there are federal penalties for noncompliance with the privacy and security rules, HHS's focus is to encourage voluntary compliance. You can ask questions and get guidance on privacy at www.hhs.gov/ocr and questions and guidance on security at www.cms.gov/hipaa.

What to do:

Begin implementing security measures now. It's the law. Use the final Security Rule as your guide to what you need to do.

How to do it:

- Begin examining your security measures now. The Security Rule was printed in the *Federal Register* on February 20, 2003, and you must be compliant with this rule by April 21, 2005. Don't wait until the last minute to comply. HIPAA will require every healthcare provider to put several layers of safeguards in place.

- Conduct your own security risk analysis and make a list of security-related questions to ask your vendor. We will show you in Chapter 4 what you need to do in your security risk analysis and give you references to the National Institute for Standards and Technology (NIST) and other documents to get much more information.

- Your practice may already have appointed a security official who is conducting a security risk analysis. If you have an interest in this area, ask if you can be a contributing member of the security team.

- Ask what "reasonable and appropriate" administrative, technical, and physical safeguards are in your office. If you are in a rural area, your physical security risks will be different than if you were in a high-risk urban area. Your security risks will also differ by the degree to which you employ technological applications in your practice, whether you perform these applications in your practice or outsource them, and whether or not you use networks and other communication links. Whereas one location may need a lock, another location may require more sophisticated alarm systems.

- Read Chapter 4 to learn more about security policies and procedures.

- Beginnings aren't easy. As your office moves from manual to automated processes, ask how you can help. Remember, everyone goes through a learning cycle when moving from manual to automated processes, some faster than others. Once in place and with workforce familiarity and ease of use, the practice will thrive, and you'll help improve the cash flow needed to stay in business.

National Identifier Standards

HIPAA has provisions for four national identifiers: provider, health plan, employer, and individual. The final employer and proposed provider identifier standards have been published, but the health plan and individual standards have not.[6]

The purpose of the identifiers is to provide electronic numeric or alphanumeric addresses for the movement of electronic transactions. For example, the physician and clearinghouse need the health plan's electronic address so that they can send claims to the health plan (primary payer). Similarly, the health plan and clearinghouse need the provider address so that they can send remittance advice for payments. Some providers maintain more than 30 payer-assigned provider identifiers, so simplifying that number to one could make billing much easier. But one identifier number also creates problems for physicians with multiple responsibilities.

Take a look at your checkbook. Each check has a routing number to the bank and, immediately after it, your unique account number. Credit card numbers also provide unique address information pertaining to the account. Your e-mail address is unique, too. That is the idea behind unique identifiers that will facilitate the movement and direction of electronic healthcare transactions.

When in place, some of these identifiers will be kept in a central depository, with access to entities in the healthcare industry on a "need-to-know" basis. Because of Medicare and Medicaid, the federal government likely will operate or outsource development of a national provider identifier database. Others will be decentralized. For example, when a patient visits a physician's office, he or she will show a benefits card that will have the "electronic" address on where to send the claim. The identifier system will only work if the numbers are kept current.

The relatively slow development of the identifier system shows that implementation of Administrative Simplification and realizing its benefits will not happen overnight.

What to do:

Watch for updates on provider identifier standards.

How to do it:

- Your state and national medical societies will likely keep information on their web sites.
- The employer identifier standard is the federal Employer Identification Number (EIN), which will require compliance by July 30, 2004.

---

6. Congress has put a hold on the HHS's conducting regulatory activities pertaining to the individual identifier. The de facto individual identifier has been the Social Security number. There are privacy concerns with use of this number, in part because it has been used in the past for many data sets and can provide a link between individual data, medical information, and other information that could undermine privacy. Further, a number of states, including California as of 2002, strictly limit the use of the Social Security number in data sets, including health-related data sets.

FIGURE 1.1

Are You a Covered Entity?

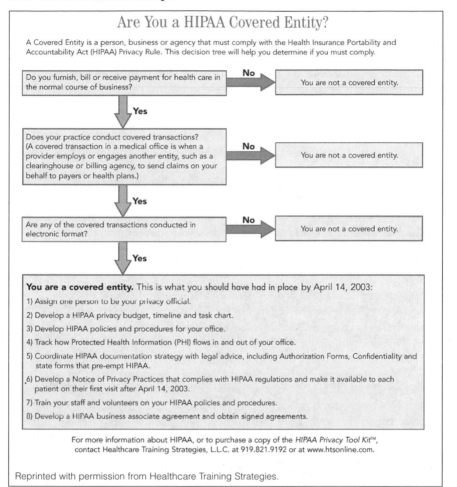

Are You a HIPAA Covered Entity?

A Covered Entity is a person, business or agency that must comply with the Health Insurance Portability and Accountability Act (HIPAA) Privacy Rule. This decision tree will help you determine if you must comply.

Do you furnish, bill or receive payment for health care in the normal course of business? **No** → You are not a covered entity.

Yes ↓

Does your practice conduct covered transactions? (A covered transaction in a medical office is when a provider employs or engages another entity, such as a clearinghouse or billing agency, to send claims on your behalf to payers or health plans.) **No** → You are not a covered entity.

Yes ↓

Are any of the covered transactions conducted in electronic format? **No** → You are not a covered entity.

Yes ↓

You are a covered entity. This is what you should have had in place by April 14, 2003:

1) Assign one person to be your privacy official.

2) Develop a HIPAA privacy budget, timeline and task chart.

3) Develop HIPAA policies and procedures for your office.

4) Track how Protected Health Information (PHI) flows in and out of your office.

5) Coordinate HIPAA documentation strategy with legal advice, including Authorization Forms, Confidentiality and state forms that pre-empt HIPAA.

6) Develop a Notice of Privacy Practices that complies with HIPAA regulations and make it available to each patient on their first visit after April 14, 2003.

7) Train your staff and volunteers on your HIPAA policies and procedures.

8) Develop a HIPAA business associate agreement and obtain signed agreements.

For more information about HIPAA, or to purchase a copy of the *HIPAA Privacy Tool Kit*™, contact Healthcare Training Strategies, L.L.C. at 919.821.9192 or at www.htsonline.com.

Reprinted with permission from Healthcare Training Strategies.

WHO MUST COMPLY?

Healthcare businesses affected by HIPAA are defined as *covered entities* and *business associates. Covered entities* must comply with HIPAA, and they include health plans, healthcare clearinghouses, and healthcare providers that transmit any health information about an individual in electronic form. To determine whether you are a covered entity, do two things: first, go to www.hhs.gov/ocr, and click on "Am I a Covered Entity?" Answer the set of questions to determine your status. That same set of questions is included in the flow chart in Figure 1.1 for healthcare providers. Use this chart to determine if you are a covered entity.[7] If you are unsure or operate under unusual circumstances, be sure to consult with your attorney.

---

7. Content from www.hhs.gov/ocr/hipaa, "Are You a Covered Entity?"

Most covered entities fall into these categories:

- hospitals, including academic medical centers;
- nursing homes;
- hospices;
- pharmacies;
- physician practices;
- dental practices;
- chiropractors;
- podiatrists;
- osteopaths;
- physical therapists;
- alternative medicine (eg, acupuncture, massage therapists);
- laboratories;
- health plans (payers); and
- healthcare clearinghouses.

Business associates are not covered entities, but covered entities must obtain and execute contracts or agreements with business associates that conduct specified activities on behalf of a covered entity. In these contracts, business associates must ensure that they will implement processes to safeguard protected health information. Part of your agreement should include recourse for your practice if a business associate accidentally or intentionally releases PHI that you have entrusted to it for business purposes.

The Privacy Rule included a sample business-associate agreement, which is included in the appendix of this book.[8] There are certain requirements that must be included in the business associate agreement, which may be part of a trading-partner agreement or contract or a separate document. Your privacy official may wish to review the required contents of a business-associate agreement recapped here.

- List of permitted and required uses and disclosures of protected health information by business associate. These will be specific to each business-associate agreement, depending upon the business relationship between the provider (covered entity) and business associate.
- Prohibition of use and further disclosure of protected health information other than as permitted or required by contract or as required by law.

___

8. See the Model Business Associate Agreement that includes these requirements: "Appendix to the Preamble—Sample Business Associate Contract Provisions," in *Federal Register* (Part V: Standards for Privacy of Individually Identifiable Health Information; Final Rule), August 14, 2002, pp. 53264-53266. Available at: http://www.hhs.gov/ocr/hipaa/privrulepd.pdf.

- Requirement that the business associate use appropriate safeguards to prevent uses or disclosures of protected health information other than those allowed by contract.
- Obligation of the business associate to report to provider any uses and disclosures that violate contract.
- Requirement that the business associate ensure that its agents and subcontractors who are given protected health information agree to follow restrictions and conditions imposed on the business associate by contract.
- Requirement that the business associate make available protected health information for patients' requests for access to, and amendment of, their protected health information and for accounting of disclosures of that protected health information.
- Requirement that the business associate make its internal practices, books, and records relating to provider's protected health information available to HHS for purposes of determining a health plan's compliance with privacy rules.
- Statement that upon termination of the business-associate agreement, the business associate will, if feasible, return or destroy all protected health information, or if such return or destruction is not feasible, extend the protection of contract to such protected health information and limit further uses and disclosures to those parties that make return or destruction infeasible.
- Authorization of termination by the provider if the business associate violates a material term of contract.

Examples of the types of activities that business associates would conduct on behalf of covered entities include, but are not limited to:

Dictation and transcription	Practice management
Claims processing	Repricing
Data analysis	Legal
Processing or administration	Accounting
Utilization review	Consulting
Quality assurance	Data aggregation
Billing	Accreditation
Benefit management	

Table 1.2 recaps the compliance deadlines for covered entities.

TABLE 1.2

Important Administrative Simplification Compliance Deadlines

Date	Deadline
October 15, 2002	Deadline to submit a compliance extension form for electronic healthcare transactions and code sets.
October 16, 2002	Electronic healthcare transactions and code sets—all covered entities except those who filed for an extension and are not a small health plan.
April 14, 2003	Privacy—all covered entities except small health plans.
April 16, 2003	Electronic healthcare transactions and code sets—all covered entities that requested a one-year extension must have started electronic transactions standards testing.
October 16, 2003	Electronic healthcare transactions and code sets—all covered entities who filed for an extension and small health plans.
April 14, 2004	Privacy—small health plans.
July 30, 2004	Employer identifier standard—all covered entities except small health plans.
July 30, 2005	Employer identifier standard—small health plans.
April 21, 2005	Security compliance for covered entities other than small health plans.
April 21, 2006	Security compliance for small health plans

BENEFITS TO THE PRACTICE CAN BE SUBSTANTIAL

Many of us remember a time when a bank accepted checks only from its own customers. If you were traveling, out-of-town checks were rarely accepted. Today, because of standard electronic formats, you can travel nationally and internationally and manage financial transactions at automatic teller machines (ATMs), via the Internet, or via toll-free telephone lines.

Retail customers often experience the benefits of online shopping. Today, you can purchase online anything from a book (including this book at www.amapress.org), records, clothing, and furniture to a car. Typically, a customer selects a product or service, enters a secure site, and presents credit-card information. Then, through a process of computers talking to each other, the purchase is approved, and someone from shipping sends your product out within a few days. The retailer is immediately reimbursed for your product.

In health care, the billing process contains many more layers of approvals and transactions with several U-turns, side roads, yields, and mismatched codes. Ultimately, it may take a slew of consultants to determine where some of the income due the physician's office has been lost.

The greatest legacy of Administrative Simplification may be that the healthcare system replicates the most efficient practices of banking or online shopping. (See Table 1.3.) Ideally, a provider could go back to caring for patients, and everyone in the office could streamline your administrative processes. Chapter 2 talks more about how that is happening and how you fit into that HIPAA plan.

TABLE 1.3

Benefits at a Glance of Administrative Simplification

Standard	Benefit
Transactions	■ Better off economically as a result of effective claims process.
	■ Eliminates multiple claim formats.
	■ Potential to reduce fraud claims.
	■ Less staff time spent on claims.
	■ Get payment from patients that you mistakenly assumed were eligible through insurance.
	■ Eliminate costly time spent in eligibility checks.
	■ Increase direct deposit into practice's account.
	■ Fewer denied claims.
Privacy	■ Accreditation, litigation, and legal exposure reduced by following specific policies.
	■ Reduce gray areas. Use the Privacy Rule to explain to patients what you can and cannot do.
	■ Patients may shop for physicians with strong privacy policy.
	■ Patients have increased trust.
	■ Staff has clarity on privacy practices.
Security	■ Office less vulnerable to patient information loss and litigation.
	■ More reliable information systems.
	■ Information accessible and useable on demand.
	■ Information not made available or disclosed to unauthorized parties.
	■ Information not altered or destroyed in an unauthorized manner.
	■ Risk assessment framework provides mechanism for practice to identify and mitigate system vulnerabilities.

IMPLEMENTATION MAY TAKE A WHILE

In 2001, national health expenditures totaled more than $1.424 trillion.[9] Physician and clinical services represented 22 percent of that total, or $313.6 billion.[10] In 2002, the projected national health expenditure totaled about $1.546 trillion, with physician and clinical services representing about the same percentage of the total as the year before, or $336 billion.[11] By 2011, when the baby-boom generation starts to turn 65 years of age, national health expenditures are expected to total $2.816 trillion, with physician and clinical services representing just over 21 percent of that total, or $593.3 billion.

Health care didn't get big in just a few years, but it is expected to almost double in less than eight years. It may take until the baby boom generation starts to turn 65 in 2011 before the efficiencies of Administrative Simplification begin to be realized in a significant way in the healthcare system as a whole, for example, with overall administrative costs materially smaller as a percent of national health expenditures. The Administrative Simplification process is starting to be implemented this year in terms of compliance, and you will begin to notice measurable changes in late 2003 and 2004. Companies that completed their testing phase will have more confidence in the transaction and code sets system, and physicians will have a better sense of how HIPAA is working inside the office.

> **CRITICAL POINT**
> You will begin to notice measurable changes from Administrative Simplification in late 2003 and 2004.

With change as big as HIPAA, it is normal to ask a lot of questions. HIPAA has a lot of gray areas, so physicians and the privacy and security officials may not have all the answers. This book and the references herein will help you get a handle on HIPAA. But HIPAA is a two-way street, and the federal government officials at HHS want to know your concerns. If you have concerns or questions, use the HIPAA administrative-simplification question e-mail formats at www.hhs.gov/ocr (privacy) and www.cms.hhs.gov (transactions and code sets and security).

---

9. Katharine Levit, et al. "Trends in U.S. Health Care Spending, 2001," in *Health Affairs,* v. 22, n. 1, January/February 2003, pp. 154-164.

10. In the preceding year, 2000, the latest year for which data are available, there were more than 823 million visits to physician offices in the United States. Of these, 57 percent were paid by private insurance, 20 percent by Medicare, 9 percent by Medicaid, and 5 percent through self-pay. Donald Cherry, et al., "National Ambulatory Medical Care Survey: 2000 Summary," *Advance Data* No. 328. Hyattsville, MD: Centers for Disease Control and Prevention, National Center for Health Statistics, June 5, 2002.

11. Stephen Heffler, et al. "Health Spending Projections for 2001-2011: The Latest Outlook," in *Health Affairs,* v. 21, n. 2, March/April 2002, pp. 207-218.

CRITICAL POINT
HIPAA is a two-way street and HHS wants to know your concerns.

What to do:

The practice isn't HIPAA compliant just because you've written and been trained on your policies and procedures. Now you must implement them. The first line of defense is you! If you have regular patient contact, whether in the reception area, on the telephone, or in the examining room, you are the practice's privacy ambassador.

So after the lawyers have had their say, and the privacy training officer says your practice has met its training requirement, the real secret to an effective program is what you do with your say.

How to do it:

■ Ask if you can serve on the privacy and security teams.

■ Develop a process that reinforces and motivates staff to implement HIPAA.

■ Be systematic about implementing HIPAA.

■ Don't assume smooth sailing. Expect reaction among the staff. New regula tions almost always create resistance. Discussing contingency scenarios and how the staff as a team will deal with them will help to break down resistance and forge a common goal of making HIPAA a success in the practice.

CRITICAL POINT
All of us came into HIPAA from somewhere else. Stay with us. No one gets to be compliant first. We can only do this together.

All of us came into HIPAA from somewhere else. Each person, from the most prominent speaker to the patient walking in your door, has gone through a learning curve. Stay with us. No one gets HIPAA compliant alone. We can only do this together, and you're part of health care's success story.

ENFORCEMENT

Enforcing HIPAA will be an overwhelming task, so HHS has divided the task of monitoring and enforcement between two federal agencies, the Centers for Medicare and Medicaid Services (CMS),[12] and the Office for Civil Rights (OCR). As shown in Table 1.4, OCR has enforcement authority for the privacy rule and CMS has enforcement authority for the other HIPAA Administrative Simplification standards, including transactions, code sets, identifiers, and security.

---

12. Within CMS, the Office of HIPAA Standards is responsible for all HIPAA standards and enforcement except privacy.

TABLE 1.4

HHS Agency Responsible for Enforcement

Standard	Enforcement Agency
Transactions and Code Sets	Centers for Medicaid and Medicare (CMS) (www.cms.gov)
Security	CMS
Employer Identifier, Provider Identifier, Health Plan Identifier	CMS
Privacy Rule	Office for Civil Rights (OCR) (www.hhs.gov/ocr)

HHS published its interim final enforcement rule on April 17, 2003.[13] This is the first installment of the final rule and will be revised before its expiration date of September 16, 2003. The revised enforcement rule, when issued, will specify "procedural and substantive requirements for imposition of civil money penalties."[14]

The importance of the interim rule is that it signals the healthcare industry on the approach that HHS will take to civil enforcement relating to HIPAA Administrative Simplification standards. According to the interim final rule on enforcement, with respect to the Privacy Rule: "OCR will seek the cooperation of covered entities in obtaining compliance with the Privacy Rule, and may provide technical assistance to help covered entities voluntarily comply with the Rule…. OCR will seek to resolve matters by informal means before issuing findings of non-compliance, under its authority to investigate and resolve complaints, and to engage in compliance reviews."[15] With respect to CMS's enforcement of the other HIPAA Administrative Simplification standards: "Enforcement activities will focus on obtaining voluntary compliance through technical assistance. The process will be primarily complaint driven and will consist of progressive steps that will provide opportunities to demonstrate compliance or submit a corrective action plan."[16]

CMS and OCR also will conduct outreach activities to HIPAA-covered entities including healthcare providers and insurers to "make sure they are aware of the requirements and to help them comply." However, a CMS/OCR

---

13. Department of Health and Human Services, Office of the Secretary, "45 CFR Part 160: Civil Money Penalties: Procedures for Investigations, Imposition of Penalties, and Hearings." *Federal Register,* v. 68, n. 74, April 17, 2003, pp. 18895-18906. This document is available electronically at www.hhs.gov/ocr/hipaa/ or www.cms.gov/hipaa/hipaa2. Citations to this document hereafter are in the standard reference format of volume *Federal Register* pages(s). (eg, 68 *Federal Register* 18895).

14. 68 *Federal Register* 18895.

15. 68 *Federal Register* 18897.

16. HHS Press Release, October 15, 2002. See www.cms.gov/hipaa/hipaa2.

nationwide outreach campaign is daunting. By the end of March 2003, one month before the Privacy Rule's April 14 compliance deadline, OCR had presented seminars in San Diego, Atlanta, New York, and Chicago. The Workgroup for Electronic Data Interchange (WEDI) and Finch University of Health Sciences/Chicago Medical School jointly sponsored OCR's one-day National Conference on the HIPAA Privacy Rule in Chicago, on a snowy Sunday, March 2, 2003. With only several weeks notice, more than 1,200 attendees, many providers from Illinois and surrounding states, spent their Sunday in a hotel ballroom seminar on privacy. That is testament to the growing interest in HIPAA.

But there are still many covered entities that have not yet addressed HIPAA. So who is going to pick up the slack on outreach, particularly in underserved and rural communities? There's the good, the bad, and the questionable. Plenty of consultants are spreading the word about HIPAA compliance, but consultants can be costly. In the early days of HIPAA, some consultants simply gave bad advice based on fear and a flurry of miscommunications. Most of those consultants have gone out of business, or they've correctly updated their content.

But we question outreach efforts from some privacy advocacy groups, the same ones that have raised privacy issues for more than a decade. They are a vital contributor to advising policy makers on privacy, and they have raised the profile of privacy nationally and internationally. Always double-check the authenticity of privacy stories. Raise your antenna when you hear results of polls or privacy violations. Ask about the dates of these "violations," especially if they predate HIPAA Privacy Compliance (April 14, 2003).

Truth be told, you are going to end up being your best source of information on HIPAA by engaging in the implementation process, regularly accessing the HIPAA administrative-simplification web sites maintained and updated frequently by HHS, and building your own risk analyses and reviewing and updating them at least yearly. No one knows your business practice better than you. When you ask the right questions, you will get the right results. It is important to remember that, especially when dealing with your vendors.

What to do:

Implement your HIPAA privacy plan.

How to do it:

- Be certain your Notice of Privacy Practices (NPP) tells patients to contact you first if they have a complaint. Provide the name of your contact person in the NPP. You do not have to name the privacy official in the NPP, unless the privacy official is also the contact person. In Chapter 3 of this book, you'll find key Privacy Rule requirements that you must include in your Notice of Privacy Practices.

- Establish and use your policies and procedures for handling patient complaints. They should give you specific guidance on what to do when a patient files a grievance.

- Be informed of patient rights. Read Chapter 3 of this book for details about those rights. Watch for news stories about patient privacy. The patients coming into your office today may know more about privacy than you, and yesterday's news story will be the focus of today's chatter.

- Develop an internal and external communication plan. You can learn more about how to implement a plan by reading Chapter 5 of this book.

- Learn the facts about enforcement. The federal government has sanctions in place for noncompliance. The government has limited resources for enforcement, has announced that it seeks to achieve voluntary compliance, and has tools available for you to attain compliance. But the most important sanction is not going to come from the federal government if you are not compliant. Rather, it is going to come from your patients who will walk away from a noncompliant environment and will pass the word very quickly in the community, as always happens. Compliance will lead to customer satisfaction!

EVERYONE HAS A SPECIFIC ROLE

HIPAA will affect everyone in your office in some way. People with the greatest exposure to patients should carefully read and discuss Chapter 3 of this book. Privacy is what the public finds most interesting in HIPAA regulations, and patients will scrutinize privacy the most, regardless of what they've learned about HIPAA's Privacy Rule. Each person in the office must be held accountable for his or her activity regarding patient privacy. You must have sanctions for your workforce pertaining to privacy breaches and security incidents.

CRITICAL POINT
Know your policies and procedures that sanction staff for privacy breaches and security incidents.

The privacy official, a HIPAA-required position, may feel overworked in the first year, but privacy officials may have a competitive edge in the marketplace because of their insider knowledge of privacy regulations. Seasoned privacy officials have a library of HIPAA books, manuals, tapes, and training materials. If you are assuming the role of a new privacy official, or you have been named the deputy privacy official, this book can be a condensed version of the HIPAA library.

CRITICAL POINT
Patients will be candid about privacy questions with nurses, physician assistants, and nurse practitioners.

Nurses, physician assistants, and nurse practitioners may field the greatest number of privacy and security questions. Patients often feel that these providers have more time to spend with them, and patients are open about asking nurses nonclinical questions. Your nursing staff should be knowledgeable about patient rights so that they won't be caught off guard if someone seems confrontational or ill informed.

Coders will find Chapter 2 of this book to be fairly basic, but everyone in the practice should understand the claims and billing process. Understanding the complexity of coding before and after HIPAA will help you deal with your practice-management software vendor and understand why HIPAA will move health care forward into an efficient electronic age.

The practice's office-management team has the greatest responsibility of all. It is their responsibility to empower and support the privacy official, to approve policies and procedures, and to be disciplined enough to implement them systematically and fairly among themselves and the staff. If there is a privacy breach at the management level, it takes a stalwart privacy official to bring that breach to the boss's attention.

RISK MANAGEMENT

HIPAA presents significant challenges, from disaster-recovery planning to vendor testing and certification to documentation management and system security. But the greatest risk for physicians is that their staff will not have a unified plan of action.

Table 1.5 provides ideas for getting started with HIPAA. Table 1.6 takes planning a bit further. Each step will be discussed in more detail as you read through this book.

TABLE 1.5

What You Can Do If You're Just Getting Started

What to do	How to do it	Follow up
Appoint a privacy official.	The privacy official may be the office manager or another person appointed by the practice.	Build a privacy team to help implement the new regulations.
Review privacy official responsibilities.	See the appendix.	Periodically review list, and train and delegate tasks to privacy team.
Identify protected health information (PHI) in the office and identify privacy risks.	Make a list of where PHI is found and share the list with others who have patient contact.	Ask each person to bring a sample of PHI to a group meeting. No two samples can be alike. Continue to watch for PHI when it's out in the open and available for others to see.

continued

T A B L E 1.5 (continued)

What You Can Do If You're Just Getting Started

What to do	How to do it	Follow up
Write and implement a Notice of Privacy Practices. Include how you will handle patient rights.	Your Medical Society may have one. (See Chapter 3 of this book.)	Train everyone on the contents of this document. It is your privacy promise to patients.
Implement necessary forms.	Ask your attorney about consent and authorization forms.	Train staff when to use these forms. See Chapter 3.
Develop forms for patient requests.	Consult AMA's *Policies and Procedures Desk Reference* (2003) for a complete set of forms.	Customize the forms for your office.
Develop policies and procedures.	Consult AMA's *Policies and Procedures Desk Reference* (2003) for a complete set of forms.	Train your staff on HIPAA policies and procedures.
Determine who can use and disclose PHI.	Identify persons or job titles that must have access to PHI to do their job. Limit access to PHI.	Develop a policy to prevent unauthorized use, including disciplinary actions.
Identify business associates.	Read Chapter 3 of this book.	Obtain signed business-associate agreements.
Train staff on policies, procedures, and Notice of Privacy Practices.	Conduct HIPAA awareness training, then train employees with direct patient contact.	Document physician and staff training. Also document volunteer training.

T A B L E 1.6

What to Do If You've Been Implementing HIPAA

What to do	How to do it	Follow up
Assess where you are with compliance.	Conduct periodic walk-throughs and spot checks.	Identify risk areas and discuss with staff.
Track use and disclosure.	Consult and follow your policies and procedures on use and disclosure. Read Chapter 3 of this book.	Maintain logs and regularly check that they are used.
Analyze security measures.	Conduct a security "gap analysis" or risk analysis.	Develop process to close the gaps and mitigate risk.

T A B L E 1.6 (continued)

What to Do If You've Been Implementing HIPAA

What to do	How to do it	Follow up
Evaluate policies and procedures.	Consult AMA's *Policies and Procedures Desk Reference* (2003) for a complete set of forms.	Expect staff to follow through with policies and procedures. Identify topics that need clarity. Reinforce good behavior.
Train everyone on staff, including volunteers and part-time employees.	Go beyond awareness. Hold a regular training day once a month.	Ask for suggestions on topics. Go beyond what is mandated. Be creative and have fun.
Review budget for privacy and security.	Consult practice-management consultant.	Set aside funds if necessary.
Evaluate Notice of Privacy Practices (NPP), considering changes, revisions, and languages other than English.	Ask if more than 5 percent of your population speaks another language. Put your NPP on audio tape as a literacy aid.	Seek a service to translate NPP into other languages.
Train as new staff comes on board and as existing staff assumes new responsibilities; test personnel periodically.	Provide one-on-one, online, or group training.	Keep a training log, including who attended and topics presented.
Continually implement administrative, technical, and physical safeguards	See Chapters 3 and 4 in this book on safeguards.	Make safeguards a matter of routine.
Sanction employees when there are breaches.	Make sure employees understand expectations. Be fair and equitable.	Retrain employees as needed and test their understanding of policies and procedures at issue.
Evaluate status of patient rights.	Keep records of patient requests. Read Chapter 3 of this book.	Talk to patients if they have concerns.
Track status of signed documents.	Periodically conduct an internal audit of documents.	Put the next review on your calendar.
Consult with business associates on their signed contracts.	Communicate commitment to privacy with your business associates.	Renew contracts on anniversary dates.
Reevaluate and adjust plan.	Document any adjustments and notify staff of changes.	Maintain a log of adjustments and employee communications.
Handle routine and unusual inquiries.	Develop an internal and external communication plan. See Chapter 5 of this book.	Make sure everyone knows the plan, what to say, and what to do.

From Patient Eligibility to Claim Payment

T his chapter focuses on the HIPAA electronics-transaction process from patient eligibility through claim for payment. In most cases, the person or organization managing the eligibility and claim payment process, whether on paper or electronically, does not ever meet the patient. Coders and billing specialists are dependent upon the staff's eyes, ears, and data-collection skills. Once the patient leaves the office, it becomes more difficult to correct incomplete or invalid information.

To help you better understand your role in the patient eligibility to claim payment process, please review each section and watch for ways you can help make the business of health care easier to manage.

CRITICAL POINT
The payment process works when you are the ears, eyes, and data collector before the patient leaves the office.

What You Will Learn in This Chapter:

■ What is involved in the claim payment process.

■ A brief overview of coding and transactions.

■ What are transactions and code sets?

■ Who are coders, and what do they do in your practice?

■ What you can do to help coders do a better job.

■ Likely coding and transaction partners.

■ How information flows in other industries and in health care.

■ The HIPAA-compliant transaction.

■ The certification process and how it affects your cash flow.

■ Questions to ask vendors, payers, billing services, and clearinghouses.

■ Will Administrative Simplification work?

Key Terms

The following definitions have been simplified for ease of understanding. They should not be considered legal definitions of key terms. Find the legal definitions at www.hhs.gov.

Access controls: The policies and procedures you follow to control access, including the verification process and granting or denying the request.

Access request: A request by the patient that your practice permit the patient to inspect or copy records about the patient. This also includes requests made by personal representatives of the patient.

Code set: Any group of codes used to encode data elements, such as tables of terms, medical concepts, medical diagnostic codes, or medical-procedure codes. A code set includes the codes and the descriptors of the codes.

Confidentiality: The condition that data or information is not made available or disclosed to unauthorized persons or processes.

Designated record set: Records maintained by or for a covered entity, including a provider's medical records and billing records about individuals; a health plan's enrollment, payment, claims adjudication, and case or medical management record systems; records used by or for the covered entity to make decisions regarding an individual.

Electronic data interchange (EDI): Intercompany, computer-to-computer transmission of business information in a standard format.

Healthcare clearinghouse: A public or private entity that "processes or facilitates the processing of information received from another entity in a nonstandard format or containing nonstandard data content into standard data elements or a standard transaction"; or "receives a standard transaction from another entity and processes or facilitates the processing of information into nonstandard format or nonstandard data content for a receiving entity."[1]

Individually identifiable information: Information that is used to identify an individual, such as name, address, phone number, e-mail address, photo ID, or driver's license number.

Transaction: An electronic exchange of data between computers in a specified format.

THE ELIGIBILITY TO CLAIM PAYMENT PROCESS

When a patient comes into the medical office, several activities must happen before, during, and after the visit, so that the physician's office can file a claim and get reimbursed for treating the patient. You play an important role in the success of the payment process.

CRITICAL POINT

You play an important role in the success of the payment process.

---

1. 65 *Federal Register* 50366.

FOCUS ON CLAREDI

www.claredi.com

HIPAA Problem

Identify and correct errors before adopting new formats. As a practice that submits electronic transactions, you want to identify and correct errors before entrusting your business to healthcare transactions based entirely on the new, electronic formats. Between April 16, 2003, and October 16, 2003, the Administrative Simplification Compliance Act (ASCA) requires that you test your HIPAA transactions for compliance. WEDI-SNIP (Strategic National Implementation Process) recommends the following seven types of transaction compliance testing:

Type 1: Integrity testing (X12 syntax)

Type 2: Requirement testing (implementation guide syntax)

Type 3: Balancing

Type 4: Situation testing (implementation guide "situational" requirements)

Type 5: Code set testing (CPT®, HCPCS, ICD9, and so on)

Type 6: Specialty or line of business testing

Type 7: Business associate-specific requirements in the implementation guide for Medicare, Medicaid, and several other payers

On a monthly basis (and at least quarterly), you should retest to see if any of the requirements or your own system's capabilities have changed. If you use a new set of codes, retest to make sure the codes will be accepted and that your claim will not be rejected.

HIPAA Solution

You may ask your clearinghouse or other vendors to submit transactions on your behalf to Claredi to have them tested for HIPAA compliance. Even if your vendor or clearinghouse is already Claredi-certified you cannot assume that your transactions will be compliant. It is easy to have your clearinghouse transactions certified by Claredi. Simply establish an account that designates your clearinghouse. Claredi automatically notifies your clearinghouse and requests the clearinghouse to submit files on your behalf. This certification process actually tests your specific capabilities when using the clearinghouse. And because Claredi certifies the specific transactions sent by the clearinghouse on your behalf, both you and your trading partners can be assured that the clearinghouse route you are using is fully compliant.

Typical Users

Hospitals, physicians, other healthcare providers, clearinghouses, vendors, and billing services companies.

continued

Focus on Claredi, continued

Is It Affordable?

Claredi charges a fee. Other companies offer testing at no charge.

Contact Information

Kepa Zubeldia, MD
President and CEO
498 North 900 West, Suite 120
Kaysville, Utah 84037
(801) 444-0339 ext 205

Creating New Patient Records

When a new patient arrives, the front office obtains business, financial, and personal information about the patient, including evidence of insurability by copying information from the patient's healthcare benefits card. Healthcare transactions become difficult to manage when routine information is not provided on arrival. That information, called individually identifiable information, includes:

- Contact information: Name, address, zip code, phone number at work and home, number at mobile phone, and e-mail address.
- Insurance information, including name of policy member and relationship to patient.
  - □ Insurance details such as certificate and group numbers, telephone numbers, copy of insurance card, and secondary insurance if any.
  - □ Medicaid or Medicare numbers, if applicable.
- Driver's license information, state and number.
- Person responsible for payment and the billing address.
- Emergency contact information.
- Health history.

After obtaining this information, the office staff usually runs an eligibility check (described in the next section) to learn details of the patient's coverage, including co-payments and deductible. If you used the telephone or fax, these eligibility inquiries can take 30 to 40 minutes each, and often, the patient had visited the doctor and left the office without the staff knowing whether insurance would pay for treatment. HIPAA's standardized transactions make it much easier for practices to check eligibility electronically.

Verifying Records for Returning Patients

Most practices request that a patient update individually identifiable information each time the patient returns to the office. Follow your office's privacy policy about updating this information. The receptionist can simply ask, "Has any information changed, such as address, phone number, or insurance carrier?"

If "yes," do not ask for the information orally when other patients in the waiting room can hear. Rather, give the patient a printed patient information profile, and ask the patient to verify information or make changes on the form. Be sure to verify that you have the current information on

■ address,

■ phone numbers,

■ emergency contact information,

■ insurance carrier,

■ change in coverage,

■ change in secondary insurance, and

■ changes in payment and billing address.

Whether the patient is new or returning, the information provided (except for the health history) becomes the financial portion of the patient's designated records set. Financial information should be in a separate file on your computer and should be password protected. For more information about HIPAA's computer-security requirements, see Chapters 3 and 4 in this book.

CRITICAL POINT
Financial information should be in a separate file on your computer. The file should be password protected.

Understanding the Medical Record

When the patient and provider meet in the exam room, the provider reviews the information provided on the paper or electronic file to get a quick overview of the patient's personal and health information. During the consultation or exam, the provider makes notes of what was observed, and how the patient will be, or has been, treated medically. This record includes information the patient provides and details the physician observes concerning current symptoms, medical history, requests for or results of lab tests or x-rays, referrals and authorizations, diagnoses and treatment plans.

The physician then either makes a diagnosis or orders more tests and indicates the findings on a "superbill." The front of the superbill typically lists evaluation and management codes that describe the extent of service in the office or the lab tests ordered by the physician, diagnosis, and follow-up appointments, if needed. A list of codes that correspond with the diagnosis are often listed on the back. This list contains the most common illnesses or injuries treated in your own office. Diagnostic codes used in an OB-GYN office, for example, will be different from the codes used in an orthopedic surgeon's office.

When leaving the office, the patient or physician brings the superbill to the front office or billing office, depending on your office structure. Before the patient exits, the billing clerk conducts a final review of information for accuracy. This is the last good opportunity to make sure all the individually identifiable information is correct. Many reimbursement processes, whether paper or electronic, slow down simply because the medical office didn't have current information.

Before the patient exits, staff should double-check the patient's information for accuracy.

Ensuring Quality Control of Health Information

Medical-records and health-information technicians review the medical charts to ensure that they are complete and properly identified and signed and that all necessary information has been stored either on paper or electronically. Sometimes, health-information technicians ask for clarification or get additional information and then assign a code to each diagnosis and procedure. Other times, they may assign the patient to one of several hundred "diagnosis-related groups," or DRGs, which determine the amount the medical office will be reimbursed if the patient is covered by Medicare or other types of insurance plans.

Rather than writing out in detail the physician's notes to be sent to the insurance company, the coding specialist provides key words, along with codes that may include modifiers, so that the payers will know the patient's medical problem and the recommended solution. When the codes for symptom and treatment don't match the diagnosis, the health plan, which may be administered by an insurance company or a third-party administrator, rejects the claim, sending it back to the physician. The physician doesn't get paid until the codes are corrected. When information about the patient is missing, such as plan number, subscriber name, correct address, and phone number, and the coder submits the claim with incorrect information, the payer doesn't recognize the data, rejects the claim, sends it back to the physician, and the physician doesn't get paid until the codes are corrected.

The problems described here highlight one of the advantages of electronic-claims submission. Whether a provider sends an electronic claim directly to a payer or through a clearinghouse, the payer or clearinghouse system that receives the claim generally has built-in editing capabilities that can detect the error and return it in a timely manner to the provider for correction, which speeds up the claims process for both provider and payer.

Coders have a lot of patience to do what they do. They also coordinate knowledge of disease processes with keen investigative instincts to find both the right code and the one that accurately pays for services. Coders are held to a very high ethical standard to avoid accusations of fraud and abuse against the practice. So you should consider celebrating a Take Your Coder to Lunch Day.

Why Coding Matters

Work with a coding specialist to see how you would code the following cases:

Simple

Bobby, a very active 5-year-old, is brought into the office with a sore and swollen wrist. He had been playing in the park with his friends when he fell from the monkey bars and landed on his side. His mother brings him into the hospital, and the doctor sends him downstairs to the lab to get a set of x-rays. The x-rays show that Bobby's arm has a slight fracture. The doctor and mother agree that Bobby's arm needs to be in a cast. He is covered by Blue Cross and Blue Shield, and his family's deductible has been met this year. His mother covers the $10 co-payment.

- What code would you use for the diagnosis and treatment?
- What additional information do you need to complete the coding process?
- What billing and payment problems do you foresee?

Complex

Joseph, an 86-year-old man, was brought into the doctor's office with symptoms that resembled a stroke. He was nauseous, weeping, and confused about his surroundings. He had a fever of 102°, and his blood pressure was 240/160. When you examined him, he was very irritable.

You are quick to call in the doctor, who also examines Joe, and suspects the patient is in the process of having a stroke. Joe is taken by ambulance to the hospital's emergency room.

Days later, after a cardiologist, a neurologist, and a geriatric internist review test results, Joe is diagnosed with a bladder infection. He is treated with heavy doses of penicillin and a prescription to help with memory loss, then released from the hospital. In a follow-up visit a month later, Joe is feeling better. His blood pressure is back within normal range, and he jokes with you about how you look like one of his grandkids.

Joe's primary insurance is Medicare. He also carries supplementary major medical insurance and prescription drug plans through his wife, who is still living.

- Would you code this as a bladder infection or a stroke or complication from dementia?
- What would happen to your billing based on either diagnosis?
- What additional information do you need to complete the coding process?
- What billing and payment problems do you foresee?

A BRIEF OVERVIEW OF TRANSACTIONS

A transaction in the world of e-commerce is an electronic exchange of data between computers in a specified format. You conduct transactions every day. For example, you want to withdraw money from an automatic teller machine. You cannot get convenient access to your home bank, so you visit another bank's ATM. You insert your card into an ATM, and the electronic reader recognizes data on the magnetic strip. When you enter your personal identification number (PIN), you are telling the computer of the bank you are visiting to communicate with the computer at your home bank. If you agree to pay a small fee for the transaction, and both computers agree you have money in the home bank, the visiting bank releases funds and electronically withdraws funds from your home account. Because bank computers use a standard set of data, this transaction can be sent and received through any ATM in the world.

You make similar transactions when you shop online via the Internet to purchase a book, an airline ticket, or furniture. In each transaction, you provide accurate and complete information into the computer. Then using electronic data interchange, one computer exchanges information with another computer without human involvement to complete the transaction.

A BRIEF OVERVIEW OF CODING

In its simplest form, codes are published sets of numbers that people and computers use to identify a patient's diagnosis, the physician's recommended procedures to relieve pain and, if possible, heal the patient, and the purchase of medical equipment and pharmaceuticals. Codes evolved from a murky set of patient and payment miscommunications, which eventually provided the basis for standards that tracked common illness and treatment.

In the late 1800s, there was little consistency in patient care. Patients purchased everything from castor oil to candy for its medicinal value. One bottle of "Milton," for example, healed cuts and abrasions, unstopped a stuffy nose, eliminated bad breath, cured tired feet, removed stains, cleaned tiles, removed paint, and shined woodwork. In 1913, the 60-year-old American Medical Association launched a war on quackery with a campaign known as "sickness insurance." But inconsistency still ruled. One physician would call a disease "consumption," while another called it "tuberculosis" and sometimes "cancer."

Health insurance was relatively new, but few could afford it. Many didn't see the need for it. Still in its infancy, the health-insurance industry faced its own problems. Patients filed their own claims based on physician notes and billing charges. Insurers faced nightmares of fraud, medical and personal misinformation, and appropriateness of care.

There were few standards for reimbursement. One insurer's marketing plan might get a reputation for reimbursing much more than a competitor, or another insurer would randomly deny a percentage of all health claims. After the Depression of the 1930s, the federal government sought to regulate the payment process with controversial "federally funded medical benefits legislation" for every individual and any dependents covered by Social Security.

The California Medical Association, working with Blue Cross and Blue Shield, launched a campaign for voluntary insurance. As voluntary insurance took hold nationwide, the Health Care Finance Administration (HCFA) and the National Center for Health Statistics, agencies within what is today the Department of Health and Human Services (HHS), established one set of codes so that payers and providers could identify an illness and the treatment for that illness using standard codes.

The unified coding system solved, and continues to solve, several problems:

■ Coding brings consistency to the language used to identify diseases.

■ Codes help HHS track illnesses and outbreak of diseases and will be increasingly important in this age of potential bioterrorism.

■ Codes help HHS determine which parts of the country need additional support.

■ Codes help pharmaceutical companies determine how their remedies most likely are used.

■ Codes help payers and providers make broad decisions about quality of care.

■ Codes help physicians and payers communicate in a common language so that physicians can get reimbursed.

But once the federal government established codes, so did states and counties. Medicaid, Medicare, and insurance plans for military personnel established sets of codes. Physicians voluntarily took over the process of claims billing and payment to effect continuity and accuracy. Physicians hired professional coders or contracted with a billing company so that the office staff could get paid for services. As the payment process grew, payers created additional proprietary codes, and new procedures demanded a new set of codes, until the average doctor's office searched through about 20 sets of diagnostic and billing codes just to process claims and receive payment.

For everything to move speedily through the claims payment reimbursement system, coders had to read and understand the physician's handwritten notes, understand the diagnosis and treatment plans so that they would match, correctly enter all codes, and send the claim to the appropriate payer. In the early 1990s, chances of that happening accurately were only about 15 percent, for many reasons, nearly all of them human errors: Patients didn't carry health insurance cards. Patients either didn't know their coverage or provided incomplete personal and insurance information. The physician's notes were hard to read. A billing-company

FOCUS ON PHOENIX HEALTH SYSTEMS

www.phoenixhealth.com

HIPAA Problem

A business office is transitioning from using nonstandard healthcare transactions to HIPAA-standard transactions. There is risk of lost or compromised data from insecure computer systems and disasters. The office must ensure the privacy of personal health information; keep abreast of HIPAA updates and guidance; and educate all workforce members about privacy and security requirements. The office must also keep abreast of HIPAA-regulatory developments and updates.

HIPAA Solution

Phoenix Health Systems offers the following HIPAA solutions:

- three free e-newsletters (HIPAAdvisory, HIPAAlert, and HIPAANotes) that provide news and timely guidance on HIPAA issues;
- an extensive Web site (HIPAAdvisory.com) that includes a wide variety of whitepapers, news items, and HIPAA how-to information;
- monthly public audio conferences on key HIPAA compliance issues; and
- a free daily e-mail discussion forum (HIPAAlive) on HIPAA compliance issues that has over 5,000 participants.

In addition, Phoenix Health Systems

- acts as a third-party management firm and outsources consultants to upgrade and manage information systems for healthcare provider organizations;
- trains healthcare executives, professionals, and other members of the work-force in privacy and security requirements and solutions;
- provides HIPAA Privacy compliance support, including privacy policies and compliance validation; and
- provides information security solutions, including risk analysis, solutions planning and implementation, security policies, and disaster recovery planning.

Typical Users

Hospitals, integrated delivery systems, and ancillary physician groups.

Is It Affordable?

The newsletters are free and contain valuable HIPAA information. Onsite consulting arrangements are customized to clients' needs.

Contact Information

D'Arcy Guerin Gue
Executive Vice President
Phoenix Health Systems
9200 Wrightman Road, Suite 400
Montgomery Village, MD 20886
(301) 869-7300
dgue@phoenixhealth.com

employee would key in one wrong number. Any single event could upset the patient-to-payment process.

In the information-technology decades of the 1980s and 1990s, software vendors developed innovative solutions to track and manage billing and payment problems for physicians and to help them run their practices more efficiently. But in the mid-1990s, more than 400 different claim-form types were still in use to seek reimbursement for healthcare services.

As electronic transactions began to take hold in the healthcare industry, vendors developed claim forms, vendor-specific and payer-specific codes, referral forms, prior authorizations, and explanations of benefits/explanations of payment (EOB/EOP). Yet the healthcare industry did not standardize these administrative functions—until HIPAA.

HIPAA TRANSACTIONS AND CODE SET STANDARDS

HIPAA Administrative Simplification was enacted in August 1996. Less than two years later, in May 1998, proposed transaction and code set standards were published by the federal government. On August 17, 2000, final transaction and code set standards were published by the federal government,[2] with compliance required by covered entities on October 16, 2002, except for small health plans, which had an additional year to comply (October 16, 2003).

In early 2001, there was considerable discussion in the healthcare industry that the October 2002 date did not give enough time to health plans and healthcare providers to achieve compliance. As a result, Congress in late 2001 enacted the Administrative Simplification Compliance Act of 2001 (ASCA),[3] which provided for an automatic extension to October 16, 2003, for covered entities to comply. This is the same date small health plans had to comply with Transactions and Code Sets.

CRITICAL POINT

Physicians with 10 or more full-time equivalent employees are required to file electronically for Medicare reimbursement. All physicians who file claims electronically, regardless of size, are covered entities and must comply.

ASCA included two important provisions besides the extension. First, in exchange for the extension, all covered entities that applied for the extension were required to begin testing of the electronic transaction and code set standards by April 16, 2003. Second, with regard to Medicare claims only, physicians with 10 or more full-time equivalent employees were required to file electronically for Medicare reimbursement, unless there is

---

2. 65 *Federal Register* 50312.

3. Public Law 107-105, December 27, 2001. 115 Stat 1003.

"no method available for the submission of claims in an electronic form."[4]

In this regard, it is important to note that there is no small-practice exclusion except for Medicare claims.[5] Any physician, healthcare practitioner, or healthcare facility, irrespective of size, that submits even one electronic claim for other than Medicare reimbursement is a covered entity and must use the electronic transaction and code set standards. The choice to submit non–Medicare claims electronically, or to initiate several other standard transactions electronically, is up to the healthcare provider.

HHS has published a set of three questions,[6] and if you answer yes to all of them, you are a covered entity. (See Figure 1.1 in Chapter 1.)

If the answer is yes to all three questions, the respondent is a covered healthcare provider. If the answer to any question is no, the respondent is not a covered healthcare provider.

Answering this series of questions is important for determining HIPAA compliance. For example, if a physician's office does not initiate any covered transactions in electronic form, it does not need to comply with the Transactions and Code Sets Rule.

COVERED TRANSACTIONS

HIPAA transaction standards are the rules that standardize the electronic exchange of administrative information. Healthcare providers must comply by October 16, 2003, with six sets of rules, including four of the eight covered-transaction standards:

■   General provisions

■   Code sets

---

4.   115 Stat 1007.

5.   This answer is given to the question: "Do small health care providers have to comply with the transaction standards adopted under HIPAA?" in Department of Health and Human Services, FAQs on Transaction Standards, February 2002: "All covered entities (health plans, health care clearinghouses, and certain health care providers), regardless of size, must comply with the transactions standards adopted under HIPAA: A covered health care provider…is one who transmits any health information in electronic form in connection with a [covered] transaction. Some small health care providers do not conduct any business transactions electronically and do not use a service to do so on their behalf. Such health care providers are not subject to the requirements of the transaction standards. HIPAA distinguishes only health plans on the basis of size, giving small health plans an extra year to comply." Also see Answer ID 928 to question 14, "Are small providers exempt from HIPAA?", at Centers for Medicare and Medicaid Services's Frequently Asked Questions (FAQ) section (www.cms.hhs.gov).

6.   See "Covered Entity Charts," September 27, 2002. On the CMS web site, choose *HIPAA* under *Programs*, then *HIPAA Administrative Simplification*, and, finally, *Covered Entity Decision Tools*. Visit www.cms.hhs.gov.

■ Four transaction standards:
  ☐ Healthcare claims or equivalent encounter information.
  ☐ Eligibility for a health plan.
  ☐ Referral certification and authorization.
  ☐ Healthcare claim status.

Each is discussed in turn.

General Provisions

The value of using the transaction standards is that everyone communicates in a common language: covered entities engaged in a healthcare transaction, such as a physician and payer handling a claim, or a physician inquiring of a health plan about a plan beneficiary's eligibility. As a result, covered entities are prohibited from changing data definitions or other data specifications in conducting the transaction.

To facilitate the use of the standards, implementation guides are available from several sources.[7] Unlike the implementation specifications discussed in Chapter 3 of this book and many of the implementation specifications discussed in Chapter 4, transaction implementation specifications are highly technical. Your practice-management system may already include the transactions, and your vendor for that system is probably changing the system transaction specifications so that they are HIPAA compliant.

Be sure to check with your vendor and get verification in writing that transactions are based on HIPAA standards because, as the covered entity, you ultimately are responsible for HIPAA compliance. Your system vendor is a business associate under HIPAA and must provide you with assurance that working on your behalf it is using HIPAA-compliant specifications. But compliance is based solely on implementation of standards by covered entities. The term is not directly relevant to vendors and applies only indirectly to business associates, through you as the covered entity.

If you use the four transactions electronically that are listed above, you must use the transaction standard adopted by the Secretary of Health and Human Services, with two exceptions.

First, you may use a business associate such as a healthcare clearinghouse to conduct the transaction on your behalf. This is the situation in many physician offices. If the practice does so, you must require the clearinghouse, your business associate, to follow the rules as if you were conducting the transaction

If you partner with a clearinghouse as a business associate, the clearinghouse can receive a nonstandard transaction (for example, nonstandard data content or nonstandard data format) from you but must send it on to another covered entity, such as a health plan (payer) or another clearing-

---

7. Implementation guides for each of the standard transactions are available from www.wpc-edi.org, which also is linked from HHS and WEDI web sites.

house, using the standard transaction. Similarly, as your business associate, the clearinghouse could receive a standard transaction from a payer (for example, a claim status response or remittance advice) and send it to you as a nonstandard transaction. Either way, you will pay for the conversion, which will be outlined as a value-added service in your business agreement with the clearinghouse.

The other exception is concerned with what is called direct data entry (DDE), which takes place when you directly enter the data into a payer's computer through a "dumb" terminal or enter data into a payer's computer file via the Internet. Larger physician practices and hospitals that send many claims to one payer may use DDE. The Internet provides further opportunity for small practices to enter such claims. If you use DDE, you still must meet the data-content rules specified in the transaction standard, but the data-format rule is not required.

Examples of DDE include the following.

■ You conduct an ATM transaction with your bank at one of its terminals. If you use another bank's terminal, it is not a direct data entry. It is a transaction that goes through one or more network connections.

■ You connect via the Internet to your credit-card company to make a direct payment electronically. If you connected to your bank via the Internet to make the payment, it is direct data entry to the bank to conduct the transaction but not to the credit-card company.

■ If you examine a number of ATM, bank, or credit-card sites via the Internet, you'll notice that the formats are different, based on designs and needs of the financial institutions. To conduct the transactions in the examples, however, the data-content requirements would be standardized. Otherwise, networked transactions would be difficult to conduct and complete.

Direct data entry using "dumb" terminals has been around a long time, but use of the Internet for DDE is a work in progress. As a result, there is considerable discussion about its future,[8] and DDE rules may be modified. We recommend that you periodically review the web site of the Centers for Medicare and Medicaid Services (CMS) for changes on DDE use, and ask your vendors or payers if you are using DDE.

---

8. During its March 2003 meeting in Chicago, Ill, the Workgroup for Electronic Data Interchange (WEDI) held a policy advisory group (PAG) meeting with healthcare industry representatives, including the federal government, to identify issues and develop recommendations pertaining to DDE use. See www.wedi.org. Also see North Carolina Healthcare Information and Communications Alliance (NCHICA), Transactions, Codes, and Identifiers Work Group, "Direct Data Entry Principles," March 5, 2003, pp. 1-3, which is available at www.nchica.org/hipaaresources.

FOCUS ON WORKGROUP FOR ELECTRONIC DATA INTERCHANGE (WEDI)

www.wedi.org

HIPAA Problem

More than 400 software systems translate transactions and code sets into standard formats. An estimated 30 billion healthcare transactions are routed through the translation process each year, which means more than 25 cents of every dollar spent on healthcare is spent on administrative costs.

In addition, Administrative Simplification must be implemented system-wide in a $1.4 trillion-per-year market, and payers, providers, clearinghouses, and proprietary, state, and local coding systems must agree on one set of standards.

HIPAA Solution

The Workgroup for Electronic Data Interchange activities include:

- fostering widespread support for the adoption of electronic commerce within healthcare;

- bringing together more than 6,000 payers, providers, clearinghouses, and state, local, and proprietary systems through various WEDI forums to eliminate multiple transaction formats in favor of industry standards;

- reducing transaction costs in health care by moving from a paper transaction system to an electronic transaction system; and

- serving as the strategic advisor to the secretary of HHS on the implementation process.

Typical Users

Individuals, providers, payers, payer organizations, government organizations, standards organizations, vendors, consumer organizations, and affiliates.

Is It Affordable?

Membership is affordable and reasonably escalates according to an organization's annual revenues.

Contact Information

Lisa Berretta
Director of Administration
Workgroup for Electronic Data Interchange
12020 Sunrise Valley Drive, Suite 100
Reston, VA 20191
(703) 391-2716

Code Sets

As we mentioned at the beginning of this chapter, code sets define much of the medical information or data content used in the transactions. A code set is defined as "any set of codes used to encode data elements, such as tables of terms, medical concepts, medical diagnostic codes, or medical procedure codes. A code set includes the codes and the descriptors of the codes."[9]

Local codes have been eliminated. Many of these were developed to respond to specific payer data requirements. Retaining them would contradict the basis for using a standard set of codes.

The code sets fall into four categories:

- Coding systems for diseases, impairments, or other health-related problems.

- Causes of injury, disease, impairment, or other health-related problems.

- Actions taken to prevent, diagnose, treat, or manage diseases, injuries, and impairments.

- Any substances, equipment, supplies, or other items used to perform these actions.

There are six defined code sets that underlie the transaction standards.

- *International Classification of Diseases,* ninth edition, *Clinical Modification* (ICD-9-CM), volumes 1 and 2, as updated and distributed by HHS,[10] for the following conditions:
  - ☐ diseases;
  - ☐ injuries;
  - ☐ impairments;
  - ☐ other health-related problems and their manifestations; and
  - ☐ causes of injury, disease, impairment, or other health-related problems.

- *International Classification of Diseases,* ninth edition, *Clinical Modification,* (ICD-9-CM), volume 3, Procedures, as updated and distributed by HHS,[11] for procedures or actions taken for diseases, injuries, and impairments on hospital inpatients reported by hospitals such as
  - ☐ prevention,
  - ☐ diagnosis,
  - ☐ treatment, and
  - ☐ management.

---

9. 65 *Federal Register* 50367.

10. Information on computer files of the ICD-9-CM is available via the Internet at the US Department of Commerce's National Technical Information Service (NTIS). Go to www.ntis.gov, and go to *Product Families: Health.*

11. *Ibid.*

■ National Drug Codes (NDC), as maintained and distributed by HHS,[12] for reporting by retail pharmacies on drugs and biologics.[13]

■ Code on Dental Procedures and Nomenclature, as maintained and distributed by the American Dental Association,[14] for dental services.

■ The combination of Health Care Financing Administration Common Procedure Coding System (HCPCS), as maintained and distributed by HHS,[15] and *Current Procedural Terminology*, fourth edition (CPT-4), as maintained and distributed by the American Medical Association, for physician and other healthcare services, including, but not limited to

   ☐ physician services,

   ☐ physical and occupational therapy services,

   ☐ radiologic procedures,

   ☐ clinical laboratory tests,

   ☐ other medical diagnostic procedures, and

   ☐ transportation services including ambulance.

■ The Healthcare Common Procedure Coding System (HCPCS), as maintained and distributed by HHS,[16] for all other substances, equipment, supplies, or other items used in healthcare services, with the exception of drugs and biologics, including, but not limited to

   ☐ medical supplies,

   ☐ orthodontic and prosthetic devices, and

   ☐ durable medical equipment.

An issue with regard to use of NDC and HCPCS codes was resolved with the February 20, 2003, publication of the final rule.[17] When the final Transaction and Code Sets Rule was published in August 2000, the rule said

---

12. Information on the National Drug Code is available via the Internet at the US Food and Drug Administration's Center for Drug Evaluation and Research (CDER) at www.fda.gov/cder/ndc/.

13. Retail pharmacies are required to use the NDC codes. The final rule of August 17, 2000, was modified on February 20, 2003, to eliminate the NDC standard for "reporting drugs and biologics in all non-retail pharmacy transactions."

14. The American Dental Association in Chicago, Ill, can be reached via the Internet at www.ada.org.

15. Information on computer files of the Health Care Financing Administration Common Procedure Coding System (HCPCS) is available via the Internet at the US Department of Commerce's National Technical Information Service (NTIS). Go to www.ntis.gov, and go to *Product Families: Health*.

16. *Ibid*.

17. Department of Health and Human Services, Office of the Secretary, "45 CFR Part 162: Health Insurance Reform: Modifications to Electronic Data Transaction Standards and Code Sets," *Federal Register,* v. 68, n. 34, February 20, 2003, pp. 8381-8399.

that retail pharmacy and nonretail (professional, institutional, and dental) standard transactions had to use the NDC. In the proposed modification published in May 2002, the rule was amended so that the NDC would be the standard code used for retail pharmacy transactions and HCPCS the standard used for nonretail pharmacy transactions.

The final modification does not establish a standard for nonretail pharmacy transactions but permits use of either NDC or HCPCS as consistent with standard transaction implementation guides and as specified by health plans in trading-partner agreements.[18] This use of code sets may be of limited applicability in most physician offices, because physicians generally give the prescription form to the patient to be filled in a retail pharmacy. Business managers in physician practices who execute agreements, however, should be cognizant of this exception to the code set specification standard for nonretail pharmacy transactions.

CRITICAL POINT

The code set rules will have greater meaning to your vendor, but you should be aware of the rules and the code values that are germane to your practice.

Code set rules will have greater meaning to your vendor, but you must be aware of the rules and the code values that are germane to your practice. What is important is that when physicians in Minneapolis or Albany or Seattle treat a patient for a cold, they can all use the same set of diagnostic and treatment codes to submit a claim for reimbursement, regardless of what health-benefit plans their patients carry. Sounds logical, and even sort of efficient, doesn't it?

Administrative simplification to coders means that their jobs are likely to become easier. In "downsizing" the transactions into one uniform set, though, your office may need to change some administrative processes and also invest in enhancements to an existing practice-management system or even a new system. Before executing new or amended business associate agreements, to be consistent with HIPAA transaction and code set standards, ask your vendor what is being done about standardizing code sets. Get the response in writing. Remember, your practice, as the covered entity, is responsible for making sure that the HIPAA electronic transactions that you transmit are compliant with the HIPAA standards.

CRITICAL POINT

Before creating a new HIPAA business associate agreement, ask your vendor what is being done about standardizing your code sets, and get the response in writing.

---

18. 68 *Federal Register* 8386.

Transaction Standards

As we said at the beginning of this chapter, when a patient visits your practice, you will carry out several administrative functions, including compiling patient-identifiable information with health-related information to create protected health information. A HIPAA transaction contains patient-identifiable information and health-related information using information from the code sets. Therefore, the transaction contains details about the patient and the patient's health that can be used to identify that person. If the transaction is sent electronically to fulfill an administrative function, it must be transmitted using the standard.

For healthcare providers such as physician practices, four standards of the eight in the HIPAA Transactions Rule apply to administrative processes. The practice may choose to use all, some, or none. These standards are

- health claims or equivalent encounter information,
- eligibility for a health plan,
- health claim status, and
- referral certification and authorization.

Before we turn to these transactions, we'll remind you that there are four other Transaction Rule standard transactions that generally will not apply to or be used by a physician's practice—enrollment and disenrollment in a health plan, health care payment and remittance advice, health plan premium payments, and coordination of benefits. However, the practice should bear in mind two things about these four standards: They complete the reimbursement process initiated using the standard transactions on the provider side. Payers have to be able to receive your standard transactions, if you so choose to send them, and they also must be able to respond using their four standard transactions. Together, this process when fully implemented should lead to measurable improvement in the speed of transactions and in their resolution.

Health Claims or Equivalent Encounter Information

According to the final rule,[19] the claims or equivalent encounter information transaction is defined by the transmission of either of the following.

- A request from a healthcare provider to a health plan to obtain payment for health care. The request includes necessary accompanying information, known as the data content.
- If there is no direct claim for payment, because the healthcare provider rendered services under a health plan benefits contract other than

---

19. 65 *Federal Register* 50370.

FOCUS ON MEDICAL MANAGER

www.medicalmanager.com

HIPAA Problem

- Claims processing can be costly and time-consuming, including dealing with repeated insurance claim follow-ups and patient inquires.
- Verification of HIPAA privacy requests from government agencies.
- Completing explanation of benefits (EOB) and sending them to appropriate recipient.
- Managing specific privacy authorizations and producing them for patient signature.
- Producing accounting of disclosure reports.

HIPAA Solution

The Medical Manager® Version 10 and Intergy® practice management solutions from Medical Manager Health Systems (MMHS) assist providers in managing information related to consent authorization and disclosure requirements. To assist providers in complying with the HIPAA Transaction and Code Set Regulation, MMHA offers Medical Manager Network Services (MMNS), a total EDI solution. MMNS collaborates with its own dedicated clearinghouse and communicates with payers on behalf of physicians for maximum cash flow solutions.

MMNS services to providers include:

- access to insurance providers, laboratories, pharmacies, and hospitals;
- online HIPAA-compliance inquires, such as eligibility requests, eligibility rosters, and pre-admission certifications;
- remittances and payments received and posted automatically;
- checks status of patient referrals;
- insurance eligibility requests sent automatically to the payer;
- quickly authorizes credit-card payments to ensure collection and reduce billing costs.

Typical Users

Small physician practices to large physician networks.

Is It Affordable?

MMNS is available for minimal up-front cost to MMHS customers and an affordable per-physician, per-month flat rate.

Contact Information

Contact a MMNS representative at (800) 877-3150.

charges or reimbursement rates for specific services, such as an HMO contract, the transaction is the transmission of encounter information for the purpose of reporting health care.

The transactions standard for claims and each of the other standards that we discuss below have a common origin, created under auspices of the American National Standards Institute (ANSI), a voluntary organization dating from 1918 that coordinates the development of standards in the United States.[20] Associated with each standard transaction is an implementation guide. These are available via the Internet from Washington Publishing Company (www.wpi-edi.org). These implementation guides are important documents and give instructions on the implementation specifications for the transaction standards. These implementation guides are lengthy and technical and you can happily refer them to your systems and software vendors.

A Note to Your Vendor

The standard for the professional component of the claim-encounter transaction, required on or after October 15, 2003, is the Accredited Standards Committee (ASC) X12N 837—Health Care Claims: Professional, volumes 1 and 2, version 4010, May 2000, Washington Publishing Company, 004010X098, and *Addenda to Health Care Claims: Professional,* volumes 1 and 2, version 4010, October 2002, Washington Publishing Company, 004010x098A1.[21]

Your information management or coding staff will tell you the claim-encounter transaction is the most frequently used HIPAA transaction. This claim is how the practice gets reimbursed. In this section, we won't go into details about how to file or understand payer-split claims. The *Field Guide to HIPAA Implementation* (AMA Press, 2002) is a great resource for those transaction details.

To keep it simple, the HIPAA professional claim encounter, the most widely used claim, requires four levels of information—the person or entity doing the billing, the person or entity to be paid, information about the claim, and information about the service. HIPAA allows up to 50 service lines in which your office inserts procedure codes. Note that all this information is gathered by people like you in the office before getting to the coder or billing company.

After successfully filing a claim, your office receives a remittance advice transaction that describes the payer's reimbursement. When using this HIPAA transaction, the office becomes more efficient due to easier billing, fewer resubmitted claims, and no paper coordination of benefits.

---

20. In 1979, ANSI chartered the Accredited Standards Committee (ASC) X12 to develop electronic data interchange standards for industry that have business transactions needs. The HIPAA Administrative Simplification standards were an outgrowth of work done by the Insurance Subcommittee of ASC X12, X12N.

21. 68 *Federal Register* 8398.

Eligibility for a Health Plan, Inquiry, and Response

According to the final rule,[22] the eligibility for a health-plan transaction is defined as the transmission of either of the following:

- an inquiry from a healthcare provider to a health plan, or from one health plan to another health plan, to obtain any of the following information about a benefit plan for an enrollee: eligibility to receive health care under the health plan, coverage of health care under the health plan, or benefits associated with the benefit plan; or

- a response from a health plan to a healthcare provider's (or another health plan's) inquiry.

A Note to Your Vendor

The standard for the professional component of the eligibility inquiry/response transaction, required on or after October 15, 2003, is the Accredited Standards Committee (ASC) X12N 270/271—Health Care Eligibility Benefit Inquiry and Response, version 4010, May 2000, Washington Publishing Company, 004010X092, and Addenda to Health Care Eligibility Benefit Inquiry and Response, version 4010, October 2002, Washington Publishing Company, 004010X092A1.[23]

HIPAA allows the provider to inquire (or ask) for information about patients in a batch (all at once) or individually.

Ideally, the financial staff conducts eligibility inquiries to determine financial risk the day before the patient arrives. An eligibility inquiry allows you to ask and receive information about the patient's coverage so that the physician and patient team can determine the best clinical and financial solution.

In the past, physician offices dreaded making eligibility inquiries because of the large amounts of time the staff had to spend on the telephone. HIPAA's standardized transactions should provide responses to eligibility inquiries in real time so that the practice can quickly know general details about the patient's insurance. In fact, in several years, it will likely be routine to swipe a health-plan beneficiary's benefit card much the way a credit card is swiped today and have immediate access to a beneficiary's plan benefits either directly off a memory chip or stripe on the card or via a standard transaction over a clearinghouse network to the benefit-plan computer database.

To conduct a HIPAA eligibility inquiry and response transaction, you first need four categories of information:

- **Payer:** The group or organization that holds the eligibility information.
- **Provider:** The group or person making the inquiry.

---

22. 65 *Federal Register* 50370-50371.

23. 68 *Federal Register* 8398.

■ **Subscriber/patient:** The information about the person who requests treatment.

■ **Benefits of the subscriber/patient:** The service provided.

Armed with information from these four categories, the office can create three levels of inquiries. Table 2.1 recaps inquiries and responses to them.

T A B L E 2.1

Levels of Inquiries

Inquiry Level	Inquiry	Response
Level 1	*Is this patient a member of your plan?* A yes or no answer is the bare minimum that payers are required to provide. Payers are unlikely to provide you with a Level 2 response if you ask only a Level 1 question.	If yes, indicate this response on patient record. If no, recheck patient data. One wrong number will produce a "no" response. If still no, ask patient for updated insurance info.
Level 2	*Is this type of service covered?* Service types may include: medical care, surgical, consultation, diagnostic x-ray, radiation therapy, anesthesia, surgical assistance, chiropractic, preadmission testing, diagnostic dental, home health care, hospital (inpatient), major medical, and acupuncture.	A good inquiry can produce the following response: 1. Co-pay amount. 2. Deductible amount. 3. Co-insurance percent. 4. Out-of-pocket expenses. 5. Subscriber last and first name, date of birth, ID. 6. Patient first and last name, date of birth, and ID. 7. Effective dates of coverage for service. 8. Primary-care provider. 9. Other payers.
Level 3	*Is this specific procedure code/ diagnosis covered?* A Level 3 inquiry requires a specific diagnosis or procedure code. Use this advanced inquiry if the patient has a known diagnosis or you know the procedure the patient is coming in to receive. This inquiry will likely require the most modifications to your Practice Management scheduler module.	Rejection possibilities: ■ You have not correctly identified yourself to the payer. ■ Bad dates in the inquiry. ■ Missing or invalid patient information. ■ No coverage at time of service. ■ Service is inconsistent.

Ask your practice management vendor if you can conduct a HIPAA eligibility inquiry and response transaction. Some questions to determine whether or not you can include:

1. How will the claim-status inquiry and response streamline my claim-status process?
2. Does my system allow me to submit and receive claim-status transactions?
3. Does my system have all of the necessary codes in the four information categories?
4. Does my system process the response and update the status of the claim in my accounts receivable?
5. How quickly should I get a response if I use the HIPAA eligibility inquiry?
6. Can I set up the system to "age" submitted claims? For example, if claims are older than 20 days, can I submit a claim-status inquiry?

As with all inquiries with your vendors (business associates), be sure to get responses in writing.

Healthcare Claim Status, Inquiry, and Response

According to the final rule,[24] a healthcare claim-status transaction is defined as the transmission of either:

- an inquiry to determine the status of a healthcare claim, or
- a response about the status of a healthcare claim.

A Note to Your Vendor

The standard for the claim-status inquiry/response transaction, required on or after October 15, 2003, is the Accredited Standards Committee (ASC) X12N 276/277—*Health Care Claim Status Request and Response*, version 4010, May 2000, Washington Publishing Company, 004010X093, and *Addenda to Health Care Claim Status Request and Response,* version 4010, October 2002, Washington Publishing Company, 004010X093A1.[25]

CRITICAL POINT

The claim-status inquiry/response transaction may be the most important electronic transaction that your medical office will implement.

This transaction may be the most important electronic transaction that any provider can implement. Once you file the claim, your interest is in receiving timely reimbursement. In the paper-transaction world, it is not unusual to have missing or incorrect information on a claim submission. Many of the front-end tools that clearinghouses and billing services use

---

24. 65 *Federal Register* 50371.

25. 68 *Federal Register* 8398.

FOCUS ON NORTH CAROLINA HEALTHCARE INFORMATION AND COMMUNICATIONS ALLIANCE (NCHICA)

www.nchica.org

HIPAA Problem

Electronic transactions threaten to interrupt the cash flow of the physician practice; lack of awareness of the physician community and unwarranted reliance on vendors to "fix" HIPAA for them; and physicians adopting nonstandard practices in privacy and security issues could leave the practice in the cold when it comes to showing conformance with mandates.

HIPAA Solution

A credible organization with diverse membership and neutral atmosphere, NCHICA was one of the first collaborative efforts formed at the state/regional level to solve compliance issues. NCHICA offers:

- model documents that save legal expenses for physicians available free at www.nchica.org;
- educational, professional development for physicians' trading partners (payers) and business associates (vendors, attorneys, and consultants);
- two gap analysis software tools, HIPAA EarlyView Privacy 2.0 and HIPAA EarlyView Security 2.0; and
- a unique environment in which more than 280 providers, clinics, vendors, attorneys, consultants, payers, and state and local agencies can collaborate to discuss HIPAA compliance and standards and develop best practices and strategies that work for all.

Typical Users

Practice managers, office managers, providers, privacy officials, and vendors.

Is It Affordable?

Membership is affordable and scalable by size of organization. HIPAA Early View Privacy 2.0 and HIPAA Early View Security 2.0 are inexpensive.

Contact Information

Gina VanBenthuysen,
Membership Coordinator, NCHICA
PO Box 13048
Research Triangle Park, NC 27709
(919) 558-925
gina@nchica.org

today for electronic claims identify and mitigate the time-consuming chores of fixing those errors.

But many times you do not know the status of a claim. You should be aware that payers who respond to claim-status inquiries from providers and from beneficiaries awaiting reimbursement of healthcare payments that they have made to providers find claim-status responses as costly as you do in terms of time expended that could have been more productive elsewhere.

Perhaps the claim-status inquiry and response using the electronic standard will prove of significant benefit to both payers and providers in eliminating time spent on the telephone, which is labor intensive and costly for both parties. Computer-to-computer request and response transactions about claim status save time and dollar resources for your staff and the payer.

Referral Certification and Authorization

According to the final rule,[26] the referral certification and authorization transaction is defined as any of the following transmissions:

■ a request for the review of health care to obtain an authorization for the health care;

■ a request to obtain authorization for referring an individual to another healthcare provider; and

■ a response to a request described herein.

A Note to Your Vendor

The standard for the professional component of the referral certification and authorization transaction, required on or after October 15, 2003, is the Accredited Standards Committee (ASC) X12N 278—*Health Care Services Review—Request for Review and Response,* version 4010, May 2000, Washington Publishing Company, 004010X094, and *Addenda to Health Care Services Review—Request for Review and Response,* version 4010, October 2002, Washington Publishing Company, 004010X094A1.[27]

The "referrals and prior authorizations" is the best transaction to getting the staff back to delivering patient care. This transaction facilitates exchange of information with other physicians such as specialists concerning a patient's treatment, and it also opens electronic communications with health plans concerning additional treatment or medication than originally approved.

Like the claim-status inquiry, this type of communication is more efficient and labor saving than having to do such communication on paper or by telephone.

---

26. 65 *Federal Register* 50371.

27. 68 *Federal Register* 8398.

IDENTIFIERS

Four identifiers are specified in the Transaction Rule:

- the National Employer Identifier,
- the National Provider Identifier,
- the National Health-Plan Identifier, and
- the National Individual Identifier.

When in place, these identifiers become the numeric or alphanumeric addresses for participants in healthcare sponsorship, payment, and treatment. For example, claims are to be submitted to primary payers first, so the health plan that is primary would be the numeric or alphanumeric address to which the claim is sent by the provider. If there were coordination of benefits, the first payer, following its adjudication and payment, would submit the claim to the secondary payer, using its unique identifier address, and so on. Each payer would submit electronic remittance advice using the standard to the provider using the provider's unique identifier.

As of March 2003, when this chapter was being written, only one of the identifiers, the National Employer Identifier, was a final rule. Its effective date was July 30, 2002. Covered entities must comply by July 30, 2004, and small health plans with receipts under $5 million have an extra year to comply, by July 30, 2005. The National Employer Identifier is the Employer Identification Number (EIN). The National Provider Identifier was proposed in May 1998, and a final rule may be published in 2003. The National Health-Plan Identifier in proposed form may also be published in 2003.

The National Individual Identifier is controversial. Congress has put a hold on any regulatory action. The de facto individual identifier has been the Social Security number, which is the source of controversy about requiring it as a standard. It is therefore unlikely to become the standard. Further, a number of states has passed legislation recently that restricts the use of the Social Security number as an identifier in matters other than Social Security.

You can see from the time lines on the effective dates for the National Employer Identifier and the other identifiers that have yet to be determined or defined by a compliance date that full realization of Administrative Simplification is several years away. (See Table 1.2 in Chapter 1.) That is OK—we're moving in the right direction.

Advantages to Provider of Using HIPAA Transactions and Code Sets

- Payers must accept a HIPAA standard transaction.
- A payer must respond to the provider with the appropriate electronic message in a standard HIPAA transaction.
- Payers may not delay payment because the transaction was submitted electronically.
- Providers can submit claims to any health plan in the United States.

- HIPAA transactions save time of both provider and payer.
- HIPAA transactions will lead to faster claim turnaround and payment and improve providers' cash flow.
- HIPAA transactions will lower administrative costs for both provider and payer.
- HIPAA transactions are an investment in technological processes that are successfully and cost-effectively used in other industries.

FOCUS ON BKD

www.bkd.com

HIPAA Problem

Too many HIPAA consultants and vendors offer conflicting advice on how to be HIPAA compliant.

HIPAA Solution

Through BKD, HIPAA-knowledgeable financial and healthcare consultants assist physician practices by providing information in manageable chunks so that each practice can make more informed business and financial decisions. Consultants facilitate or manage relationships with other professional business associates. Healthcare consultants also assist the office in selecting from among the many HIPAA resources available in the market. Financial and healthcare technology consultants offer cost-effective solutions on technology investments for electronic transactions and cash flow concerns.

Typical Users

Small, independent physician offices to multi-specialty groups and hospitals that own physician groups.

Is It Affordable?

Financial and business advice is tailored to the size and need of each physician practice.

Contact Information

Rodney A. Walsh
Managing Consultant, BKD, LLP
Twelve Wyandotte Plaza
120 West 12th Street, Suite 1200
Kansas City, MO 64105-1936
(816) 221-6300

The Privacy Team

B y now, most of you have developed HIPAA privacy policies and procedures, and you've conducted basic HIPAA awareness training. If you haven't yet met those goals, this chapter will show you how to do them. Or, if you are well on your way to adopting HIPAA privacy, this chapter can be the benchmark to see how you're doing. Or, use this chapter as a retraining tool when someone in the office is promoted, or a new employee comes on board.

Adopting the new privacy rules will take about six months to "get under your skin." By then, the old methods will seem nonproductive and troublesome.

What You Will Learn in This Chapter:

This chapter, loaded with lists, charts, and insider tips on how to manage patient privacy, gives you step-by-step instructions on how to implement and sustain patient privacy in your office. We've divided the building of your HIPAA privacy plan into 10 steps.

Step 1: Start with the basics: Designate a privacy official, familiarize your-self with HIPAA, and develop a budget and a time-and-task chart.

Step 2: Develop your Notice of Privacy Practices (NPP).

Step 3: Get to know the six patient rights.

Step 4: Learn how you can use and disclose protected health information (PHI).

Step 5: Review and Implement HIPAA's Administrative Requirements.

Step 6: Manage special requirements, including marketing and fundrais-ing, personal representatives, and verification.

Step 7: Develop business-associate contracts.

Step 8: Work with legal counsel to assess your compliance status.

Step 9: Train your staff.

Step 10: Implement your plan.

With each step, you'll find "What to Do" and "How to Do It" sections to use as a foundation for writing simple policies and procedures for a small to midsize physician practice. The procedures in this chapter can also be used in a long-term-care facility, and some of them can be used in home health care. Real scenarios show you how the situation may look so that you can see why the policy or procedure is necessary.

Key Terms

William Braithwaite, MD, PhD, the lead drafter of the HIPAA Privacy Rule,[1] says that in writing the rule, his team invented plenty of new terms. More detailed official definitions are available in the glossary, but these have been simplified for ease of understanding. Most terms will make sense after a quick review.

Designated record sets: The medical, financial, and other records used to make decisions about an individual.

HHS: Department of Health and Human Services, the regulatory agency that implements HIPAA.

Incidental use and disclosure: Permissible uses and disclosures, such as announcing a person's name in the waiting room or over the public address system.

Office for Civil Rights (OCR): The enforcement agency for the Privacy Rule.

Opt out: To request restrictions on use and disclosure of PHI.

Patient rights: The rights assigned to patients under HIPAA.

Personal Representative: A legal guardian, friend, or family member who has written authorization to speak and act on behalf of the patient.

Protected health information (PHI): Information that refers to individually identifiable health information.

Treatment, payment, and healthcare operations: Treatment is providing healthcare services by one or more providers. Payment is the process of getting reimbursed for services. Healthcare operations are activities related to running the medical office, such as quality assessment and improvement activities.

Use and disclosure: Use is the sharing of information inside your medical office. Disclosure is releasing information or transferring of or providing access to PHI outside the medical office.

STEP 1: START WITH THE BASICS

A Quick Overview of the Privacy Rule

Most laws allow you to do anything you want, unless there's a provision against it. HIPAA is just the opposite. You can use and disclose patient information, but you have to find a reason for each use or disclosure. The core of the Privacy Rule is that you must identify a permission, even those that come with special requirements to use or disclose patient information.

---

1. From Dr. Braithwaite's presentation to the Sixth National Compliance Congress, Washington, DC, February 2003.

CRITICAL POINT

To use or disclose PHI, you must first identify permission (or a reason).

There are 11 permissions and 9 special requirements for using and disclosing PHI. Each is discussed in plain language in this chapter. Table 3.1 and Figures 3.1 and 3.2 summarize the permissions and special requirements.

TABLE 3.1

Permissions and Special Requirements for Disclosing Protected Health Information

Permissions	Special Requirements
Required disclosures	Verification
Disclosures to the patient	Minimum necessary
Your own treatment, payment, operations	Business associates
Others' treatment, payment, operations	Personal representatives
Personal representatives (friends, family)	Marketing
Disaster relief organizations	Psychotherapy notes
Incidental disclosures	Consistent with Notice of Privacy Practices
Public purpose	Consistent with other documents
Authorization	State laws (consent or other law)
De-Identification	
Limited Data Set	

Patient Rights

Patients are learning about privacy. A groundswell of privacy-focused consumer advocate groups had privacy on their minds long before HIPAA's Privacy Rule was adopted. So count on billboard and print ads, reporters from television and periodicals, and Internet sites to educate patients about their rights. Also, count on patients coming into your office with a mixture of sort-of-accurate to just plain false information. Patients don't want to be misinformed, but too often news of breached confidentiality is so compelling that it frightens them. That's why everyone in the office must understand the basics of the Privacy Rule and help put patients at ease.

HIPAA gives patients six rights and puts them in writing. Your Notice of Privacy Practices must also indicate how you will handle these six rights. See Table 3.2 for a recap of patient rights.

FIGURE 3.1

Permissions for Disclosing Protected Health Information

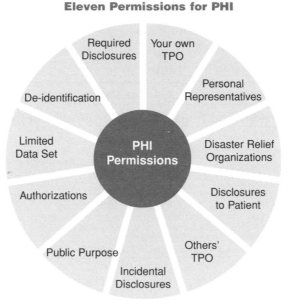

Reprinted with permission from Carolyn Hartley.

FIGURE 3.2

Special Requirements for Disclosing Protected Health Information

Reprinted with permission from Carolyn Hartley.

T A B L E   3.1

Patient Rights

Access and right to copy medical records
Request for amendment to designated record set
Request for accounting of disclosures
Request to be contacted at an alternate location
Request for further restrictions on who has access
Right to file a complaint

The Office for Civil Rights (OCR) of the US Department of Health and Human Services (HHS) has been designated by the Secretary of HHS as responsible for enforcement of the Privacy Rule. The Director of OCR, Richard Campanelli, has announced that enforcement of the Privacy Rule will be "complaint-based."[2] If your office is investigated for any reason, whether it is a criminal or civil investigation, or if a representative from HHS visits your office, you will be asked to produce significant records documenting your privacy efforts. Most of your documentation shows where you have used or disclosed protected health information. Further, HHS requires the following two disclosures:

1. disclosures to the patient while in the office, and if the patient requests access to medical records (some exceptions apply—see Step 4), and

2. disclosures to a representative from HHS who asks to review your documentation.

> **CRITICAL POINT**
> HHS requires only two disclosures: (1) to the patient and (2) to HHS upon request.

An Open Approach to the Privacy Rule

A common misconception is that the Privacy Rule was created because patients were concerned about confidentiality. That may be true, but it's not the basis for the Privacy Rule. In Chapter 2, we discussed how health care is moving into the electronic age by creating a set of standardized transactions and code sets. As medical records expand into electronic format and are transmitted electronically, HHS believes that consumers will expect privacy to be a big part of HIPAA.

What Are Patients Learning About Privacy?

For more than a decade, a groundswell of public concern has emerged about privacy and the security of private information. Do you have a sense

---

2. From Director Campanelli's presentation to the National Conference on the HIPAA Privacy Rule, Chicago, IL, March 2, 2003.

of how your patients feel about your current privacy practices? We recommend that you take a survey. You'll be surprised at what you find.

In reviewing recent surveys about privacy, we found provocative results from the Institute for Health Care Research and Policy's Health Privacy Project on the Internet at www.healthprivacy.org. A few survey results will give you an idea of what patients are thinking. We give some interesting statistics in Figure 3.3 about the public's attitude toward privacy. Figure 3.4 summarizes advice from the Health Privacy Project.

FIGURE 3.3

Consumer Attitudes about Health Privacy

- One in five American adults believes that a healthcare provider, insurance plan, government agency, or employer has improperly disclosed personal medical information. Half of these people believe that it resulted in personal embarrassment or harm.

- One in seven Americans has done something out of the ordinary to keep personal medical information confidential. To protect their privacy and avoid embarrassment, stigma, and discrimination, people withhold information from their healthcare providers, provide inaccurate information, doctor-hop to avoid a consolidated medical record, pay out-of-pocket for care that is covered by insurance, and—in extreme cases—avoid care altogether.

- Twenty-four percent of healthcare leaders polled knew of violations of patient confidentiality and could describe the violations in detail.

- Seventy-seven percent of the respondents to the poll said the privacy of their personal health information is very important; 61 percent are very concerned that their personal health information might be made available to others without their consent; 55 percent would not trust an insurance company or a managed care company to keep their personal health information private and secure.

FIGURE 3.4

Advice to Consumers from Privacy Advocates

What You Can Do to Protect Your Privacy[3]

- Read Notice of Privacy Practices carefully.
- Talk about confidentiality concerns with your physician.
- Ask how your medical information is shared in a large healthcare organization.
- Read authorization forms before you sign, and edit them to limit the sharing of information.

---

3. Condensed from content provided by Health Privacy Project, www.healthprivacy.org. Reprinted with permission.

- Register your objection to disclosures that you consider inappropriate.
- Request a copy of your medical record.
- Review your records.
- Request a copy of your file from the Medical Information Bureau.4
- Be cautious on health web sites.
- Educate yourself about medical privacy issues.

What Does It Mean to Be a Covered Entity?

Healthcare providers are covered entities under HIPAA if they submit health information electronically in a designated HIPAA transaction. The HIPAA transaction, for example, is when you or anyone in your office submits claims electronically for reimbursement. That claim contains information that can be used to identify a patient. Such individually identifiable information includes, but is not limited to, name, address, zip code, e-mail address, phone number, Social Security number, or driver's license number. A complete list is discussed later in Step 4 of this chapter. Before you can submit that electronic claim, you must complete the tasks listed in Figure 3.5 to be compliant. More important, you must also follow and practice your privacy policies every day.

F I G U R E 3.5

What a Covered Entity Must Do to Be HIPAA Compliant

Are you a covered entity? If so, you and your staff must work quickly to show your good faith effort to be compliant with the Health Insurance Portability and Accountability Act (HIPAA) Privacy Rule.

What to do:

1. Appoint a privacy official and seek initial HIPAA awareness training.
2. Develop a privacy team.
   a. Determine how your office will respond to patient requests.
   b. Develop forms for patients to fill out for each request. Include an authorization form.
3. Decide how you will manage documentation requirements for use and disclosure.
4. Conduct a "gap analysis"—find out where your privacy and security gaps might be.
5. Map out how protected health information (PHI) flows through your office.
6. Develop a Notice of Privacy Practices. After April 14, 2003, give copies to each patient on their first visit. Keep a log of patient signatures acknowledging receipt of the NNP.

---

4. Medical Information Bureau: PO Box 105, Essex Station, Boston, MA, 02112; www.mib.com.

7. Define Treatment, Payment, and Healthcare Operations (TPO) in your office. Get authorization from patients to release protected health information outside of TPO.

8. Set up business associate agreements with vendors who have access to medical or payment information about your patients.

9. Develop administrative, technical, and physical safeguards of protected health information.

10. Develop policies and procedures that describe:

a. How you will apply minimum necessary policies.

b. How you will use (internal) and disclose (external) protected health information.

c. How you will protect patient rights.

d. How you will manage requests made in the public good.

e. How you will sanction employees for intentional and accidental breaches.

f. How you will handle patient complaints.

11. Consult with an attorney about your legal documentation and ask about state law preemptions.

12. Train all staff, including volunteers, full-time, and part-time workers by April 14, 2003. Include training on how to give patients access to medical records.

13. Ask your clearinghouse to test and certify your transactions—begin April 16, 2003, and be finished by October 15, 2003. Retest at least quarterly.

14. Run a pilot test on one day. Give your NNP to patients to see if the process bottlenecks your system.

Are We a Covered Entity If We Have Fewer Than 10 Employees?

This question has tripped up many healthcare providers and their practices. You are a covered entity if you transmit health information electronically irrespective of size. CMS will allow your practice to file Medicare claims by paper if you have fewer than 10 employees. Carefully examine Steps 4 and 5 in this chapter, and also read Chapter 4 of this book.

Who's Enforcing the Privacy Rule?

We explained earlier why you must keep good records about use and disclosure of protected health information and that the Office for Civil Rights (OCR) within HHS is the agency responsible for enforcing HIPAA's Privacy Rule. It is no secret that OCR is understaffed and underfunded, even though they've received $6.4 million[5] to pay federal employees to enforce the Privacy Rule. To encourage compliance, HHS has empowered patients with a right to file a complaint with the Office for Civil Rights if a patient believes his or her rights have been breached. That form is on OCR's web site. Special-interest privacy groups are expected to help patients under-

---

5. President George W. Bush recommended $6.1 million in his FY2004 budget.

stand what it means to experience a privacy breach. Count on them to provide a direct link to OCR's complaint form.

To the patient, a privacy breach means that person believes that health information used to identify that person has been disclosed to someone who should not have access to that information.

For example, if a patient has given specific written instructions not to allow an employee in your office to see medical records, and you agreed to that request, then your office has breached confidentiality if the staff person saw the medical record.

The HIPAA Privacy Rule assigns significant penalties for knowingly disclosing protected health information. If someone in your office has been trained in the Privacy Rule and knowingly discloses PHI, a patient complaint can trigger criminal penalties up to $50,000 per incident and imprisonment for a year. Knowing disclosure, combined with the intent to use protected health information for personal gain can result in a fine of $250,000 per incident and 10 years' imprisonment.

HHS says it will handle unintentional inappropriate disclosures in the first year with a kinder, gentler approach by offering technical training and assistance. While they may identify potential penalties, HHS investigators are unlikely to impose financial penalties or jail time during the first year's ramp-up period, offering compliance assistance instead. Nevertheless, noncompliance can damage your reputation in the community, which can be worse than a monetary sanction.

Don't count on a kinder, gentler approach from patients and their attorneys. A patient who believes privacy has been breached can contact a consumer advocate group, the state's attorney general, or the American Civil Liberties Union. A patient can hire an attorney to file a complaint with OCR if the patient believes privacy has been breached. HIPAA does not provide a private right of action, which means that a patient cannot sue the physician for a HIPAA privacy breach.

Instead, a patient's attorney is more likely to build a case around state privacy laws and then use HIPAA-recommended penalties as a benchmark for penalties. Publicity that might arise from any of these sources about your noncompliance with privacy standards can damage your reputation. Follow your policies and procedures, and keep good written documentation. These are your best defense strategies if your practice is targeted for civil or criminal cases.

CRITICAL POINT
Good documentation is your best defense strategy.

Protect Patient Confidentiality

Behind examining-room doors, patients expect to find an atmosphere of confidentiality with their physicians. Patients often reveal stories about their personal, spiritual, and professional lives. In a short span of time, patient and physician develop a bond of trust that becomes the first step in the healing process.

But once the examining-room door reopens, the medical record, with detailed physician notes, may be consulted by several readers. A nurse may need to review treatment plans and administer medications or order lab tests. The medical coder will review the treatment plan and provide diagnostic and procedure codes for the payer. A licensing group may review the records for clinical credentialing purposes.

Not everyone needs access to the patient's record.

■ A receptionist may only need to know that patients have updated their patient information records or conduct front office tasks.

■ A scheduler or insurance clerk may only need to know a patient's insurance eligibility.

■ A billing clerk may only need to know the patient's co-pay and related insurance and contact information.

■ The insurance company only needs access to those portions of the medical record that pertain to the reason for the visit. For example, an insurance company does not need the entire medical record to make reimbursements for a flu vaccination.

"Need to know" is not new to many industries, but it is to health care. "Need to know" in HIPAA is called *minimum necessary*. The practice's leadership will be required to make a list of persons who have access to specific portions of patient files. The practice will also be required to establish passwords that control who on the staff has access to patient files. You'll learn much more about "minimum necessary" later in this chapter under Step 4 on use and disclosure of PHI.

As you read through this chapter, it may seem that the Privacy Rule is patient focused. It is. But the Privacy Rule also protects physicians. It spells out what a practice can and cannot do with a patient's protected health information, whether that information is in electronic, paper, or oral form.

If you have implemented the Privacy Rule, the activity list in Figure 3.5 can be a reminder of loose ends for review. If you are starting now on HIPAA, that list will get you well on your way. Keep in mind, though, that implementation is not a one-time event for you to complete over a weekend. HIPAA's Privacy Rule establishes the most far-reaching set of standards in the history of health care. You'll be expected to implement, follow, and practice HIPAA privacy for as long as the practice is in business.

Designate a Privacy Official

Your privacy official is the person who leads the privacy team and is responsible for developing and implementing the policies and procedures and privacy compliance program. This person will become the primary HIPAA expert in your office.

What to do:

Designate one person in the office to be the privacy official.

How to do it:

1. The practice's management team begins by creating a job description for the privacy official. Duties may include:

   ■ Working with management and an attorney to review state and federal laws that govern privacy.

   ■ Staying current on HIPAA regulations and work with outside organizations in compliance investigation or review.

   ■ Reporting to the practice's management and lawyer on policies and procedures, and including state laws in those policies.

   ■ Conducting periodic assessments of privacy and security risks.

   ■ Participating in creating business-associate agreements.

   ■ Overseeing patient complaints.

   ■ Educating the practice's management about HIPAA's nonretaliatory mandates against persons who file a complaint.

   ■ Educating and overseeing the practice's compliance activities.

   ■ Overseeing privacy relationships with business associates.

2. Establish qualifications. The privacy official must be familiar with the clinical and administrative functions of the office, willing to take on new responsibility, including fast-track learning of HIPAA content, highly ethical, exhibit strong organizational and communication skills, and work well with management and staff.

3. Establish a reporting structure. The office manager and privacy official, even though they may be one and the same, may report to two different supervisors.

4. Discuss salary or bonuses for taking on the additional responsibilities. The salary for privacy officials in medical offices ranges from $40,000 to $65,000, depending on size and responsibilities.

5. Document the level of independent decision making given to the privacy official. The privacy official needs authority to oversee some activities but should consult the management team for approval on others.

6. Consult with an attorney on documentation that you can create and documentation that you will need to review before presenting any outside the practice. Much of HIPAA compliance is about documentation, but keep in mind that your documentation could become evidence in a criminal or civil enforcement proceeding. Be careful what you put into written form.

7. Privacy officials may wish to obtain a privacy designation offered through URAC, also known as the American Accreditation HealthCare Commission (www.urac.org), or through the American Health Information Management Association (www.ahima.org).

Designate a Privacy Team

The privacy official cannot handle privacy implementation independently. There is too much work to be done. In addition, the privacy official cannot be the "privacy watchdog" for the office. Privacy is a team activity and requires support from many levels. Consider the following as candidates for the privacy team: your head nurse, billing supervisor, receptionist, management, and insurance clerk.

Develop a Budget and Time-and-Task Chart

Do you need a budget to implement HIPAA? Richard Campanelli, a former trial attorney in the special litigation section of the Civil Rights Division, U.S. Department of Justice, and now director of the HHS Office for Civil Rights, said that a covered entity's budget for HIPAA implementation was an indication that the entity was serious about its good-faith efforts to implement HIPAA.[6]

But how big should your budget be? That depends on when you started and how fast you moved through the compliance process. If you've been working on compliance for more than six months, you've saved significantly by dividing the work among your staff. If you're rushing to get compliant before someone finds out you're not, consulting fees, training packages, lawyer fees, potential penalties, and desk references can run you upwards of $15,000, or even more, for a small practice.

Few physician practices have kept accurate records of the cost of HIPAA implementation. If time is money, and assuming that the average privacy official spends six to eight months implementing HIPAA in the office, then the privacy official's time alone, if billable, would be worth $30,000 to $40,000—money well saved.

Use the HIPAA To Do List in Figure 3.5 and assign a timeline to those tasks. Meet regularly to review your progress. If you're just getting started, and many physicians are, consult with your attorney and determine what needs to be done immediately.

Start Now—Right Now

If you are beginning your privacy activities as you read this, you are well behind the deadline. You are not alone. Some industry experts have predicted that 35 to 50 percent of healthcare providers will have begun HIPAA compliance activities after the April 14, 2003, deadline. If you are one of the latecomers, you must begin to show good-faith efforts that you will protect patient privacy.

---

6. From Richard Campanelli's speech at the Fifth HIPAA Summit, Washington DC, October 2002.

STEP 2: DEVELOP YOUR NOTICE OF PRIVACY PRACTICES

Your privacy official should take the lead in developing a Notice of Privacy Practices (NPP), also called a Notice of Information Practices. The NPP is a detailed document that spells out:

- how your practice will use and disclose protected health information with or without a patient's consent for treatment, payment, and health-care operations; how medical information about the payment may be used and disclosed; and how the patient can gain access to his or her medical information;
- what the staff will do to protect the patient's privacy; and
- the patient's rights under HIPAA's Privacy Rule.

You can find sample NPPs that have been drafted by lawyers on many web sites. Some of the most useful are at:

- North Carolina Health Care Information and Communications Alliance (www.nchica.org). A Spanish version of this NPP is available at Healthcare Training Strategies (www.htsonline.com)
- American Medical Association (www.ama-assn.org)
- HIPAA Collaborative of Wisconsin (www.hipaacow.org)
- Pacific Retirement Services (www.retirement.org/hipaa)

What to do:

Few providers can afford to hire a lawyer to develop an NPP. Evaluate several NPPs and develop one that works best for you.

How to do it:

In reviewing the sample NPPs at the web sites referred to, keep in mind that these are sample documents. There is a risk in relying on someone else's document, unless you understand what it means and how the content will affect your office personnel. In a civil or criminal case, a lawyer will use your NPP as "Exhibit A" if you are called to defend your privacy practices.

- Edit the NPP to accommodate your practice, but do not edit out required language in the NPP.
- Ask your attorney to be certain that the language in your NPP matches the language in your policies and procedures.
- If you add or delete any content, it must be written in plain English. If you are in a culturally diverse area, you may wish to have your NPP translated into another language, but HHS does not require you to do so. Consider also putting your NPP on cassette tape for patients who have difficulty reading. Some practices are also developing the NPP in Braille.
- Develop a one-page summary of your NPP in plain language.
- Develop an acknowledgment form for patients to sign when they have received and reviewed their NPP. A copy of an acknowledgment form is in the appendix of this book. HHS does not dictate what the acknowledgment

form should look like—only that you obtain signatures acknowledging receipt.

- Ask the privacy team and management teams to review the NPP you've selected.

- Include a statement indicating that you reserve the right to amend the NPP.

- Follow established procedures for distributing and documenting the NPP.

- Be certain every employee understands the NPP before posting it or giving it to patients.

- Keep in mind that patients will expect you to do what you say you will do in your NPP.

Know How and When to Distribute the Notice of Privacy Practices

Any person, whether a patient or not, may request your NPP. The Privacy Rule grants all persons the right to shop around and review NPPs from any covered entity, including nursing homes, home health agencies, physicians' offices, or hospitals, before deciding to become a patient.

What to do:

Distribute your Notice of Privacy Practices to each patient on the first day of service after April 14, 2003, whether that visit is in person or through other means, such as electronic, via web site or e-mail, or by telephone.

How to do it (first visit is in person):

- Post your NPP where it can be easily seen in a common area, such as the waiting room.

- Keep extra copies of the NPP in a file in the front office so that you can easily distribute them.

- Present the NPP when an individual first arrives, along with other information you need to gather (updated contact information, insurance information, and so forth).

- Ask the individual to read and sign the acknowledgment form at the end of the NPP. The acknowledgment form does not ask the person to agree to the NPP's contents, only to acknowledge receipt. Your NPP is not subject to patient revisions. The patient may choose to exercise one of the patient rights before leaving the office. You can learn more about patient rights in Step 3.

- You must make a good faith effort to have the individual acknowledge receipt of the NPP. If the individual refuses to sign, keep a log of that person's response. Signing the NPP acknowledgment is not a prerequisite for treatment. You cannot deny care to a patient who refuses to acknowledge receipt.

- If an individual who is not a patient requests an NPP, give the individual a copy of your NPP. Also ask the person to sign an acknowledgment of receipt of the NPP.

- Place a copy of the signed acknowledgment in the patient's file.

How to do it (first visit is via web site):

- If your practice maintains a web site that provides information about your medical practice, you must prominently post your NPP on your web site.

- Include an "acknowledgment" button similar to software-agreement buttons so that the patient can acknowledge that he or she has read and reviewed your NPP. Keep an electronic log of patient responses.

- If possible, print a copy of the acknowledgment and place in patient's record.

How to do it (first visit is via e-mail):

- After April 14, 2003, if a patient's first visit is through e-mail, the NPP must be automatically provided at the electronic point of care (you are providing medical advice via an electronic means).

- Send an e-mail message to the patient asking if he or she can receive and open documents electronically. If so, ask if you can send a copy of the NPP.

- If the e-mail message fails, a paper copy must be provided. You can mail the NPP to the patient's address.

- Print a copy of the e-mail message with patient acknowledgment and place in patient's medical record.

How to do it (first visit is by telephone):

When speaking to a patient by phone, you do not have to provide the NPP before scheduling an appointment. Follow your policies and procedures if the first visit is by telephone. If your policies are not yet in place, and the provider gives medical advice over the telephone, do the following steps:

- Send a copy of the NPP by mail along with an acknowledgment form on the same day the provider speaks to the patient.

- Ask the patient to sign the acknowledgment form and return it to the office.

What to Do if Patient Refuses to Sign

Privacy officials tell us that at least one or two persons each week refuses to sign a form or log acknowledging receipt of the NPP. The most common reason is, "That NPP is just another one of those government forms and I'm not going to sign it." Remember, by signing an acknowledgment form or log, the patient is not agreeing to the NPP content, only that they received the NPP.

What to do:

If a patient refuses to sign an acknowledgment of receipt of the NPP, make a notation in your records of that decision.

How to do it:

- On the acknowledgment form or log, indicate the patient's decision, the reason for the patient's decision if known, and the date.
- The patient's refusal to sign an acknowledgment of receipt of the NPP does not mean he or she cannot exercise patient rights, and you cannot refuse to treat someone solely on this decision.
- Place a copy of the patient's acknowledgment of receipt of the NPP in the patient file.
- The patient is still allowed to request and keep a copy of your NPP.

Revising the Notice of Privacy Practices

Let's say that months after you begin issuing your NPP, you realize that you have a conflict with one of the sections.

What to do:

Your NPP is a legal document. Carefully reconstruct the language you want to change and consult an attorney.

How to do it:

- Be certain your NPP includes a statement that your practice reserves the right to make a revision, and that it describes how the practice will provide recipients of its NPP with the revised version. A "material change to the uses or disclosures, the individual's rights, the covered entity's legal duties, or other privacy practices" cannot be implemented prior to the effective date of the notice.
- If the practice decides to make a material change to how it uses and discloses PHI, it must follow a legal process, including resending the revised NPP to all patients who have already acknowledged receipt in writing.
- Post the revised NPP in a common area, along with the date it was revised.
- Continue to offer it to individuals who come into the office for the first time.

STEP 3: GET TO KNOW THE SIX PATIENT RIGHTS

For the first time in the history of organized health care in the United States, HIPAA's Privacy Rule grants federally recognized rights to individuals so that they can have some say in who has access to their patient information. Each right begins with a patient request, either by or on behalf of a patient. The patient's request is just that—a request. If the request is reasonable, you will be obligated to follow through on the request. As you respond to each request, the staff faces certain additional responsibilities.

FOCUS ON MOREHEAD MEMORIAL HOSPITAL

www.morehead.org

HIPAA Problem

You are not sure how to display the entire Notice of Privacy Practices in a public area; how to provide the NPP to other members of the partial Organized Health Care Arrangement (OHCA) which includes physicians, specialists, and long-term care facilities; and how to let patients know what would happen if they opted out of a hospital or medical directory.

HIPAA Solution

Morehead Memorial Hospital developed a HIPAA task force of 10 staff members to develop and design an NPP that would be durable and also could be placed in many locations through the facility. The taskforce also worked with in-house graphic designers to produce an NPP on an 8 x 11 spiral, laminated pad with 10 layers. Each layer features specific content from the NPP so that readers could flip to that content without having to read through all eight pages.

For Spanish-speaking patients, the taskforce published the corresponding content in Spanish on the back of each page. For vision-impaired patients, the taskforce produced an audiotape of the NPP.

To solve questions on opt-outs of hospital directories, hospital staff created a small card that indicates what opting out of a directory means—no flowers, no cards, no visitors, and so forth.

The products and some documents developed by the task force are also available to their physician groups, including pathologists, radiologists, anesthesiologists, and also to the physician practices and nursing home owned by the hospital.

Is It Affordable?

The only out-of-pocket cost was to produce the NNP as a spiral, laminated document.

Typical Users

Patients and physician groups.

Contact Information

Annette White, RHIA, Privacy Official
Mary Barrett, Task Force Coordinator
Morehead Memorial Hospital
117 E. Kings Highway
Eden, NC 27288
(336) 623-9711
awhite@morehead.org
mbarrett@morehead.org

We'll discuss each right in more detail in this step. Table 3.3 serves as a good reference and quick reminder. Most patient rights contain exceptions that are presented in the discussion that follows.

A Patient Can Make a Request to Any Staff Member

Patients usually go to one person outside the clinical staff to ask non-medical questions. At some time, everyone on your staff will be asked to explain a patient right—all the more reason you should make sure everyone in your office has a clear understanding of patient rights and understands the procedures for following up on each request.

Review Table 3.3. Talk to your privacy official about how the staff and privacy team will handle each request and include that process in your policies and procedures. See Step 4.

T A B L E 3.3

Patient Rights and What Each Means to You

Patient Right	What It Means	Documentation	
		Required	Recommended
Further restrictions, also called "opt-outs"	Patient requests that protected health information is not made available to specific persons, groups, or organizations.	No	Strongly
Alternative communications	Patient requests to be contacted at a location other than work or home.	No	Strongly
Access to information and making of copies	Patient asks to have access to medical record and to make copies.	No	Strongly
Amend PHI	Patient has a right to request a provider amend PHI in the patient's record set.	Yes, if you agree to amend	

T A B L E 3.3 (continued)

Patient Rights and What Each Means to You

Patient Right	What It Means	Documentation	
		Required	Recommended
Accounting of disclosures	Patient has a right to request a list of where you have disclosed PHI.	Yes	
File a complaint	Patient has a right to file a complaint if he or she believes privacy has been breached.	No	Strongly

In describing each patient right, we offered suggestions on what to do, and how to do it. If you have already developed your HIPAA privacy policies and procedures, and the procedures in this book are in conflict with your procedures, you are obligated to follow your own procedures. Consult your privacy official if you have a question about your HIPAA policies and procedures. You can also analyze how best to develop your own policies using the AMA's *HIPAA Policies and Procedures Desk Reference,* which offers a complete and affordable reference of policies and procedures for the medical office. Obtain a copy at www.amapress.org.

Patient Right #1: Requests for Further Restriction

An individual can request the practice to agree that it will not allow certain persons or entities to have access to medical information.

Example: A patient's sister-in-law is the receptionist at the physician's office, and the patient does not want her relatives to have access to her medical record. You assure her that according to the HIPAA Privacy Rule the receptionist does not have access to patient information, but the patient insists that you put her further restriction in writing.

What to do:

Obtain the further restriction in writing.

How to do it:

- In a private setting, give the patient a copy of an opt-out form (also called patient restriction form). One is available for you in the appendix of this book.
- Ask the patient to write the specific restriction and the reason for the request.
- Tell the patient that you will present the request to the privacy official.

- Follow your policies and procedures manual on who will respond to the request, and how the response will be made. If you have not yet developed your policies and procedures manual, outline a process to manage further restrictions as you write them.

- Document the request and also document whether you agreed to comply with the request.

- If you comply with the patient's request, you must do what the patient asked.

CRITICAL POINT

You do not have to comply with the patient's request to restrict disclosures, but if you agree, you must comply with the request.

Patient Right #2: Request for Alternative Communications

A patient has a right to request that you contact him or her at a location other than home or work. You must honor this request if it is reasonable. You cannot deny the request because you think the reason lacks merit.

Example: Sam frequently travels, and when he is in town, he's usually reached on his mobile phone. He also has three teenagers and doesn't want them to pick up messages from anyone, especially his doctor's office. He also does not want his bills sent to his home but to his work address.

What to do:

Obtain a request for alternative communications from Sam.

How to do it:

- Tell the patient you can accommodate his request and that he is not required to give a reason for the request.

- Ask the patient to put the request in writing.

- Make a notation in the patient's electronic medical record, and also make a paper notation for staff members who do not have access to the patient's electronic medical record.

- You can put a condition on this request: You can ask that the patient explain how payment will be handled, which is particularly important if the patient wishes only to be contacted by mobile phone.

CRITICAL POINT

If you accept the alternative communications request, you must follow through and contact the person at the alternate location.

Patient Right #3: Access to Information and Right to Copy

Individuals have a right to see portions or all of their designated records set and to make copies. A designated record set contains billing records, clinical records, and other records that you maintain to make decisions about the individual. A "personal representative" can also make a request to access personal records.

Use common sense when responding to this request. Often, patients are just curious, or they want to check on payment or treatment procedures. If you are doubtful, ask the patient why he or she wants to see the records.

There are exceptions to the right of access. Patients do not have access to:

- psychotherapy notes;
- to records if they are being compiled for a civil, criminal, or administrative action; or
- if the record is exempt from the Clinical Laboratory Improvement Act of 1988 (CLIA). That law requires clinical laboratories to disclose test results or reports only to authorized persons—usually the person who ordered the test.

Example: Jennifer received a soccer scholarship to attend college, and she signed a form giving the university's health system permission to have access to her medical records. Now she wants to know what is in her records.

What to do:

Unless there is an exception, allow the patient to have access to his or her designated record set.

How to do it:

- If there is a policy and a procedure already in place, follow them.
- Unless you know the patient, ask for a driver's license or other document that proves she is who she says she is.
- Check to be sure that you have the medical record in your office.
- Ask the patient to put the request in writing. (You can use the Request for Records Access form included in Appendix A of this book.)
- Submit the request to the privacy official, unless your policies and procedures tell you to consult someone else.
- If the records are on site, you have 30 days to comply. If your practice didn't create the record, be helpful and redirect the patient. If the records are off site, you have 60 days to comply. Your practice can request a 30-day extension if you send the individual a written notice explaining why you need more time and also give the date you'll deliver the records.
- Provide what you can. The information must be readable in hard copy or electronic format depending on what the patient requested.

- If medical records are in two locations, you only have to produce PHI from one location.

- The practice may provide the individual with a summary if the patient agrees to pay for the time spent in writing the summary.

- Record this activity, along with the request in a Request to Access Records log.

- Arrange a convenient time and place for the patient to review the medical records. You can mail copies of the PHI if the individual requests this.

- You may charge a reasonable fee for making copies or a summary report. You cannot charge for time spent retrieving the record.

CRITICAL POINT

Granting patient access to medical records is a required disclosure, unless you believe that access will do harm to the patient.

What If You Decide to Deny Access?

There are valid reasons to deny the request. If you deny the request, your decision may or may not have to go through a review process. A review process is initiated when the patient challenges your decision that he or she cannot have access to his or her medical records.

Some decisions are nonreviewable, meaning that the patient cannot challenge your decision to deny access:

- Exceptions to right of access, listed earlier in this step.

- The patient is an inmate.

- You obtained the PHI through clinical research that includes treatment. This only applies during the research and only if the limitation on access is agreed to in advance.

- The PHI is a government record.

- The PHI was obtained under a promise of confidentiality.

The following are reviewable, and the patient can challenge your decision to deny access:

- The patient may be endangered if he or she sees the medical record.

- Someone else is referred to in the record, and that person may be harmed.

- The person making the request is not the patient but a personal representative, and you believe that giving that representative access may cause harm to the patient or someone else.

What to do:

Provide a reason to the patient for the denial. If the denial is reviewable, the patient can challenge your decision.

How to do it:

- Refer the denial process to the privacy official.

- If you are the privacy official, put the reason for the denial in writing and submit it to the patient within the time allowed (30 days or 60 days, depending on the location of records).

- The patient can still challenge your decision by asking another licensed healthcare professional to review your denial. If this happens, ask for a request to review the letter from the "reviewing" professional for your protection and documentation. Your practice or the patient must follow the recommendations of the reviewing official.

Patient Right #4: Request to Amend Protected Health Information

A patient has a right to request that a provider amend PHI or amend information about the individual.

Example: After reviewing her records, Alice sees that her physician has identified her as being a Class II diabetic, but her only diabetic episodes occurred during the third trimesters of pregnancy when carrying her second and third children. Alice believes that her records should indicate her diabetes was gestational and not a permanent condition. She wants that portion of her records corrected.

What to do:
Unless certain grounds exist to deny the request, you must make the amendment.

How to do it:

- If you don't know the patient, ask for identification, such as driver's license or other picture ID.

- Refer the request to the privacy official. Some privacy officials want to see all requests, and others delegate it to the head nurse or another staff member.

- Record the request in an amendment log, including the date and deadline to respond.

- If you are the privacy official, give the patient a request-to-amend form. A sample form is provided for you in the appendix of this book.

- Ask the patient to identify what she wants amended and put that in writing. Ask her to put the reason for the amendment in writing, too.

- Ask the patient how she wants to be contacted about the amendment.

- Tell the patient you will respond to her request in a timely manner. You have 60 days from the date of the request.

- Take the request form to the provider who made the original notation for approval.

- If the provider agrees with the revision, make the amendment. Attach the amendment to the medical record.

- If others have received the patient's information, and the information could be a detriment to the patient, ask the patient to identify who else should receive the amendment. If your practice has sent PHI that is part of this amendment to another party, even if the patient doesn't know about this earlier transaction, you must also notify the third party of the amendment.

- If another covered entity made the amendment and you also maintain PHI on the patient, you also must make the amendment.

- For questions about amendments, consult your HIPAA policies and procedures or consult your Privacy Official.

CRITICAL POINT

Consult your privacy official on all amendment requests.

When to Deny an Amendment

There are four permitted reasons to deny a request to amend:

- The information is accurate and complete.
- Your office did not create the PHI.
- PHI to be amended is not part of the designated record set.
- The patient did not have the right to inspect the medical records.

What to do:

Inform the patient that the amendment cannot be made.

How to do it:

- In writing, let the patient know the reason the amendment cannot be made.
- Include language explaining that the patient can submit a statement disagreeing with your decision and can also file a complaint to the practice and/or the Secretary of HHS. Include the name and address of the contact person in your office who receives complaints.
- If the individual submits an objection, you can offer a rebuttal.
- In your rebuttal, identify the records or PHI that is the subject of the dispute. Attach the correspondence to the record that contains PHI.

Patient Right #5: Accounting of Disclosures

A patient has a right to request and receive an accounting of where you have sent (disclosed) the patient's PHI. There are several disclosures you are not required to account for:

- The PHI was used for treatment, payment, and healthcare operations.
- You sent PHI to the patient.

- The patient signed a HIPAA-compliant authorization.
- The patient is listed in a facility directory. A facility directory in a hospital, for example, lets visitors know your room number but cannot reveal details about your health condition.
- You disclosed PHI to a person involved in the patient's care or treatment.
- PHI was used for national security or intelligence purposes.
- A correctional institution or law-enforcement official has lawful custody of the individual.
- The disclosure was made before April 14, 2003.
- You made proper "incidental" disclosures (discussed in this step) mentioned in your policies and procedures.
- PHI was de-identified for clinical research purposes.

Example: Robert is one of three finalists to be hired as a senior executive with a large public company that trades on the New York Stock Exchange. In making the final decision, the company will conduct a due-diligence background check of his personal records. Damaging health information could put the company at risk and cause him to be disqualified. He wants to know where your office has disclosed his medical records.

What to do:

If you agree to this request, provide Robert with a list of the disclosures.

How to do it:

- Refer this request to your privacy official, or follow your policies and procedures for responding to this request. If you have not developed your policies and procedures you can do the following:
  - ☐ If you don't already know the patient, ask for verification to make sure the patient is who he says he is. Do the same for a personal representative.
  - ☐ Check the disclosure list to determine whether you can make a disclosure.
  - ☐ Record the disclosure request in a disclosure log.
  - ☐ Tell the patient you will respond to the request, and you have up to 60 days to provide the disclosure list.
  - ☐ Review the patient's chart and the practice's disclosure log.
  - ☐ Contact your business associates to see if they have made any disclosures.
  - ☐ Compile a list of disclosures from multiple locations and provide the date of the disclosure, the name of the entity or person and address that received the information, a brief description of the PHI disclosed, and a brief statement about the purpose of the disclosure.
  - ☐ Ask for someone else to review the report.
  - ☐ Make a copy of the disclosure report for the patient's file.
  - ☐ Send the disclosure report to the location requested by the patient.

FOCUS ON BOYCE-WILLIS CLINICS

HIPAA Problem

Attempting to centralize patient records in paper and electronic formats and following through on patient requests when the medical practice has agreed to them. This clinic has 60 providers at six different locations throughout the county and patients often go to the most convenient clinic, regardless of whether their records are there.

HIPAA Solution

The practice administrator established a numbering system to identify patient security levels. A "1" means that the patient had not made any particular requests, and a "7," the highest, means the patient had many security issues. A box on the Misys' practice management software allows for this ranking. The numbering system can also be used to refer the reader to notes in the practice management system.

For nurses reading paper files, the privacy official placed a red stamp on the outside of the chart to indicate that the patient had requested restrictions.

In training, staff adopted policies and procedures that mandated that the medical records are updated once a week to include disclosure requests.

Typical Users

Practice administrators, clinical staff, and physicians.

Is It Affordable?

Yes. The practice administrator worked with software already in place.

Contact Information

Allison Jenkins
Boyce-Willis Clinics
P.O. Box 7200
Rocky Mount, NC 27804

Note that you cannot charge the individual for the first accounting request in each 12-month period. You may charge a reasonable fee if the patient makes this request a second time within 12 months.

CRITICAL POINT
Inform your privacy official of any request for an accounting of disclosures.

Patient Right #6: File a Complaint

Your practice must provide a process for patients to file a complaint, and you must also identify that process in your Notice of Privacy Practices. In the past, you've handled patient complaints, and your process may already be in place. But the Privacy Rule mandates that you document and respond to requests in a specific way.

Example: When Jennifer gets to college, she learns that her soccer scholarship has been put on hold because the university's coach questions her health record. In her application, Jennifer was forthcoming that she'd had knee surgery, but the medical record sent to the university coach contains detailed medical language that the coach cannot read, and now he believes that her surgery was more serious than he originally thought. Jennifer did not sign an authorization and did not know that the coach had requested her medical record. She has filed a complaint with the head nurse, but she is angry that her files were forwarded without her permission. She may also file a complaint with the Office for Civil Rights.

What to do:

Work with the patient to resolve this complaint.

How to do it:

- If you received the complaint, refer it to the privacy official.
- Document the complaint on a privacy complaint log.
- Tell the patient that you will respond promptly after the practice has reviewed and investigated the complaint.
- Evaluate the severity of the complaint and determine how best to solve it.
- Respond in writing to the patient.
- Mitigate any events that may cause a detriment to the patient.

CRITICAL POINT

Invite patients to file complaints with you, rather than with the OCR. It is a critical first step encouraged by the OCR. Work with the individual to resolve the complaint. By doing so, you will enhance patient satisfaction with your practice.

No Retaliation

HIPAA requires your practice to have a policy against retaliation. You cannot intimidate patients or other persons for filing a complaint. You cannot retaliate, intimidate, threaten, coerce, or discriminate against a patient or other persons who exercise their rights under the Privacy Rule.

What to do:

Establish a policy that says you will not retaliate or discriminate against a patient for filing a complaint.

How to do it:

- In your Notice of Privacy Practices, include a statement that says the practice will not retaliate, intimidate, threaten, coerce, or discriminate against a patient or other persons who exercise their rights under the Privacy Rule.

CRITICAL POINT
You cannot intimidate an individual for exercising a patient right.

No Waiver of Rights

HIPAA also requires that you cannot require a patient to waive his or her patient rights, including the right to file a complaint to the Secretary of HHS, as a condition of treatment, payment, participation in a health plan, or eligibility of benefits.

What to do:
Establish a no-waiver-of-rights policy.

How to do it:

■ A no-waiver-of-rights policy must be included in your Notice of Privacy Practices. Specifically, it says that the practice will not refuse to treat an individual if that person chooses to exercise one of the six patient rights, including filing a complaint with the Secretary of HHS.

CRITICAL POINT
You cannot ask an individual to waive patient rights in exchange for treatment.

STEP 4: USE AND DISCLOSURE OF PROTECTED HEALTH INFORMATION

When you were reviewing the six patient rights in Step 3, it may have seemed as though the Privacy Rule was written just for patients. The content in Step 4 outlines how the Privacy Rule protects physicians. The rule gives physicians specific guidelines for when to disclose PHI. The heart of the Privacy Rule rests in Step 4. The basic principle is that a healthcare provider and its employees, as a covered entity, cannot use or disclose protected health information, except as permitted or required by the rule.

Map Out How Protected Health Information Flows Through Your Office

To "use" PHI means that you or your staff uses patient's protected health information internally. To "disclose" PHI means that you send information about the patient's protected health information outside the office.

Until now, we've introduced a broad description of protected health information. Now, it's time for a more specific definition of PHI. First, to determine if information about a patient is "Protected Health Information," begin by asking three questions.

1. Is the information created or received by a healthcare provider, health plan, or healthcare clearinghouse? *(Did you create the information?)*
2. And does the information relate to the past, present, or future diagnosis or treatment of a physical or mental condition? *(Does the information relate to the patient's diagnosis or treatment?)*
3. Or does it relate to a payment claimed or paid for a past, present, or future diagnosis or treatment of a physical or mental condition? *(Will the information be used to file a claim or get paid for services?)*

Next, ask yourself if the information is individually identifiable. *(Can you identify the person using specific information about the patient?)* Individually identifiable information includes:

- name,
- zip codes,
- date of birth and date of treatment,
- telephone numbers,
- fax number,
- e-mail addresses,
- Social Security number,
- medical record numbers,
- health plan beneficiary numbers,
- birth certificate and driver's license,
- vehicle identification number and license plate number,
- web site address,
- finger prints and voice prints, and
- photos.

Information that contains one or more of these identifiers may be individually identifiable. To use (look at it internally) or disclose (send it to someone outside the practice) this information, you must first determine whether you need permission to disclose it.

There are several types of permitted disclosures—meaning that you can send PHI externally without written permission or authorization from the patient. (See Table 3.4.) Contact your privacy official for any questions about permitted disclosures in your state. HIPAA defers to state laws if a relevant state law is more stringent.

TABLE 3.4

Permitted Disclosures without Authorization

Permitted Disclosures (check with state laws)	What It Means
Disclose PHI to the patient	Talk to the patient about his or her diagnosis, treatment, and medical condition.
Disclose PHI for treatment	Treatment may include talking to the patient, coordinating care, consulting with another provider about the patient's condition, prescribing medications, ordering lab tests, scheduling surgery, and so forth.
Disclose PHI for payment	Payment refers to the process of obtaining information about the patient's eligibility or coverage, inquiring about co-pays, billing, and claims management, reviewing medical necessity, obtaining preauthorizations for treatment, filing balance due to a credit agency, and so forth.
Disclose PHI for healthcare operations	Healthcare operations refer to the activities the provider participates in that relate to the business functions, such as quality assessments, case management, and care coordination, contacting providers and patients with information about treatment alternatives, certification, accreditation, licensing or credentialing, medical reviews, legal services, and auditing, including fraud and abuse detection (see definition of health care operations in the glossary of this book)

Permitted Incidental Disclosures

When the Privacy Rule became effective in April 2001, a lot of confusing information spread quickly through the healthcare industry about what you can and cannot do. Stories made for quirky images—people sitting in waiting rooms with paper sacks over their heads to hide their identity, physicians purchasing pagers to avoid calling patients by name. Confusing stories and inaccurate advice also added desperation to HIPAA implementation. Then, in December 2002, HHS released a guidance document that dispelled many myths and clarified "permitted incidental disclosures."[7] Some of those permitted disclosures include:

- Staff members at a nursing station may coordinate care if they speak in a low voice.

- Nurses or other staff can talk to the patient by phone or discuss treatment of the patient with another provider on the phone if these discussions are conducted in low voices and away from listeners.

---

7. December 4, 2002, guidance can be found at www.hhs.gov/ocr/hipaa.

■ Lab results can be discussed with patients or other professionals in a joint treatment area if you take precautions.

■ You can leave a message for a patient on an answering machine or with family members, but you should limit the information to the amount necessary for the purpose of your call.

■ You may ask patients to sign in and call patients by name in waiting rooms, but you shouldn't ask them to sign the reason for visit.

■ You can announce the patient by name in a waiting area or use a public-address system to request a patient to come to a specific location.

■ You may use an x-ray light board at a nursing station if it is not publicly accessible.

■ You may place patient charts outside exam rooms if you use reasonable precautions—face charts to the wall or provide a cover that conceals the chart when it is in place.

CRITICAL POINT
Some incidental permitted disclosures are allowed. Implement safeguards when discussing PHI.

What to do:
Track the flow of protected health information through the practice.

How to do it:
■ Start with an awareness exercise. At an office meeting, ask everyone to bring a sample of protected health information found in the office, but be certain you know where it came from so you can return it. No two persons can bring the same item. (Recall from previous definitions that protected health information contains health information and at least one patient identifier.)

■ Using a simple list, track one or two of the samples of PHI as it travels through the office: how it arrived in the office; how it was entered into the medical record; if it was used in a referral, in administrative functions, or to process a claim; and whether it should have been destroyed.

■ Ask if this could have been temporarily misplaced in or out of the office, and what you could do to keep track of the PHI.

■ Develop a log procedure that tracks PHI either on paper or in a software program.

When Are You Required to Obtain Permission to Use or Disclose Protected Health Information?

Your practice has probably adopted policies that say you will disclose PHI as required by the Privacy Rule. Your privacy official will give you specific guidance that helps you determine when you can disclose PHI. Table 3.5 gives permissions at a glance.

What to do:

Disclose PHI as required by the Privacy Rule and state laws.

How to do it:

- Check your HIPAA policies and procedures to determine whether the use or disclosure fits within one of the Privacy Rule permissions. A list of permissions is provided at the beginning of this chapter in Table 3.1.

- Use or disclose protected health information only as each permission allows. Unless there are specific exceptions, you are required to disclose PHI to the patient and to the Department of Health and Human Services if HHS is reviewing your facilities, books, records, and accounts to determine HIPAA compliance.

- You can use and disclose PHI for treatment, payment, and healthcare operations without the patient's written consent or authorization, except where a specific "authorization" is required, such as psychotherapy notes.

- Evaluate whether the use or disclosure must comply with Special Requirements. A list of special requirements is provided at the beginning of this chapter in Table 3.1.

- Before making a use or disclosure, double-check your decision with the privacy official.

- Document the use or disclosure.

TABLE 3.5

Permissions at a Glance

What's Happening	What You Can/Cannot Do	Is Written Permission Required?
A representative from HHS wants to visit you and asks to see your books, records, accounts, and other PHI documents.	Ask for credentials. The Privacy Rule requires you to permit HHS officials access to your records.	No
A patient requests to see the medical record.	Ask for identification. Unless there are reasons not to allow the patient to see medical records (see Step 3, Patient Right #3), the Privacy Rule requires you let the patient see the record.	Recommended
A friend or relative has legal authority over the patient and wants to see the record.	Ask for identification. Ask to see the legal document. Unless there are reasons not to allow the relative to see medical records (see Step 3), the Privacy Rule requires that you let the patient see the record.	Recommended

T A B L E   3.5 (continued)

Permissions at a Glance

What's Happening	What You Can/Cannot Do	Is Written Permission Required?
The patient requests treatment from another provider for a health condition.	You can use and disclose information for treatment to another provider in your practice, and if you are referring the patient, you can disclose information to the referring physician. You cannot disclose PHI for marketing if the PHI includes psychotherapy notes or when state laws require written permission.	Recommend a HIPAA consent form.
The patient gives you an insurance card so that you can process payment.	You do not need written authorization from the patient to file an insurance claim for payment. State laws require a consent to disclose. Most practices obtain consent to file insurance claims.	No
The patient wants to know if a specific treatment will be covered by insurance.	You do not need written permission from the patient to do an eligibility check or check for authorization to treat.	No
A patient requests a list of where your practice has disclosed protected health information.	Ask for identification. Ask if there are specific disclosures of interest. Inform the patient that you have up to 60 days to consult the records and complete the request.	Recommended
A mother wants access to her teenage daughter's medical records.	Consult the privacy official. Ask for identification. Then ask the following: Does the mother have authority to act on behalf of her daughter? (yes) Are there state laws prohibiting the parents' access? (no) Do you suspect abuse, neglect, or endangerment? (no) Are there special HIPAA considerations? (no)	Document the mother's request. If the mother's answers match the answers given in the parentheses, you may give permission. If any answer doesn't match, consult the privacy official.
A physician wants specific patients to participate in a clinical trial.	Ask the patients to sign an authorization.	
A physician is referring a patient to another physician.	You may use and disclose PHI to another provider without consent or authorization unless another law (such as a state law) applies.	No

continued

T A B L E   3.5 (continued)

Permissions at a Glance

What's Happening	What You Can/Cannot Do	Is Written Permission Required?
A pharmaceutical company wishes to inform patients when a new drug will be available.	Contact specific patients, and ask if they wish to be contacted. Ask patients to sign an authorization allowing the pharmaceutical company to contact them.	Yes
An outside company is doing quality assessments.	Ask for credentials if the visit is a surprise. In most cases, the visit has been prearranged.	No, this is a function of healthcare operations.
You want to send medical records to your transcription service.	Make certain the transcription service has signed a business-associate agreement.	No, this is a function of healthcare operations.
Your transcription service is overseas and you want to send medical records to them.	This is not recommended. If privacy is breached, you have no clear recourse to recover the lost files.	Not yet, but if you're using an overseas transcription service, it may become a significant patient issue if files are lost.
You wish to have a conversation about a patient with your attorney.	Be certain your attorney has signed a business-associate agreement.	No, this is permitted under the business-associate agreement.
The state public health department is investigating an outbreak of hepatitis B.	Ask for verification of the public health official. Provide relevant files, but only to the extent that it will help the public health official determine hepatitis B outbreak. Remove individual identifiers unless public health asks for specific records.	No, this is in the public good.
You want to contact a family member about a patient's condition, ie, she fainted in the office.	You can provide information to a family member to the extent that you limit information to the current condition.	No, this is permitted.

Uses and Disclosures for the Public Good

There may be times when you are asked to disclose protected health information for the "public good." If a state law does not prevent you from releasing specific PHI, the Privacy Rule allows this type of disclosure without the patient's authorization. Table 3.6 explains uses and disclosures for the public good.

What to do:

Release PHI to a public authority if you have verified the request as being for the public good and if a state law does not prohibit or restrict you from doing so.

How to do it:

■ Ask for identification from the authority that requests PHI.

■ Document the request for PHI.

■ Present the request to the privacy official, who will determine whether the disclosure is for the public good. There are 16 circumstances in which you would release PHI to a public authority.

T A B L E 3.6

When to Release PHI for the Public Good

Public Good Circumstance	Special Requirement
Required by law	Limit the PHI to the requirements of the law. Verification is required.
Public-health authority	A public-health authority is authorized by law to collect information to prevent or control disease, injury, birth, death, investigations, or interventions.
Child abuse or neglect	A public-health authority is authorized by law to receive reports of child abuse or neglect.
Victims of abuse, neglect, or domestic violence	If the practice reasonably believes a patient is a victim of abuse, neglect, or domestic violence, you can disclose information if: ■ the disclosure is required by law; ■ the individual agrees to the disclosure; or ■ the disclosure is necessary to prevent serious harm, or the individual is physically or mentally unable to agree to the disclosure.
Food and Drug Administration	You may disclose PHI to the FDA for safety, quality, or effectiveness, such as reporting adverse events, product defects, product recalls, or monitoring patient response to a drug.

continued

T A B L E 3.6 (continued)

When to Release PHI for the Public Good

Public Good Circumstance	Special Requirement
Communicable diseases	Disclose PHI to a person who may have been exposed to a communicable disease or is at risk of spreading a disease if you are authorized by law to notify that person.
Employee workplace medical surveillance	You may disclose PHI to a patient's employer if you meet certain requirements. Consult the privacy official for those requirements.
Health oversight activities	Disclose PHI for oversight activities, such as audits, investigations, inspections, licensure, or disciplinary actions. You cannot disclose PHI if the individual is the subject of the investigation.
Judicial and administrative proceedings	You've received a court order to release PHI. Special circumstances apply. Consult the privacy official if you receive a subpoena or court order.
Law enforcement	Eight types of circumstances apply: 1. Required by law such as gun shot wounds, child abuse or neglect, domestic violence; 2. Warrant or process; 3. Government agency request; 4. Identifying a suspect or material witness; 5. Victims of a crime; 6. Suspicious death; 7. Crime on the premises; and 8. Medical emergency. Consult your privacy official if a law enforcement official requests PHI.
Coroners and funeral directors	You may disclose PHI to a coroner or medical examiner to identify a deceased person and to funeral directors to help them carry out their duties.
Organ, eye, or tissue donation	Disclose PHI from a cadaver if the organ is used for donation or transplant.
Research	Specific conditions apply, so consult your privacy official if you are asked to provide PHI for research.
Avert a serious and imminent threat to health or safety	Disclose PHI if in good faith the practice believes the disclosure is necessary to avert a serious threat or to prevent harm. Consult the privacy official if a patient makes a suspicious statement.
Special government functions	Special circumstances apply to military and veterans activities, inmates, and other government functions. Consult the privacy official if a federal agency requests PHI.
Workers' compensation	Disclose PHI that complies with state workers' compensation laws.

FOCUS ON CABARRUS GASTROENTEROLOGY

HIPAA Problem

Keeping track of HIPAA documents for each patient.

HIPAA Solution

This practice printed a HIPAA tab to be used as an index separator in each patient's medical record. As patient requests, authorizations, or public good requests are received, each is filed behind the HIPAA tab. Authorized personnel have been trained to review content behind the HIPAA tab before releasing patient information outside of treatment, payment, and healthcare operations.

Typical Users

Office managers, physicians, nurses, and other authorized personnel.

Is It Affordable?

The tabs cost just pennies per folder.

Contact Information

Vickie Burrage
Cabarrus Gastroenterology
200 Medical Park Drive, Suite 257
Concord, NC 28025

Minimum Necessary

HHS says a covered entity must develop policies and procedures that allow for appropriate individuals to have access to PHI, including the entire medical record. Not everyone needs access to the patient's designated record set. A designated record set contains a group of files that may include

- medical and billing records;
- eligibility, enrollment, payment, or case management records; and
- information used to make decisions about the individual.

What to do:

Evaluate how you meet the "minimum necessary" requirement.

How to do it:

- Use common sense when looking at a patient record. Ask yourself, "Will the information in this file help me do my job?" If the answer is "no," or "I'm not sure," then close the file.
- Minimum necessary is scalable. A solo practitioner will have different minimum-necessary standards than a network of physicians with several locations.

- The privacy official must make a working list of persons or classes of persons who must have access to specific portions of the designated record set to fulfill their duties.

- The privacy official then must specify how much access is needed for each class of individuals. For example, a physician or nurse will need full access to a patient's health information, but a receptionist does not require as much to fulfill the front office tasks.

- For access via electronic media, assign passwords to each person. Do not share passwords. A nurse may not want a physician making patient notes while the nurse is logged in on the patient file.

- Some types of business associates, such as transcriptionists, may need routine access to medical records. Include those routine disclosures in your policies and procedures.

CRITICAL POINT

"Minimum necessary" means that you will receive information necessary to complete your tasks. If you see something that you think is not relevant to your job, close the file.

STEP 5: REVIEW AND IMPLEMENT HIPAA'S ADMINISTRATIVE REQUIREMENTS

The Privacy Rule requires your office to perform several tasks to manage privacy. You may have already implemented these tasks. But if you are doing them for the first time, here is a list for your review and development.

What to do:
- Designate a privacy official and a contact person for complaints.
- Develop and distribute your Notice of Privacy Practices.
- Develop your HIPAA policies and procedures.
- Develop documentation procedures.
- Train your workforce on your policies and procedures.
- Develop internal sanctions if an employee breaches privacy policies.
- Develop a process to mitigate breaches.
- Develop safeguards that provide for administrative, technical, and physical safeguards of PHI.

How to do it:
We'll review these one at a time in the following discussion.

Designate a Privacy Official

The Privacy Rule requires your office to designate a privacy official. The privacy official may be the office manager, a contractor, or a new hire, but the practice is not required to hire a full-time person to fill this position. You can learn more about this responsibility in Step 1 of this chapter.

Designate One Person to Be the Contact Person to Receive Complaints

The contact person may also be the privacy official in a small office. In many offices, the contact person can be the receptionist, the head nurse, or another person with good customer-service skills who is also trustworthy and can keep confidences. The name and phone number of the contact person must be provided in the Notice of Privacy Practices.

The contact person plays a critical role in managing complaints for several reasons. Providers want to know what patients are thinking, and providers prefer to learn first hand if patients have a concern, so that they can manage problems internally. This is an important part of providing good customer service.

Few of us welcome a complaint that has been filed against us with a federal agency. A phone call from the Office for Civil Rights following up on a patient complaint wouldn't sit well with the practice's leadership. Explore ways in which you can direct complaints to your practice's contact person.

It's unlikely that the Office for Civil Rights will have the personnel to follow up on each complaint, and there is talk about hiring a contractor to follow up on complaints.

Perhaps the best reason for an effective contact person is that complaints filed internally will keep the plaintiff's lawyers at bay. Often unhappy patients just want to be heard. If your office can provide an empathic listener at the source of pain, you could prevent costly investigative downtime and lawsuits.

How to do it:
- Appoint one person to be the contact person.
- Include the contact person on your privacy team.
- Train the contact person so that he or she is well informed about the Privacy Rule.

Develop HIPAA Policies and Procedures

Privacy compliance is the responsibility of everyone in the office. The privacy official is responsible for getting policies and procedures in place but will not have time to write and coordinate the development of these documents. The privacy official therefore has several solutions:

- Delegate the task of writing policies and procedures to the privacy team.
- Purchase one of several inexpensive policies and procedures manuals to review and adapt to your office:
  - ☐ The *HIPAA Policies and Procedures Desk Reference* contains 59 forms and 39 policies and procedures, quick reference guides, and a privacy summary and costs less than $200.00 at www.amapress.com.
  - ☐ The Workgroup for Electronic Data Interchange's Strategic National Implementation Process (SNIP) initiative has developed a set of policies and procedures. Find them at www.wedi.org/snip.
  - ☐ HIPAA Gives (Government Information Value Exchange for States) provides HIPAA content for state governments (www.hipaagives.org). Price not listed.
  - ☐ The Boundary Information Group (BIG) has developed 100 policies and procedures at www.hipaainfo.net. Price includes on-site development and implementation.
  - ☐ WebMD/Medical Manager offers a HIPAA Compliance Package that includes a Privacy Tool Kit and policies and procedures reference for $798.00 at www.medicalmanager.com.
  - ☐ Siemens Health Center offers an electronic set of HIPAA policies and procedures at www.siemens.com.
  - ☐ A complete list of training organizations can be found at the Workgroup for Electronic Data Interchange at http://snip.wedi.org/public/articles/HIPAASolution.pdf.
- Call your state medical society, AMA Press, or HIPAA statewide organization to find policies and procedures you can buy.

The previous list of manuals is designed to provide a policy and procedure for nearly every event that can happen in the office. But policies and procedures are scalable according to size. A small practice with fewer than 10 employees may find that a 30- to 50-page document adequately guides the staff in privacy compliance. On the other hand, a multi-specialty practice with 10 locations may need 100 to 150 pages with a variety of specific forms. Discuss scalability (how much is enough) and HIPAA compliance policies and procedures with your lawyer.

CRITICAL POINT
You can purchase sample policies and procedures and then customize them to your office policies. Be certain that your policies and procedures are consistent with your Notice of Privacy Practices.

Revising Your Policies and Procedures

You must update your policies and procedures as necessary each time there are changes in the Privacy Rule. HHS can revise the Privacy Rule no more than once a year. Cross-reference any changes with provisions in the Notice of Privacy Practices.

If you find that you quickly adopted a set of policies and procedures and aren't following them because they don't work, you should:

- Make a list of which policies and procedures aren't working.
- Ask your lawyer which of the ineffective policies and procedures are cross-referenced in the NPP.
- If you revise your policies and procedures, you must retrain your staff in the new policies.

Develop Documentation Procedures

The Privacy Rule requires specific documentation to be in writing. Required documentation must be maintained for six years from either the date it was created or from the date when the record was last in effect, whichever is later. Examples of required documentation include:

- HIPAA policies and procedures,
- a Notice of Privacy Practices (NPP) in plain English,
- acknowledgment of receipt of NPP,
- authorizations,
- agreed upon restrictions,
- accountings of disclosures,
- complaints, and
- sanctions.

All covered entities are also required to permit HHS access to facilities, books, records, accounts, and other sources of information that will help the secretary of HHS's Office for Civil Rights determine whether the entity is complying or compliant. In addition, most health-law attorneys strongly recommend that providers document patient requests.

What to do:

Establish a documentation process.

How to do it:

- Follow your policies and procedures if you already have them. If you are using this book to design your HIPAA documentation, consider the list above.
- Keep HIPAA documentation in a separate HIPAA patient file for each patient.

- When developing documentation for legal review, ask your attorney if the information you provide will be accorded the attorney-client privilege. You'll want to make sure the attorney isn't required to report your state of compliance, or noncompliance, to an enforcement agency.
- If you ask a patient to provide documentation to you in writing, your practice must maintain that documentation for six years.

CRITICAL POINT
If you're not sure whether to document or not, the decision should be "Yes, document."

Workforce Training

HIPAA's Privacy Rule requires that you train your staff, including volunteers and part-time employees, on your HIPAA privacy policies and procedures. Many organizations begin with HIPAA awareness—a great idea because it prepares staff and volunteers for the policies and procedures. The regulations, however, say that you must train your staff on your HIPAA policies and procedures.

HIPAA also requires that you train new employees within a reasonable amount of time after they have been hired and also train employees when they assume new responsibilities.

HIPAA privacy training is discussed in detail in Step 9 of this chapter.

CRITICAL POINT
You are required to train staff on your HIPAA privacy policies and procedures.

Develop Internal Sanctions if an Employee Breaches Privacy Policies

Another name for *internal sanction* is *disciplinary action*. Most physicians intend for their employees to come to work every day and do an exceptional job each day. Yet keep in mind that no hospital, no medical practice, no nursing home will be 100 percent compliant all the time. This portion of the rule is subject to a practical and flexible standard. The Privacy Rule requires your practice to put in writing the disciplinary actions you'll take if an employee violates a privacy policy and procedure. The rule doesn't specify what those sanctions should be, only that the staff knows the consequences of a breach of privacy.

What to do:
Follow your policies and procedures if they are already in place. If not in place, you can use some or all of the following. The privacy official should identify situations that require an internal sanction and establish consequences.

How to do it:

- If a patient files a complaint, refer the complaint to the privacy official.

- The privacy official will evaluate whether the breach involved protected health information. If the breach did not contain PHI, the complaint is not a HIPAA complaint.

- The privacy official or the practice's management team will investigate and evaluate the complaint to determine whether there was a violation.

- If the complaint has merit, the privacy official will follow the procedure for internal sanctions. That procedure may include suspending a workforce member, putting a written document in the employee's file, or conducting a meeting with the employee and supervisor.

- Neither the privacy official nor practice management can take any action against a "whistleblower." A whistleblower is a member of the workforce or a business associate who discloses PHI in the good-faith belief that either the practice has engaged in unlawful conduct or violates professional or clinical standards or the care, services, and conditions of the practice endanger one or more patients, workers, or the public.

- If a member of the practice is a victim of a criminal act and discloses PHI to a law-enforcement official, no disciplinary action may be applied if the PHI is about the suspected perpetrator of the criminal act.

- The practice is not required to monitor business associates, but you must take steps to address a problem if you are aware that a business associate has violated an individual's privacy. Contact the privacy official immediately if you suspect this has happened. Business associates are discussed in Step 9 of this chapter.

CRITICAL POINT

Policies and procedures must provide sanctions for privacy breaches and security incidents.

Develop a Process to Mitigate Breaches

To mitigate something is to make it less harsh, less painful, or less severe. The Privacy Rule does not specify what steps you must take to resolve or mitigate harm to a patient from a privacy breach, but the rule does require the practice to try to resolve a complaint if the patient believes it has caused harm.

The normal human reaction is to try to mend a breach before the complaint goes to a supervisory level. Keep in mind that all of us came into HIPAA privacy from somewhere else. We've all had to go through a significant learning curve. If you are on the front end of your learning curve, the best answer is to go directly to your privacy official if you believe the practice needs to undo potential harm. HHS expects the privacy official to be knowledgeable about privacy and support you in your privacy efforts.

If a patient files a complaint with you and has chosen you as the person to blame, don't say, "I'm so sorry I did this to you." Don't say, "You're out of your mind. That didn't happen." And don't say, "It's no big deal. No one cares about your health issues but you anyway." Do say, "Let's take this to the privacy official so that you can tell her what happened."

Once you've presented the patient's complaint to the privacy official, step out of the picture. The privacy official is usually the only employee who can make mitigation recommendations.

What to do:

Leave all mitigations to the privacy official.

How to do it:

- Document your conversation with the individual making a complaint.
- Do not offer any solutions.
- Tell the privacy official what happened. Explain your part as honestly as you remember it.
- If the privacy official cannot see the complaining patient at this time, make an appointment for them to meet.
- Ask the privacy official if there is anything else you can do to help.
- Common mitigation responses may include:
  - ☐ An apology.
  - ☐ Retrieving the protected health information from where it was sent.
  - ☐ Adopting policies and procedures that clarify a situation that wasn't addressed before this incident.
  - ☐ Retraining workforce members.
  - ☐ Sanctioning an employee.

Most privacy violations are not intentional, but they do need to be corrected. If the violation was intentional, mitigation procedures can get complicated.

- Attorneys may become involved.
- An employee may get fired.
- Consumer advocates may make inquiries.
- Reporters will cover and publicize intentional breaches.
- Law-enforcement officials may get involved.
- OCR investigators may also get involved.

CRITICAL POINT

OCR prefers that physicians mitigate breaches before an individual files a complaint with HHS.

Develop Administrative, Technical, and Physical Safeguards

HHS refers to "safeguards" as the measures you take to protect confidential information. For example, do you lock your doors at night? Can any employee in the office gain access to medical and billing charts? Are nosy patients allowed to walk around and see another person's chart? Does the office manager know and use the physician's password? Do business associates have a specific user ID that they must use to gain access to your records?

The Privacy Rule presents mandates for administrative, technical, and physical safeguards pertaining to oral, paper, and electronic protected health information (PHI). Chapter 4 of this book goes into much more detail about administrative, technical, and physical safeguards of electronic PHI. In that chapter in particular, we discuss requirements from HIPAA's final version of the Security Rule that was published in the *Federal Register* on February 20, 2003.

> **CRITICAL POINT**
> You cannot have privacy without first having security.

HIPAA obligates you to protect the security of health information in your practice. Security is about controlling access to PHI. Privacy is about controlling what information is permitted to be used and disclosed and to whom.

When you lock the doors every night, or when you require employees to use passwords to gain access to PHI, you are meeting security safeguards. When the patient requests access to medical or billing information, or when you provide permitted medical information to a family member, you are meeting the privacy regulations.

Your medical records are an asset to your practice. If a physician wanted to sell his or her practice, certified valuation analysts would evaluate several aspects of the practice, including the medical records. So it makes good business sense to protect that asset and place limits on who can have access to that information.

The medical records also contain confidential financial and health information about patients, and patients expect that information to remain private. But once a medical record leaves the physician's hands, the information in that record may be used for many purposes, such as filing for claim payment, ordering additional tests, analysis for additional treatment, referral to another physician or surgeon, and so forth. Patients expect other providers to analyze confidential health information to provide the best treatment, but patients don't expect someone who shouldn't have access to it to see confidential health information.[8]

---

8. The final Security Rule also provides compatible standards for privacy safeguards that will help your practice mitigate the risk of privacy breaches.

Administrative Safeguards

The Privacy Rule requires covered entities to perform 10 administrative tasks to protect the privacy of health information. These are decisions that the practice's management team must take action on. You can ask an outside consulting firm to help you meet the administrative requirements, but all of them must be adopted internally. Table 3.7 outlines the required administrative tasks.

TABLE 3.7

HIPAA Privacy Administrative Tasks and How to Do Them

What to Do	How to Do It
Appoint a privacy official and a contact person	The Privacy Official may also be the office manager. The privacy official is responsible for developing and implementing the privacy policies and procedures. Delegate a privacy team to help the privacy official, although the privacy official is accountable for privacy. The privacy official also may be the designated security official, as required by the Security Rule (see Chapter 4).
	Appoint a contact person to receive complaints.
	Send the privacy official to training. Expect at least a six- to eight-month learning curve.
	Keep the privacy official in contact with a health-law attorney for legal advice.
Develop HIPAA policies and procedures	Develop your own or adopt and revise a set of policies and procedures from a vendor. Your policies and procedures can be scaled—if you're a small practice, you don't need 200 pages of policies and procedures. The policies and procedures that you adopt must ensure compliance.
	You must follow your policies and procedures. If you amend them, keep the old policies for six years, and retrain in the new policy or procedure.
Develop and implement safeguards	It's one thing to write a policy that tells staff to lock the doors at night or to keep voices down so that other patients can't hear, and another thing to practice privacy all the time.
	Safeguards prevent unintended uses and disclosures. Safeguards include the administrative, technical, and physical processes in this section.

T A B L E   3.7 (continued)

HIPAA Privacy Administrative Tasks and How to Do Them

What to Do	How to Do It
Develop a documentation process	Develop new documentation habits that put into writing how you use and disclose patient information, patient activities and requests, and document policies and procedures.
	Keep documentation for six years from the date the record was created or six years from when it was last used, whichever is later.
	Some samples of documentation to keep include:
	■ Patient receipt of Notice of Privacy Practices.
	■ Patient request to access medical or billing records.
	■ Persons or entities for whom or to whom protected health information has been used and disclosed.
	■ Policies and procedures.
	■ Employee or volunteer receipt of policies and procedures.
	■ Business-associate agreements.
	■ Signatures from employees who attended training.
	■ Test results from HIPAA privacy training.
	■ Specific authorizations from patients.
	■ Patient complaints.
	■ Employee incidents and sanctions.
	■ Mitigation activities.
Train your staff	HIPAA requires that you train your staff on your policies and procedures. Set aside one to two hours to train employees in appropriate groups:
	■ Persons with direct patient contact,
	■ Persons with little or no direct contact, and
	■ Persons with management responsibilities.
	Keep a record of who attended training and test them for understanding.
	Retrain if there are unintentional breaches.
	Train staff members when they accept new responsibilities.
	Train new staff when they come on board.
	Ask staff members to sign a confidentiality agreement or acknowledgment at the completion of training. These agreements should state that PHI cannot be disclosed even after the employee leaves the practice.

continued

T A B L E   3.7 (continued)

HIPAA Privacy Administrative Tasks and How to Do Them

What to Do	How to Do It
Develop a process for complaints	Include a process for making complaints in your Notice of Privacy Practices so that patients will complain to you rather than the Secretary of HHS.
	Identify this process in your policies and procedures:
	Who should receive the complaint?
	Who follows up on complaints?
	What is the process if the complaint is significant?
	How do you mitigate serious complaints?
Develop sanctions	Develop a policy and procedure that sanctions employees and volunteers for intentional breaches and unintentional incidents.
Mitigate breaches	Develop a policy and procedure for mitigating any harmful effect that comes from a privacy violation. This includes breaches caused by business associates. Your privacy official is most likely the person to follow this policy.
Do not allow intimidation or retaliation	Develop a policy that says you will not intimidate, harass, or retaliate against any patient for exercising any right under the HIPAA Privacy Rule, including the right to file a complaint.
Do not ask patients to waive rights	Develop a policy that says you will not ask patients to waive their rights before you will treat them.

Technical Safeguards

Most employees use technology every day without giving much thought to technical safeguards. Technical safeguards issues may involve:

- **Sharing passwords.** Even sharing of passwords between physicians and office managers is no longer allowed.

- **Internet shopping.** Computers left open to the Internet can leave medical records exposed to outsiders.

- **Friends and family e-mail lists.** Do you send and receive personal e-mails at the office? Each time you receive an e-mail from a non-secure site, such as AOL, Earthlink, or Juno, you are exposing your computer to viruses.

- **Computer games.** Do you know what is on each employee's desktop? Are there games that can crash your network? Games may contain viruses that damage network data.

- **Remote access.** Do the physicians download medical records from home via nonsecure Internet providers, update the records, and e-mail them back to the office?
- **"Minimum necessary."** Who has access to the medical records? Your password should give you the level of information you need to do your job.

This discussion covers technical safeguards in general, but you should also read Chapter 4 of this book. If you have an interest in more advanced technical safeguards, Chapter 4 can lead you in the right direction.

To the average worker, technical safeguards sounds complicated, but it's much easier to understand when put into simple language. Table 3.8 defines some terms often used when discussing computer security.

TABLE 3.8

Technical Safeguard Terms[9]

Technical Safeguard Term	What It Means
Access control	A system of policies, procedures, and electronic codes that determines who has physical access to protected health information and at what level.
	Access control includes policies and procedures to allow staff members access using one password only and to guarantee that each person's password is not shared by others.
Audit controls	A person or a software program that checks to make sure the right people have access to the right information.
Authentication	A process to make sure the person logging on really is that person.
Contingency planning	The plan you follow if something happens to your electronic data.
Encryption	Similar to a locked door, but instead of using a key to enter, the program uses random bits of information with different lengths.
Passwords	The unique set of numbers and letters that identifies you as the user. Do *not* share your password.
Security incident	A breach.
	Someone may hack into the system, but more likely, an employee has shared information that should not have been shared.

continued

---

9. Definitions for these terms have been simplified for understanding. Consult the Security Rule at www.cms.gov for a full review of legal terms and definitions.

T A B L E 3.8 (continued)

Technical Safeguard Terms

Technical Safeguard Term	What It Means
Media controls	Receiving and removing information from hardware and software in and out of a facility. When you donate used computers to the local college, for example, you must eliminate the "media" or data on your computer before it goes to someone else.

What to do:

Discuss technical safeguards with your information-technology department head or contractor. Then develop and follow your policies and procedures for maintaining technical safeguards.

How to do it:

- Appoint a security official. The security official should be someone with excellent people management skills and some computer knowledge who understands—and maybe even likes—computer activities.

- The information technology specialist or contractor for your office should read Chapter 4 of this book.

- Conduct a risk analysis and other implementation specifications included in the Security Rule's administrative safeguards. The Security Rule requires that you do this, and Chapter 4 of this book tells you how.

- Establish user passwords for part-time and full-time employees and business associates.

- Develop emergency access procedures.

- Audit the integrity of your information.

- Develop a process that authenticates the user.

- Develop and follow policies and procedures that maintain technical safeguards.

- Train the staff on your technical policies and procedures.

- Develop a wish list of items you'd like your vendor to provide.

Physical Safeguards

Physical safeguards refer to the measures you take to physically protect patient health information. Physical safeguards include:

- **Doors and windows.** Do you lock them at night?
- **Laptops and handheld computers.** Are they put into a safe or locked up when you're away?

- **Computer screens.** Who can see them when you step away from the computer?

- **Patient files.** Are they protected from access by non-authorized persons?

- **Building maintenance.** Do maintenance workers have access to medical records? Have you trained personnel about HIPAA or had them sign a confidentiality agreement?

- **Media controls.** Do you erase everything from the computers when you change them or donate computers to a school? Is the information really deleted or is just the file name erased?

- **Fire, theft, or disaster.** Do you have a plan to handle partial or full disasters? A partial disaster could be loss of telephone service or electricity, while a full disaster could be a fire.

Physical safeguards focus on protecting the facility as much as they do on replacing the data if it were lost. Your security official is required to conduct a risk analysis and regular audits to determine the physical safety of patient information. You'll learn much more about that in Chapter 4 of this book.

What to do:

Implement security procedures that are included in the Privacy Rule for three reasons. (1) It's the law. (2) It will protect your office assets. (3) As you build your Security Rule compliance program, implementing the security components in the Privacy Rule will get you well on your way. Remember, though, that the Security Rule covers protected health information in electronic form but that the Privacy Rule covers protected health information in electronic, oral, and written forms.

How to do it:

- The security official's responsibility is to manage and supervise physical security measures. The security official may want to delegate some of that responsibility.

- Develop a policy and procedure that explains how you will receive and remove data from hardware and software.

- Establish a policy that defines who is allowed on the premises and where they have access to information. For example, are patients allowed in the medical-records room?

- Establish timeout policies for your computers. For example, if you need to step away from the computer, should the screen turn black within five minutes or two minutes? Do you need to log back on after 10 minutes or 5 minutes? Should you install biometric readers?[10]

- Train the staff in your physical-safeguards policies and procedures.

---

10. Biometric readers identify users by a signal from the user's body (a thumbprint, the iris, a voice print, and so on).

Create a Medical Practice Black Box

To assist in recovering critical data about your medical practice, assemble several items and put them into a *black box* to be stored off site. Critical items in your black box could include:

- backup software to rebuild computers,
- backup data of patient records,
- inventory of items in the medical office (could include video or photos of contents),
- list of staff telephone numbers,
- insurance agent and contact information, and
- other items that you would have difficulty recreating.

STEP 6: SPECIAL REQUIREMENTS

In Step 4, we discussed how each use and disclosure of PHI fell within one or more permissions. But before using or disclosing PHI, you may also need to review any special restrictions that you agreed to or special requirements, such as for marketing and fund raising. These special requirements are presented here.

Verify the Identity of the Person Who Requests Access to Protected Health Information

Kahili calls on the phone and says she's in the orthopedist's office. She asks that you fax a copy of her medical record to this doctor. Kahili hasn't been in the office for more than a year, and frankly, you can't remember who she is or what she looks like.

What to do:

Ask for verification and other details before faxing the information.

How to do it:

Follow your policies and procedures. If you haven't developed policies and procedures, follow this process:

- Use common sense. If this sounds like a legitimate request, then proceed.
- Ask the patient for personal information that you can verify from the medical record. That information could be the Social Security number, driver's license number, insurance number, or mother's maiden name.
- Call the general telephone number of the orthopedist's office and not the direct-dial number given to you.
- Verify that the patient made the request.

- Ask for the fax number at the other physician's office and inform the physician's office that you are faxing the patient's medical record. In some states you may want to ask for an authorization from the patient.
- Fax only what the patient requested from the patient's medical record.
- Request confirmation by e-mail or phone call acknowledging that the fax was received.
- Make a notation, including relevant paper work, in the patient's record of this transaction.

CRITICAL POINT

If you don't know the individual making the request, ask for verification.

Verify Personal Representatives

Mia holds legal and medical power of attorney over her father, who is a patient in your office. He has dementia and also is on medication for cardiac arrhythmia. Her father is in an assisted-living facility and has had a severe reaction either to something he ate or to complexities from medication. Her father has been stabilized, but Mia wants to review her father's medical records to see if she or the emergency-room physician can determine what caused his reaction. You know her father, but you don't know Mia.

What to do:

Ask for verification and other details before delivering the medical record to the daughter.

How to do it:

Follow your policies and procedures. If you haven't developed them, follow this process:

- Ask to see a copy of the power of attorney. It should be on official letterhead or should include the stamp from a notary public.
- Ask for picture identification from the personal representative, such as a driver's license.
- If the patient's request is by fax, follow the processes for the patient in the scenario above.
- Use common sense. If this request feels reasonable, follow through after you've satisfied the verification requirement.
- Make a written notation, including copies of the paperwork, in the patient's file.

CRITICAL POINT

Do not be afraid to ask for identification from callers or visitors whom you do not know before releasing PHI. In fact, as politely as possible, insist on verifying identification.

Minimum Necessary Special Requirements

Ginger, a patient in the office, is a victim of domestic violence, and she has requested that you not send a report of her visit to her husband's insurance company for fear her husband will do harm if he learns she has talked about him. Ginger wants to see the billing information before you send it to the insurance company.

What to do:

If a patient makes a request in writing, and you have agreed to that request, you must honor it.

How to do it:

Follow your policies and procedures. If you have not developed them, use this process:

- Check the medical record or log to see if a special requirement applies.
- Consult with the privacy official on this special request.
- Use the "minimum necessary" standard and determine the minimum amount of information necessary to send to the insurance company.
- If you agree to the request to view the records before they are sent to the insurance company, set an appointment and ask the patient to stop in to review the billing record.

Special Requirements for Marketing

In your practice, you see several children with type A diabetes. A pharmaceutical company that you have worked with announces that the Food and Drug Administration has approved its compact insulin pack that can be implanted in children over three years of age. A sales representative who has become a good and reliable resource for you stops into your office and demonstrates how the implant works and also shows you a video of kids who are living with diabetes without insulin injections. The physicians in your office would love to do something for the kids they treat. The company would like to send a brochure to each of your patients with juvenile diabetes and tell them about this implant. It could be a significant change for the kids, their parents, and siblings.

What to do:

Determine whether this is "marketing" or "communications for treatment purposes." Communication that merely promotes health in a general manner and does not promote a specific product or service from a particular provider does not meet the general definition of marketing. Communications, such as mailings reminding women to get an annual mammogram and mailings providing information about how to lower cholesterol, about new developments in health care (new diagnostic tools), and about health or "wellness" classes, support groups, and health fairs are permitted, and are not considered marketing.[11]

How to do it:

Follow your policies and procedures. If you don't have them, follow this process:

■ Consult your privacy official before sending out any messages to patients.

■ This communication is about a specific product and meets the general definition of marketing. While it also falls into treatment, it does promote a specific product.

■ In a face-to-face communication, a physician does not need an authorization to communicate about this product with the patient or patient's family.

■ If the physician wants other parents to learn about the implant, send the families a letter and ask if they wish to receive information about the product. Ask for a signature on an authorization form.

■ Keep a record of each signed authorization, and send the families with signed authorizations the information about the product.

Psychotherapy Notes

Psychotherapy notes receive special protection under HIPAA's Privacy Rule. A medical practice may not use or disclose psychotherapy notes for any purpose, including most treatment, payment, or healthcare operations, without a written authorization signed by the patient.

As with all laws, there are exceptions. Authorizations are not necessary for the following purposes:

■ The originator of the notes wants to review them.

■ In a training program, the medical practice can use or disclose PHI to students, trainees, or other mental-healthcare personnel for learning under supervision to improve their skills in group, joint, family, or individual counseling.

■ The medical practice can use or disclose psychotherapy notes to defend itself in a legal action or other proceedings brought on by the patient.

■ The Secretary of HHS wants to review them.

■ The use or disclosure is required by law.

■ You need to avert a serious threat to health or safety, under specific conditions.

---

11. From Office for Civil Rights, OCR Guidance Explaining Significant Aspects of the Privacy Rule, December 4, 2002, available via the Internet at www.hhs.gov/OCR/hipaa/privacy.html.

Policies and Procedures Consistent with Notice of Privacy Practices

Your Notice of Privacy Practices, authorization, and acknowledgment forms can be made available for the public to read and determine how you plan to use and disclose patient information. Your HIPAA policies and procedures, which are internal documents, are your road map of what to do and how to do it in those public documents. Your public documents and your internal documents must be consistent.

What to do:

Make your internal policy and procedure documents consistent with your public documents such as the NPP.

How to do it:

■ If your medical office describes how it will use and disclose PHI in the NPP, you must describe how you will manage that use or disclosure in your policies and procedures. For example, if you plan to contact patients to provide reminder appointments, you must tell the patient in the NPP that you will do so.

■ If a patient makes a special request, your policies and procedures should tell you how to follow that request.

■ Contact your privacy official if you have any questions about how to implement a privacy policy.

State Laws

If a state privacy law is more stringent than HIPAA's Privacy Rule, then you must follow the more stringent state law. Otherwise, with some exceptions, HIPAA's Privacy Rule provision defers to the state-law provision.

What to do:

If the state law conflicts with HIPAA and the state law is more limiting, follow the state law.

How to do it:

■ Work with medical societies or your attorney to determine what state laws define what you can and cannot do under HIPAA.

■ Develop a list of circumstances in your state that require a consent form or written authorization before you can use or disclose confidential medical information.

■ Train your staff on those more stringent privacy laws.

■ Develop a consent form compatible with your state law.

CRITICAL POINT

You must follow a state law rather than HIPAA if the state law is more stringent.

FOCUS ON HIPAA CAAT

www.hipaacaat.com

HIPAA Problem

Keeping track of and maintaining compliance records (disclosures, patient signatures, special requests such as alternative communications, opt outs, access to medical records, amendments, updated documentation, forms and authorizations); generating reports without bogging down staff workflow or computer systems; and ensuring the physical and electronic security of protected health information.

HIPAA Solution

HIPAA CAAT is an Internet-based compliance automation and tracking tool for single and group physician offices. It is a secure tool that enables a reporting mechanism to determine status of information. It is easy to set up and easy to use.

Typical Users

Single-physician practices to large multi-specialty groups.

Is It Affordable?

It costs $995 to install with no additional licensing fees for users, and an annual subscription fee of $199. Discounts are available to members of some medical societies.

Contact Information

Dave Ronis
(866) 703-CAAT (2228)

STEP 7: DEVELOP BUSINESS-ASSOCIATE CONTRACTS WITH YOUR VENDORS

Every medical practice needs one or more business associates to help keep the practice running smoothly. Business associates are contractors hired to do the work of or for a covered entity. A business associate may be an attorney, a practice-management consultant, a transcription service, a billing company, and many more. If that business associate handles protected health information, your practice is required to enter into a business-associate agreement. In that agreement, the business associate ensures that it will provide safeguards that protect confidential patient information.

Employees and volunteers usually aren't business associates. This list provides a good overview of the types of business associates that provide professional services:

- Claims processing or administration.
- Data analysis.
- Processing.
- Medical transcriptionists.
- Utilization review.
- Quality assurance.
- Billing.
- Benefit management.
- Practice management.
- Repricing entities. ´
- Lawyers.
- Accountants and bookkeepers.
- Data aggregation.
- Management consultants.
- Administration.
- Accreditation services.
- Financial services.[12]

You are not required to have business-associate contracts with people or companies that have no reason to be in contact with protected health information. For example, in the December 4, 2002, Guidance on business associates issued by OCR, HHS indicated that you do not need business-associate agreements with plumbers, electricians, or photocopy machine technicians because they do not need access to PHI to perform their services, "or any access to protected health information by such persons would be incidental, if at all."[13] However, a software company may be a business associate if it hosts software containing patient information on its own server or if it accesses patient information when trouble-shooting a software function.

---

12. A business-associate agreement is not required in the following circumstances: "When a financial institution processes consumer-conducted financial transactions by debit, credit, or other payment card, clears checks, initiates or processes electronic fund transfers, or conducts any other activity that directly facilitates or effects the transfer of funds for payment of health care or health plan premiums. When it conducts these activities, the financial institution is providing its normal banking or other financial transaction services to its customers; it is not performing a function or activity for, or on behalf of, the covered entity." Office for Civil Rights, OCR Guidance Explaining Significant Aspects of the Privacy Rule, December 4, 2002, available via the Internet at www.hhs.gov/OCR/hipaa/privacy.html.

13. *Ibid.*

Contents of the Business-Associate Agreement

The Privacy Rule spells out specific contents that must be included in your business-associate agreement. That content includes the following list of items.

- Establish the permitted uses or disclosures of PHI.

- A business associate cannot use or disclose PHI if the medical practice is also not permitted to disclose it.

- A business associate cannot use or disclose PHI except as permitted in the agreement.

- A business associate must report to you any use or disclosure incidents that were not permitted by the agreement.

- A business associate must use appropriate safeguards to prevent use or disclosure of PHI.

- A business associate must ensure that its own agents or subcontractors agree to the same restrictions.

- A business associate must make PHI available if an individual requests to see, amend, or receive an accounting of disclosures.

- A business associate must make its books, records, or practices available to the secretary of HHS for a compliance audit.

- The practice can terminate the agreement if the business associate violates the agreement.

- If the agreement is terminated, the business associate must return or destroy all PHI at contract termination.

Deadline for Business-Associate Agreements

Business-associate agreements must have been in place by April 14, 2003. But there is an exception. If your practice has written agreements, such as a confidentiality agreement, already in place, and you do not otherwise modify or amend the agreement, you will be considered "compliant" if you update the agreement and include the items above by April 14, 2004, or on the contract's renewal date, whichever comes first. If you modify or amend the agreement prior to April 14, 2004, you must include the business-associate provisions in the agreement.

STEP 8: WORK WITH LEGAL COUNSEL TO ASSESS YOUR COMPLIANCE STATUS

HIPAA is federal law. You need an attorney to assist you in final review of your documents. You can take the lead in creating these documents from over-the-counter products or documentation you've seen on web sites, but before implementing any documentation, discuss it with your lawyer. Be certain to ask for attorney-client confidentiality before presenting any documentation to an attorney. Your attorney should be well versed in health law and knowledgeable about HIPAA.

- *Ask your attorney to review the following:*
    - Internal documents and processes.
    - Policies and procedures.
    - Your documentation process.
    - Your confidentiality agreement to be signed by staff members.
    - Unusual complaints or mitigation procedures.
    - Your use or disclosure processes.
- *External documents and processes.*
    - Notice of Privacy Practices.
    - HIPAA informed-consent form (not required by all states and not the same as a "consent to treat").
    - Business-associate agreement.
    - Authorization form.
    - NPP acknowledgment form.

In most cases, a good attorney will advise you that HIPAA is about using common sense. No practice can afford to use an attorney for all of its documentation, but no practice can afford to put documents out for public scrutiny without an attorney's review.

STEP 9: TRAIN YOUR STAFF

Many people believe that HIPAA training will wind down after April 14, 2003. But HIPAA insiders believe it will only escalate after the deadline because excessive privacy breaches discovered by consumers will force healthcare staff into more focused retraining. HIPAA requires that you train new staff within a reasonable amount of time after each person is hired. Any time someone in your office is promoted or changes job position, you must provide privacy training according to new job responsibilities.

Focused training will keep your staff from making mistakes, and if there is a privacy breach, your trained staff will know how to handle the problem before it becomes an issue. Don't let the fear of breaches drive your training program. Fear usually results in confused thinking and knee-jerk responses.

FOCUS ON HEALTHCARE TRAINING STRATEGIES

www.htsonline.com

HIPAA Problem

HIPAA regulations are too complicated for the office staff to understand. The staff understands the basics of privacy and security but needs to know how to implement HIPAA in day-to-day experiences. The practice has little or no computer access to online training. Individual learning styles are not compatible with online reading and testing.

HIPAA Solution

Healthcare Training Strategies provides:

■ simplified training materials in a multimedia, scenario-based format that make it easy to learn the safeguard requirements and how staff should respond to patient requests and administrative requirements;

■ "Pocket Guides," "101 Guides," and wall charts that translate complicated legal language without compromising legal integrity;

■ materials that assist in implementing change; and

■ test questions designed for group discussions.

Typical Users

Privacy officials selecting multimedia training materials for staff, staff with direct patient content in physicians, and long-term care facilities.

Is It Affordable?

Cost of complete set of training materials is less than $600. No licensing is required for additional users. Items in kit may be purchased separately.

Contact Information

Denise Kustka
Account Manager
Healthcare Training Strategies
617 Hillsborough Street
Raleigh, NC 27602
(919) 821-9192
denise@htsonline.com

Training must be to the extent necessary for each employee to carry out his or her work functions. How much training is enough? That is the subject of much debate.

■ What approach to training is right for your audience?

■ Should you use an online trainer?

■ Should you bring in a speaker and conduct a half-day seminar?

■ Should you purchase multimedia materials that physicians' offices are accustomed to using?

The truth is that no single training philosophy works all the time for all employees. Determine how extensive your training should be by dividing your staff into three categories (see Table 3.9).

TABLE 3.9

Training by Job Category

Patient Contact Category	Amount of Training Needed
1. Employees with direct patient contact: Physicians, nurses, office manager, privacy official	Extensive training, with regular updates and reminders throughout the year
2. Employees with some patient contact: Receptionist, billing and insurance clerks, medical-records staff, lab technicians, volunteers, coders	Awareness training with regular updates and reminders throughout the year
3. Employees with little or no patient contact: Maintenance staff, housekeeping	Awareness training, with reminders or posters where they will see them

A good training program, whether you develop it yourself or use an outside resource, will include the following topics:

■ Part I: HIPAA awareness (30 minutes to 1 hour).
  □ Overview of HIPAA privacy.
  □ The practice's approach to protecting patient privacy.
  □ Patient rights and how the practice will honor those rights.
  □ The role of the privacy official.
  □ How the practice plans to enforce the Privacy Rule.
■ Part II: Your HIPAA policies and procedures (2 hours).
  □ Key terms.
  □ Permissions for use and disclosure of protected health information.
  □ Special requirements for use and disclosure of PHI.
  □ Patient rights.
  □ Privacy management.
■ Part III: Year-round training (15 to 30 minutes once a month).
  □ Include training exercises and contingency scenarios as part of monthly staff meetings.
  □ You'll find a comprehensive training program, including year-round topics for discussion and an action approach to changing behavior, in Appendix A.

As part of each training session, you should also:

■ Test for understanding, and keep records of each person's test.
■ Have employees sign an attendance register, and maintain records and date(s) of attendance.

FOCUS ON TRAIN FOR HIPAA

www.trainforhipaa.com

HIPAA Problem

Healthcare organizations have a variety of educational dilemmas, from training staff about job-specific requirements to training clinical and management professionals about privacy, security, and transactions and code sets requirements. As such, healthcare organizations require content adaptable for multiple audiences; the ability for staff to be trained at multiple locations, customized for specific facilities; and continual appraisal of updated content based on HHS revisions.

HIPAA Solution

Train for HIPAA provides an array of HIPAA training and education solutions, including Internet-based HIPAA courses, on-site trainers, and job-related content. In addition, Train for HIPAA provides

- audioconferences,
- the HIPAA Summit Conference series,
- the Harvard HIPAA Colloquium, and
- customized products and services specific to the institution, both in content and appearance. (Many categories of healthcare training can offer continuing education credit to participating students.)

Training categories are divided into the following sections:

- basic curriculum,
- role-based curriculum,
- advanced training modules, and
- a special HIPAA policies and procedures implementation course.

Typical Users

Privacy officials or clinical professionals with some health information management experience. Content is somewhat academic, but can be understood by health information professionals.

Is It Affordable?

Each segment costs $95 per class per user, and volume discounts are available for multiple users.

Contact Information

Matt Feigenbaum
Train for HIPAA Corporate Headquarters
15344 Barrett Road
Mount Vernon, WA 98273

- Ask employees and volunteers to sign a confidentiality agreement at the end of HIPAA training.

- Review confidentiality provisions with employees as part of training at least once a year.

Note: In Appendix A, you'll find a detailed month-by-month schedule of training topics that can be very helpful to you as you build a privacy program in your medical practice.

STEP 10: IMPLEMENT YOUR PLAN AND EVALUATE YOUR COMPLIANCE STATUS

The day-to-day challenges of making privacy a major aspect of your medical office will come from making mistakes and then fixing those mistakes. No office can avoid all privacy violations, but you can show good faith that you are trying to make the office violation free.

What to do:

Evaluate your implementation process.

How to do it:

- Read the HIPAA To Do checklist in Figure 3.5 of this chapter and assess how you are doing.

- Evaluate the privacy official's workload. Should some of this work be delegated or reassigned?

- Communicate with everyone on staff about how they are doing.

- Tell your patients how you are managing patient privacy. Keep in mind that your patients and your staff have different approaches to privacy, but both desire the same outcome. Physicians and their staff have always believed that they practiced confidentiality. Patients believe what they read or hear or see. If patients hear how you protect their PHI, they will believe you. If they see that you are taking measures to protect PHI, they will believe you. However, if you defer the privacy message to an outside Internet site, or to an outside privacy advocate group, patients will likely get up in arms and distrust the process. Nothing can derail your implementation plan faster than distrustful and irritated patients. Trusting and content patients make for good customer service and customer satisfaction and strengthen your foundation for successful HIPAA privacy implementation.

- Evaluate your training status. Do you have new employees? Have current employees taken on new responsibilities that require retraining? Have your policies and procedures or HIPAA rules changed? You will have to retrain the workforce in the changes.

- Conduct a monthly checkup. HHS calls it an audit. Are you using your new documentation procedures? Are patients signing the NPP acknowledgment? Are you honoring patient requests that you have agreed to?

- Have patients commented on your new privacy procedures? What kind of feedback are you getting from them? Read Chapter 5 of this book to help you manage the HIPAA communication process. Talk to your patients before someone else talks to them.

FOCUS ON ADMINISTAFF

HIPAA Problem

Office managers and privacy officials are so distracted by employer responsibilities that they do not have time to properly balance ongoing patient care with requirements like HIPAA compliance.

HIPAA Solution

Administaff serves as an off-site, full-service human resources department for busy physicians and business owners across the nation. Administaff's Personnel management SystemSM provides administrative relief and high-performance HR solutions through a comprehensive range of services that include benefits management, government compliance, employment administration, employer liability management, recruiting and selection, performance management, training and development, and owner support.

Clients find more time to focus on practice management and HIPAA compliance, while accessing the HR resources needed to select, train, and retain quality employees and better manage employer liability issues.

Typical Users

Small to mid-size practice with a minimum of six employees.

Is It Affordable?

Yes. The fee is a percentage of a client's annual gross payroll.

Contact Information

For more information, call (800) 465-3800.

Security

T he purpose of this chapter is to provide you with a basic under-
standing of the final HIPAA Administrative Simplification
Security Rule that was published in the *Federal Register* on
February 20, 2003.[1] Compliance with the Security Rule is required by
April 21, 2005.[2]

What You Will Learn In This Chapter:

- The basic structure of the Security Rule.

- How the Security Rule relates to the Privacy Rule.

- Why the Security Rule is technologically neutral and scalable.

- How the Security Rule is designed to provide scalability and flexibility.

- How to conduct a risk analysis.

- What the difference is between required and addressable implementation specifications that underpin the security standards, and how to
manage those terms when implementing the Security Rule.

- Why reasonable and appropriate actions provide the framework for the
Security Rule, irrespective of size, complexity, or environment in which
the covered entity operates.

- What the characteristics are of administrative, physical, and technical
security safeguards.

- Why cost is a consideration in exercising its responsibility to comply
with the Security Rule, but that "cost is not meant to free covered entities from this responsibility."[3]

---

1. Department of Health and Human Services, Office of the Secretary, "45 CFR
   Parts 160, 162, and 164: Health Insurance Reform: Security Standards; Final
   Rule," *Federal Register,* v. 68, n. 34, February 20, 2003, pp. 8333-8381. Citations
   to this document hereafter are in the standard reference format of volume
   Federal Register page(s): (eg, 68 *Federal Register* 8333).

2. Small health plans have an additional year to comply, by April 21, 2006.

3. 68 *Federal Register* 8343.

Key Terms

Administrative safeguards: Administrative actions, and policies and procedures, to manage the selection, development, implementation, and maintenance of security measures to protect electronic protected health information and to manage the conduct of the covered entity's workforce in relation to the protection of that information.

Availability: The property that "data or information is accessible and useable upon demand by an authorized person."

Confidentiality: The property that "data or information is not made available or disclosed to unauthorized persons or processes."

Covered entities: Health plans, healthcare clearinghouses, and healthcare providers that transmit any health information in electronic form under the transaction standards.

Electronic protected health information (EPHI): Protected health information (PHI) that meets requirements (i) and (ii) of the PHI definition, namely, information that is (i) transmitted by electronic media or (ii) maintained in electronic media.

Electronic media: Electronic storage media including memory devices in computers (hard drives) and any removable or transportable digital memory medium, such as magnetic tape or disk, optical disk, or digital memory card; or transmission media used to exchange storage media, including, for example, the Internet, extranet (using Internet technology to link a business with information accessible only to collaborating parties), telephone voice response and faxback systems, leased lines, dial-up telephone lines, private networks, and the physical movement of removable or transportable electronic storage media. Certain transmissions, including of paper, via facsimile, and of voice, via telephone, are not considered to be transmissions via electronic media, because the information exchanged was not in electronic form before the transmission.

Encryption: An algorithmic (mathematical) process to transform data into a form in which there is a low probability of assigning meaning without use of a confidential process or key. Decryption is using a confidential process or key to take encrypted data and transform it into original data.

Implementation specification: A required or addressable implementation specification provides instruction to a covered entity with respect to actions that must be taken to comply with a particular standard.

Integrity: The property that "data or information has not been altered or destroyed in an unauthorized manner."

Physical safeguards: Physical measures, policies, and procedures to protect a covered entity's electronic information systems and related buildings and equipment from natural and environmental hazards and unauthorized intrusion.

Protected health information (PHI): Except for three exclusions listed in the glossary of this book under this definition, PHI is individually identifiable health information that is (i) transmitted by electronic media; (ii) maintained in electronic media; or (iii) transmitted or maintained in any other form or medium.

Required or addressable: A required implementation specification requires implementation by the covered entity, whereas an addressable implementation specification allows the covered entity to determine the reasonableness and appropriateness of the implementation specification, implement it if it is reasonable and appropriate, and implement an alternative equivalent measure if reasonable and appropriate, with the covered entity documenting its decision making.

Security incident: The attempted or successful unauthorized access, use, disclosure, modification, or destruction of information or interference with system operations in an information system.

Technical safeguards: The technology and the policy and procedures for its use that protect electronic protected health information and control access to it.

ABOUT HIPAA'S SECURITY RULE

The Security Rule became effective April 21, 2003, and requires compliance no later than April 21, 2005, for most covered entities: healthcare providers who transmit any health information in electronic form in connection with a standard transaction, health plans, and healthcare clearinghouses.[4]

However, the Privacy Rule, which required compliance by covered entities other than small health plans by April 14, 2003, also required that administrative, technical, and physical safeguards of electronic, oral, and paper PHI be in effect as of that date.[5] As a result, the Privacy Rule accelerates the need for implementation of security provisions, and the final Security Rule provides guidance for the "appropriate" (security) safeguards required under the Privacy Rule.

In the coming months, the Centers for Medicare and Medicaid Services (CMS) likely will issue guidance on the Security Rule. In addition, organizations such as the Workgroup for Electronic Data Interchange (WEDI) will be conducting analyses of the Security Rule and offering implementation specification information, based on experiences of its membership, through its Strategic National Implementation Process (SNIP).[6]

Unlike the Privacy Rule, which applies to protected health information in electronic, oral, and paper media, the final Security Rule applies only to *electronic* protected health information. Both rules cover protected health information "at rest" (storage) and "during transmission." The Privacy Rule defines authorized and required uses and disclosures of such information, and the rights patients have with respect to it.

---

4. 68 *Federal Register* 8334.

5. "164.530(c)(1): *Standard: safeguards.* A covered entity must have in place appropriate administrative, technical, and physical safeguards to protect the privacy of protected health information." See US Department of Health and Human Services, Office for Civil Rights, for Privacy of Individually Identifiable Health Information (Unofficial Version): Regulation Text," October 2002, p 29.

6. WEDI's SNIP initiative can be accessed via the Internet at www.wedi.org/snip.

FOCUS ON KRYPTIQ

www.kryptiq.com

HIPAA Problem

Guarding privacy of patients in an electronic environment has the potential to make work processes inefficient. For example,

- inefficient work flow automation with too many systems can create "islands of information";
- documentation to track use and disclosures of PHI can be filed in several folders;
- reports on accounting of disclosures take time to create;
- staff can lose track of alternative methods of communication;
- minimum necessary may differ from one practice to the next; and
- e-mail messages to and from patients may be unsecured.

Providing a secure e-mail environment is addressable in HIPAA Security Rule, and must be safeguarded per the HIPAA Privacy Rule.

HIPAA Solution

As part of the solution, Kryptiq can install a secure e-mail environment that delivers protected health information into one central database that enables information sharing. In addition, Kryptiq can also

- attach secure patient files to e-mail referrals;
- gather secure lab results without being printed or faxed;
- obtain alerts of abnormal and urgent lab reports;
- obtain pre-visit questionnaires in a secure environment from patients;
- send secure messages to e-mail, PDA, database, or cell phones;
- prevent too many systems from creating "islands of information";
- manage and track the use and disclosure of PHI; and
- create reports of PHI disclosures.

Typical Users

Clinics affiliated with hospitals and academic medical centers.

Is It Affordable?

This is a long-term investment. Cost is customized to each practice's needs.

Contact Information

Tyler Blitz
Director of Product Marketing
Kryptiq Corporation
1920 NW Amberglen Parkway, Suite 100
Beaverton, OR 97006
(503) 906-6300

The Security Rule defines protections for such information. Three key definitions of properties comprise the foundation for security of electronic protected health information: *integrity, confidentiality,* and *availability*.

■ **Integrity** is the property that such information has "not been altered or destroyed in an unauthorized manner."

■ **Confidentiality** is the property that such information is "not made available or disclosed to unauthorized persons or processes."

■ **Availability** is the property that such information is "accessible and useable upon demand by an authorized person."

These properties, and other security attributes, are embodied in three types of security standards: administrative safeguards, physical safeguards, and technical safeguards.

Within administrative, physical, and technical safeguard categories are standards and implementation specifications. These will be examined in detail in this chapter. Covered entities are required to comply with the standards and to follow the implementation specifications, which define what needs to be done to achieve compliance with the Security Rule. Implementation specifications are categorized as either *required* or *addressable*, which will be discussed in the next section, "Security Standards."

It is important to note several characteristics of the Security Rule.

■ "In general, the security standards will supersede any contrary provision of State law."[7]

■ The security standards establish "a minimum level of security that covered entities must meet."

Accordingly, compliance with the Security Rule is designed to provide "a floor of protection of all electronic protected health information" but take into consideration that covered entities are of different size and complexity, and, thus, likely to require different means to achieve protection of electronic protected health information. As a result, the Security Rule is considered "technologically neutral."[8]

---

7. 68 *Federal Register* 8355.

8. "The standards do not allow organizations to make their own rules, only their own technology choices." 68 *Federal Register* 8343.

The foundation of the Security Rule is that security protections must be "reasonable and appropriate," as assessed in a required risk analysis and study of risk-management measures. The Security Rule is designed to be "scalable and flexible." As a result, a small physician practice will have a different array of security protections than a large practice, clinic, or hospital, with the selection of security protections determined by the risk analysis. Many of these protections will be reflected and documented in written policies and procedures that must be kept current (although they may be in electronic form), with such documentation retained for six years from date of creation or date last in effect. Similar documentation must be created and maintained that memorializes "actions, activities, and assessments" pertaining to the Security Rule. Both types of documentation must be made available to members of the practice workforce who are responsible for or affected by the Security Rule. See Figure 4.1 for a sample risk analysis.

Risk Analysis

Before you examine the standards and implementation specifications, think about security in the context of your daily life. In the aftermath of the events of September 11, 2001, and as a result of new initiatives on homeland security in the United States, you probably are more security conscious.

If you travel commercially, you are used to enhanced security activities, especially in airports. You may have used the relatively new electronic boarding pass kiosks, which you access using a credit card or frequent flyer card, each encoded with your personal information, to gain access to the flight-reservation database and print a boarding pass and ticket receipt.

Without thinking about security, you probably use an automated teller machine routinely now to get cash or make check deposits. You may make electronic payments over the Internet through your bank or directly with your credit-card company. You likely have eaten in a restaurant, and given your credit card to a waiter who disappeared from your view for a period of time while he completed an electronic transaction through a swipe box. Each of these activities has a security risk, and each has a set of protections designed to mitigate that risk. In each of these activities, you have made or make at the time of activity, implicitly or explicitly, a risk analysis based on a variety of factors.

The Security Rule requires you to carry out the same type of analysis, using a variety of factors, to assess your risks in protecting electronic protected health information (EPHI). This is information that you create, receive, transmit, or maintain in an electronic media storage device.

You likely will find that you already have a number of administrative, physical, and technical security protections in place that meet the standards and implementation specifications.

The required risk analysis is an important document and should be carefully constructed, documented in writing, updated as appropriate, and retained for six years in accordance with HIPAA's documentation standard. This exercise will help you mitigate liability associated with risk, provide a foundation for enhanced productivity, and strengthen your corporate culture by focusing the staff's attention on mitigating potential business risks and finding solutions that will be of benefit to the workforce.

FIGURE 4.1

Sample Risk Analysis

Following is an example of a portion of a risk analysis that you might conduct in your practice. As you will see, you will have to protect passwords to computer software that gives access to databases containing EPHI.

1. Your objective is to ensure that passwords are protected.
2. You survey the workforce to determine how each person protects his password.
3. You ask each person if he or she has disclosed his or her password to another member of the workforce.
4. You observe computer stations to note if there are any posted password reminders.
5. Based on the findings of the survey and observations, you assess the practice's vulnerability.
6. You determine if there have been any database intrusion security incidents as a result of a breakdown in password protection.
7. You prepare policies and procedures for protecting passwords, based on mitigating past, existing, or potential vulnerabilities.
8. You make sure that the workforce understands those vulnerabilities and policies and procedures to mitigate the risk and make password protection a key element of the practice's training.
9. You assess and update this portion of the practice's overall risk analysis periodically, as well as after any related security incident that involves a breakdown of password protection.

The National Institute of Standards and Technology (NIST), part of the US Department of Commerce, has published a number of documents on security and risk assessment. Risk is defined here as "the likelihood of a given threat-source's exercising a particular potential vulnerability, and the resulting impact of that adverse event on the organization."[9] We outline nine steps in Table 4.1, with inputs and outputs at each step that would comprise a risk analysis that you would perform in your practice.[10]

---

9. Gary Stoneburner, Alice Goguen, and Alexis Feringa, *Risk Management Guide for Information Technology Systems,* Special Publication 800-30. Washington, DC: NIST, October 2001, p. 14.

10. Entries in Table 4.1 are based on information drawn from two NIST studies: *ibid,* p. 15, and Marianne Swanson and Barbara Guttman, *Generally Accepted Principles and Practices for Security Information Technology Systems,* Special Publication 800-14. Washington, DC: NIST, September 1996. Each of these studies provides valuable guidance on preparing a risk assessment. The studies are available via the Internet at www.crsc.nist.gov/publications.

TABLE 4.1

Steps to Follow in a Risk Analysis

Step	Inputs	Outputs
1. Examine technical and nontechnical system characteristics, determining scope and methodology of each system	Hardware in practice. Software in practice. System interfaces inside/outside practice. Medical data and information responsibility and accountability of practice staff and outsiders such as vendors and business associates using systems. Mission and goals of each system used in practice.	System boundary. System functions. System and data criticality. System and data sensitivity.
2. Threat identification	History of any system attacks (eg, errors, fraud, disgruntled employees, fires, water damage, electrical failure, hackers, viruses). Source of medical data and information in systems. Asset valuation.	Threat statement, including consequence assessment.
3. Vulnerability identification	Assess weaknesses. Reports from prior risk assessments. Audit comments. Security requirements. Security test results.	List of potential vulnerabilities.
4. Control and safeguard analysis	Effectiveness of current controls and safeguards. Potential effectiveness of planned controls and safeguards.	List of current and planned controls and safeguards.
5. Likelihood determination	Threat-source motivation. Threat capacity. Nature of vulnerability. Current controls. Assessment of probabilities of threats occurring.	Likelihood ratings for potential threats.

6. Impact analysis
  a. Loss of integrity
  b. Loss of availability
  c. Loss of confidentiality
	Mission impact analysis. Asset criticality assessment. Data criticality. Data sensitivity.	Impact rating.

7. Risk determination	Likelihood of threat exploitation. Magnitude of impact. Adequacy of planned or current controls.	Risks and associated risk levels. Levels of risk the practice is willing to accept, taking cost of controls as a factor into account.

T A B L E 4.1 (continued)

Steps to Follow in a Risk Analysis

Step	Inputs	Outputs
8. Control recommendations		Recommended controls.
9. Results documentation		Risk assessment report.

SECURITY STANDARDS

As this chapter is written, just several weeks following the publication of the final Security Rule in the *Federal Register* on February 20, 2003, there is scant commentary and interpretation on the details of the final Security Rule, other than in the preamble to the final Security Rule. The proposed Security Rule published in the *Federal Register* on August 12, 1998,[11] is not of much help in this regard, as the final Security Rule is considerably different from the proposed rule.

As a result, the standards and implementation specifications in this chapter are reproduced from the final Security Rule, with word changes in several instances to enhance clarity. The language is straightforward in most instances and closely aligns with the language used in the Privacy Rule. We provide commentary where we think it germane to help you with implementation. It is important for you, in the months before the Security Rule compliance date of April 21, 2005, to periodically visit the Centers for Medicare and Medicaid Services (CMS) web site for frequently asked questions and guidance that CMS will publish on the Security Rule. Refer to Figure 4.2 for an overview of the structure of the Security Rule.

F I G U R E 4.2

Structure of the Security Rule

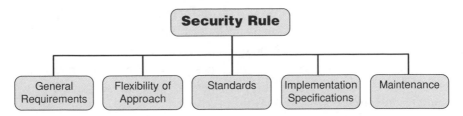

General Rules

There are five general rules in HIPAA's Security Rule:

- general requirements,
- flexibility of approach,
- standards,
- implementation specifications, and
- maintenance.

General Requirements

There are four general requirements in the general rules:

- Ensure the confidentiality, integrity, and availability of all electronic protected health information that the covered entity creates, receives, maintains, or transmits.

- Protect against any reasonably anticipated threats or hazards to the security or integrity of such information.

- Protect against any reasonably anticipated uses or disclosures of such information that are not permitted or required under Privacy of Individually Identifiable Health Information, as discussed in Chapter 3.

- Ensure compliance with the Security Rule by the practice's work-force.[12]

These requirements serve as the foundation for the administrative, physical, and technical safeguards.

Flexibility of Approach

The general rules provide for flexibility of approach in complying with the Security Rule. Because of its importance in providing a foundation for the scalability of administrative, physical, and technical safeguards, the two parts of this rule are reproduced here:

1. Covered entities may use any security measures that allow the covered entity to reasonably and appropriately implement the standards and implementation specifications as specified in Security Standards for the Protection of Electronic Protected Health Information.

2. In deciding which security measures to use, a covered entity must take into account the following factors:
   a. The size, complexity, and capabilities of the covered entity.
   b. The covered entity's technical infrastructure, hardware, and software security capabilities.
   c. The costs of security measures.
   d. The probability and criticality of potential risks to electronic protected health information.[13]

---

12. 68 *Federal Register* 8376.

13. 68 *Federal Register* 8376-8377.

CRITICAL POINT
To determine what are the reasonable and appropriate security measures for your practice, you must take these four factors (a–d) into account.

Standards
This part of the general rules requires that covered entities must comply with the security standards with respect to all electronic health information. Failure to comply leads to liability for civil sanctions and potential loss of business.

Implementation Specifications
There are two types of implementation specifications, required and addressable, and each implementation specification is so designated. If an implementation specification is designated required, a covered entity must implement the specification. The term *addressable* is more complicated and gives the covered entity options. These options are outcomes of the risk analysis that the practice conducts. When analyzing a particular addressable implementation specification for a standard, the practice must determine "whether each implementation specification is a reasonable and appropriate safeguard in its environment, when analyzed with reference to the likely contribution to protecting the entity's electronic protected health information."[14] For example, in a large physician practice, you likely would conduct a detailed background investigation of a person seeking employment (clearance implementation specification). In a solo practice with only the physician's spouse as the "workforce," a not uncommon occurrence, such a clearance procedure likely would not be considered reasonable or appropriate.

In this and other addressable implementation specifications, the covered entity must balance the safeguard specification with the degree of risk mitigation the specification affords, taking into consideration its analysis of risk, strategy for risk mitigation, security protections already in place, and cost of implementation. If the covered entity determines that the implementation specification is a reasonable and appropriate safeguard, it must implement the specification.

If your practice determines that the implementation specification is not reasonable and appropriate, you have two options, and for each of them, you must document why the implementation specification is not reasonable and appropriate. First, you must document why it is not reasonable and appropriate, and implement one or more alternative equivalent measures, or a combination of such measures, if reasonable and appropriate. Second, if you can otherwise document that the standard can be met, you may choose to implement neither the implementation specification

---

14. 68 *Federal Register* 8377.

nor alternative equivalent measure(s). In either circumstance, written documentation of the decision is critical.

Maintenance

This part of the general rules requires that covered entities review their security measures periodically and make modifications as necessary to ensure that they continue to provide "reasonable and appropriate protection of electronic protected health information."

ADMINISTRATIVE SAFEGUARDS

Administrative safeguards are "administrative actions, and policies and procedures, to manage the selection, development, implementation, and maintenance of security measures to protect electronic protected health information and to manage the conduct of the covered entity's workforce in relation to the protection of that information."[15]

There are nine administrative safeguard standards,[16] outlined in Table 4.2, each of which is discussed in turn.

T A B L E 4.2

Administrative Safeguards[17]

Administrative Safeguards Security Standards	Implementation Specifications (IS)	Required (R) or Addressable (A)
Security-management process	Risk analysis.	R
	Risk management.	R
	Sanction policy.	R
	Information system activity review.	R
Assigned security responsibility		R
Workforce security	Authorization and/or supervision.	A
	Workforce clearance procedure.	A
	Termination procedures.	A
Information access management	Isolating healthcare clearinghouse function.	R
	Access authorization.	A
	Access establishment and modification.	A

---

15. 68 *Federal Register* 8376.

16. The Administrative Safeguards are at 68 *Federal Register* 8377-8378.

17. 68 *Federal Register* 8380.

T A B L E 4.2 (continued)

Administrative Safeguards

Administrative Safeguards Security Standards	Implementation Specifications (IS)	Required (R) or Addressable (A)
Security awareness and training	Security reminders.	A
	Protection from malicious software.	A
	Log-in monitoring.	A
	Password management.	A
Security incident procedures	Response and reporting.	R
Contingency plan	Data backup plan.	R
	Disaster recovery plan.	R
	Emergency mode operation plan.	R
	Testing and revision procedure.	A
	Applications and data criticality analysis.	A
Evaluation		R
Business-associate contracts and other arrangement	Written contract or other arrangement.	R

Standard: Security-Management Process

What It Is

Implement policies and procedures to prevent, detect, contain, and correct security violations.

This standard and the four required implementation specifications "form the foundation upon which an entity's necessary security activities are built."[18] In essence, a covered entity is to evaluate and manage its security risks, provide sanctions as a disincentive for or deterrent to noncompliance, and periodically review its security controls. "Covered entities have the flexibility to implement the standard in a manner consistent with numerous factors, including such things as, but not limited to, their size, degree of risk, and environment."[19] A covered entity can find guidance for implementing these specifications from the Computer Security Resource

18. 68 *Federal Register* 8346.

19. *Ibid*.

Center (CSRC) of the National Institute of Standards and Technology (NIST), which is available via the Internet.[20]

CRITICAL POINT

"Your first priority is to develop a way to quantify and evaluate risk. You need to know what you are protecting and how much it's worth before you can decide how to protect it."[21]

Implementation Specifications

There are four required implementation specifications.

1. Risk Analysis (required)

What to do:

Conduct an accurate and thorough assessment of the potential risks and vulnerabilities to the confidentiality, integrity, and availability of electronic protected health information held by the covered entity.

How to do it:

- See Table 4.1 earlier in this chapter for a general outline of tasks in a risk analysis.

- Consult the National Institute for Standards and Technology for useful documents that will help you conduct a risk analysis. Specific documents and web-site references to download the documents are given throughout this chapter.

2. Risk Management (required)

What to do:

Implement security measures sufficient to reduce risks and vulnerabilities to a reasonable and appropriate level to comply with the general requirements of the security standards.

How to do it:

- These are threat-management outcomes of the risk analysis that you will conduct. They will provide the foundation of your policies and procedures.

- These threat-management outcomes will be reflected in policies and procedures that you will implement in your practice that take into consideration your unique environment.

---

20. See NIST, "Risk Management Guide for Information Technology Systems," NIST SP 800-30, January 2002. See Chapters 3 (Risk Assessment) and 4 (Risk Mitigation). Available online at www.csrc.nist.gov/publications/nistpubs/800-30/sp800-30.pdf.

21. Al Berg, "6 Myths About Security Policies: Leave Your Preconceptions Behind and Write Policies That Work in the Real World," *Information Security*, October 2002, p. 49.

3. Sanction Policy (required)

What to do:

Apply appropriate sanctions against workforce members who fail to comply with the security policies and procedures of the covered entity.[22]

How to do it:

- Your practice must determine appropriate internal penalties for violations of your practice's security policies and procedures by the workforce in your practice.

- Such penalties should be an incentive to comply with your practice's policies and practices and deter noncompliant actions (for example, posting passwords on computer terminals).

- Your sanction policies and procedures will be an outcome of the risk analysis and should be related to the practice's estimate of harm pertaining to a particular security incident.

4. Information System Activity Review (required)

What to do:

Implement procedures to regularly review records of information system activity, such as audit logs, access reports, and security incident tracking reports.

How to do it:

- Ask your practice-management system vendor for help in setting up system audit logs and reports.

- As part of your security-management process, identify all reporting requirements and establish procedures for compiling requisite information, creating log entries, safeguarding the documentation, and maintaining the documentation for six years.

Standard: Assigned Security Responsibility

What It Is
Identify the security official responsible for the development and implementation of the policies and procedures required by the Security Standards for the Protection of Electronic Protected Health Information.

Implementation Specification
The implementation specification is reflected in the standard and, as such, is required.

---

22. The covered entity determines the sanctions, taking into consideration "its security policy and relative severity of the violation." 68 *Federal Register* 8347.

FOCUS ON MEDABILITI

www.medabiliti.com

HIPAA Problem

The practice uses paper-intensive information-management systems and multiple systems to maintain scheduling, billing, and patient information. Confidentiality and integrity of patient information may be threatened as a result of ineffective system development and business practices. New business processes have been established without evaluating workflow efficiencies.

HIPAA Solution

MedAbiliti can:

- provide consultation services that involve the practice in the development of its systems (consultants will assess the current business and technical environment to identify true business needs, and then custom-design processes and technical solutions according to specifications provided by the practice);

- conduct process and system audits and risk analyses, and manage documentation efforts (such as accounting of disclosures, alternative communications, special patient requests) to meet HIPAA requirements;

- provide expertise in secure application development and implement online reporting capabilities where needed (scheduling, requests, disclosures, and so on); and

- provide a system that allows secure, role-based access to necessary information, based on business needs.

Typical Users

Hospitals, hospital systems, ancillary physician groups, payers, researchers, and business associates.

Is It Affordable?

MedAbiliti solutions are constructed with user input to fit client budgets.

Contact Information

Tres Watson
MedAbiliti
1040 Avenue of the Americas, 24th Floor
New York, NY 10018
(212) 730-9330
twatson@medabiliti.com

What to do:

Consult the Security Official job description in the Appendix for a description of qualifications and duties of the security official.

How to do it:

- "Final security responsibility must rest with one individual to ensure accountability within each covered entity."[23] The same person may "fill the role for both security and privacy."

- The security official must have a good understanding of technology applications and business operations in the practice; be a good writer who can communicate technical terms and concepts in lay language; and be a "people person" who can ensure enforcement of policies and procedures in a collegial work environment.

- The security official is the team leader for making sure the risk analysis is conducted, policies and procedures are developed and completed, requisite training is performed, and compliance is made inevitable.

CRITICAL POINT

You are required to appoint a security official. This person may also be your privacy official, depending on the size of the practice and the privacy official's technology background.

Standard: Workforce Security

What It Is

Implement policies and procedures to ensure that all members of its workforce have appropriate access to electronic protected health information, as provided under the next standard, "Information Access Management," and to prevent those workforce members who do not have access from obtaining access to electronic protected health information.

Implementation Specifications

There are three addressable implementation specifications:

1. Authorization and/or Supervision (addressable)

What to do:

Implement procedures for the authorization and/or supervision of workforce members who work with electronic protected health information or in locations where it might be accessed.

How to do it:

- As part of the risk analysis, determine who has need for access to electronic protected health information as part of job duties.

---

23. *Ibid.*

- Describe such needs and corresponding authorization and supervision responsibilities in job description.
- Ensure that each member of the workforce understands those responsibilities.

2. Workforce Clearance Procedure (addressable)

What to do:

Implement procedures to determine that the access of each workforce member to electronic protected health information is appropriate.

How to do it:

- Clearance will be an outcome of the risk-analysis determination and elaboration of authorization in job descriptions, just described above.

3. Termination Procedures (addressable)

What to do:

Implement procedures for terminating access to electronic protected health information when the employment of a workforce member ends or as required by determinations made as specified in the previous implementation specification, "Workforce Clearance Procedure."

How to do it:

- Establish an exit-interview format in which passwords are invalidated, terminated workforce members are informed that any authorizations are denied, and such members informed about federal penalties for unauthorized access to electronic protected health information in the practice.
- Have terminated members of the workforce sign a form indicating that they understand the exit-interview information.

These implementation specifications illustrate the concept of address-ability, especially with regard to risk analyses pertaining to small physician practices. For example, in designing a clearance procedure, the "need for and extent of a screening process is normally based on an assessment of risk, cost, benefit, and feasibility as well as other protective measures in place.... For example, a personal clearance may not be reasonable or appropriate for a small provider whose only assistant is his or her spouse."[24] Similarly, with regard to termination procedures, "in certain circumstances ... in a solo physician practice whose staff consists only of the physician's spouse, formal procedures may not be necessary."[25] Finally, "the purpose of termination procedure documentation is to ensure that termination procedures include security-unique actions to be followed, for

---

24. 68 *Federal Register* 8348.

25. *Ibid.*

example, revoking passwords and retrieving keys when a termination occurs."[26] Certainly, the procedures would be different in the solo practice example above from a multi-physician, large-staffed practice. In each case, however, given addressable implementation specifications, it is required that the standard compliant policies and procedures be documented in writing.

Standard: Information Access Management

What It Is
Implement policies and procedures for authorizing access to electronic protected health information that are consistent with the applicable requirements of Privacy of Individually Identifiable Health Information.

This standard is analogous to other HIPAA Administrative Simplification standards in the Privacy Rule that restrict access to protected health information to authorized users.

Implementation Specifications
There are three implementation specifications, one required and two addressable.

1. Isolating Healthcare Clearinghouse Functions (required)

What to do:

If a healthcare clearinghouse is part of a larger organization, the clearinghouse must implement policies and procedures that protect the electronic protected health information of the clearinghouse from unauthorized access by the larger organization.

How to do it:

This is not an implementation function that a practice will have to address directly, but the practice needs to know about it if the practice engages a healthcare clearinghouse as a business associate. In that case, the practice, as a covered entity, will be responsible for security incidents of the clearinghouse as business associate of which it becomes aware. Accordingly, a covered entity should:

■ Inquire of the clearinghouse if it is part of a larger organization.[27]

■ If so, make sure that the workforce outside of the clearinghouse operation understands security and confidentiality of EPHI and sanctions for unauthorized access to such information.

---

26. *Ibid.*

27. The required implementation specification relating to a healthcare clearinghouse that is part of a larger business organization is illustrative of the need to restrict access to only those persons with authorized access to EPHI.

- Make sure clearinghouse staffers are knowledgeable about policies and procedures to protect EPHI.
- Execute a business-associate agreement with the clearinghouse.

2. Access Authorization (addressable)

What to do:

Implement policies and procedures for granting access to electronic protected health information, for example, through access to a workstation, transaction, program, process, or other mechanism.

How to do it:

- Determine through the risk analysis which workforce members have need for access to electronic protected health information.
- Reflect the need for such access in job descriptions.
- Have the privacy and security officials jointly develop policies and procedures that are consistent on this point with both the Privacy Rule and the Security Rule.

3. Access Establishment and Modification (addressable)

What to do:

Implement policies and procedures that, based upon the entity's access-authorization policies, establish, document, review, and modify a user's right of access to a workstation, transaction, program, or process.

How to do it:

- Establish a procedure for periodically reviewing and modifying access based on a change in an authorized workforce member's changed work functions.
- Document any change in access and maintain documentation for six years.

These two addressable implementation specifications pertaining to authorizing access and a user's right of access recognize that there are alternatives to complying with this standard that may be based on a covered entity's size and degree of automation.

Standard: Security Awareness and Training

What It Is

Implement a security awareness and training program for all members of the workforce (including management).

Implementation Specifications

There are four addressable implementation specifications for this standard:

1. Security Reminders (addressable)

What to do:

Periodic security updates.

How to do it:

■ Post security reminders in work areas.

■ Periodically broadcast security reminders electronically to the workforce.

2. Protection from Malicious Software (addressable)

What to do:

Procedures for guarding against, detecting, and reporting malicious software.

How to do it:

■ Discuss protection with your practice-management software vendor.

■ Install commercially available virus detection and firewall software on practice computer systems.

3. Log-In Monitoring (addressable)

What to do:

Procedures for monitoring log-in attempts and reporting discrepancies.

How to do it:

■ Discuss monitoring with your practice-management software vendor.

■ Check the documentation for the operating system in use to determine its capability for monitoring log-in activity.

■ Acquire commercially available software for monitoring and reporting system activity.

4. Password Management (addressable)

What to do:

Procedures for creating, changing, and safeguarding passwords.

How to do it:

■ Develop a policy and corresponding procedure for password management.

■ The designated system administrator should be the only person with access to passwords of other workforce members.

■ Passwords should be changed periodically (for example, every 30, 60, or 90 days), based on threat exposures determined in the risk analysis.

■ Implement a sanction for posting of a password on or by a terminal.

Even though the implementation specifications are addressable, "Security awareness training is a critical activity, regardless of an organization's size."[28] While training is required, content and method are addressable. That the implementation specifications are addressable reflects several considerations discussed in the preamble to the Security Rule, namely, that training is: "Dependent upon an entity's configuration and security risks," and "An on-going, evolving process as an entity's security needs and procedures change." [29]

> **CRITICAL POINT**
>
> All members of your workforce, including management, are required to participate in security awareness and training.

Each person with access to electronic protected health information must be knowledgeable about and understand the appropriate security measures to reduce the risk of improper access, uses, and disclosures. Awareness is the first goal of training. Awareness is not a one-time outcome for the workforce, though, but rather a continuing responsibility as technology changes, new technology is introduced into the practice, and as policies and procedures change in response to possible modifications of HIPAA standards. The practice is not responsible for providing training to anyone outside of its workforce, but the practice is responsible for ensuring that business associates are aware of the practice's security policies and procedures. This level of awareness of policies and procedures should also be imparted to individuals who may be at your facility or facilities for a limited time, such as vendors, maintenance personnel, and others. Such individuals can be made aware of the covered entity's security requirements by giving them pamphlets or copies of security policies and procedures.

You can find guidance for implementing these specifications from the Computer Security Resource Center (CSRC) of the National Institute of Standards and Technology, available via the Internet.[30] NIST's special publication, Information Technology Security Training Requirements, identifies the importance of awareness and training programs:

■ "Awareness programs set the stage for training by changing organizational attitudes to realize the importance of security and the adverse consequences of its failure.

---

28. 68 *Federal Register* 8350.

29. 68 *Federal Register* 8350.

30. NIST, Information Technology Security Training Requirements, A Role- and Performance-Based Model, NIST SP 800-16, April 1998. See especially, Chapter 4, "Training Development Methodology." This document is available via the Internet at www.csrc.nist.gov/publications/nistpubs/800-16/sp800-16.pdf.

■   "The purpose of training is to teach people the skills that will enable them to perform their jobs more effectively."[31]

These statements highlight two important attributes of a successful awareness and training program: A change in corporate culture is required, and the payoff can be greater staff productivity. When the practice's staff works together to conduct a risk analysis, each member of the staff has a stake in the inputs and in the security safeguards. Management plays an important role in effecting change and in realizing the payoff. That's reflected in the language of the standard.

Standard: Security Incident Procedures

What It Is
Implement policies and procedures to address security incidents.

A *security incident* is the attempted or successful unauthorized access, use, disclosure, modification, or destruction of information or interference with system operations in an information system.

Implementation Specification
This standard has one required implementation specification:

1.   Response and Reporting (required)

What to do:

Identify and respond to suspected or known security incidents. Mitigate, to the extent practicable, harmful effects of security incidents known to the covered entity. Document security incidents and their outcomes.

How to do it:

This required implementation specification does not mandate reporting security incidents to outside authorities. Such decisions should be based upon "business and legal considerations."[32]

CRITICAL POINT

You are required to respond to and mitigate any harmful effects of security incidents.

---

31. Ibid, Chapter 4, p. 52.

32. 68 *Federal Register* 8350.

Standard: Contingency Plan

What It Is

Establish (and implement as needed) policies and procedures for responding to an emergency or other occurrence (for example, fire, vandalism, system failure, and natural disaster) that damages systems that contain electronic protected health information.

Implementation Specifications

There are five implementation specifications, three required and two addressable:

1. Data Backup Plan (required)

What to do:

Establish and implement procedures to create and maintain retrievable exact copies of electronic protected health information.

How to do it:

- Check with your practice-management software vendor to see if your software accommodates backup with exact-copy capability.

- With regard to data backup, a small physician's office might do a daily tape, CD, or DVD backup and maintain that electronic media offsite in a secure location.

- A large physician practice might use a more complex procedure, such as a real-time secure data stream or periodic batch duplicate data download to a secure offsite location.

2. Disaster Recovery Plan (required)

What to do:

Establish (and implement as needed) procedures to restore any loss of data.

How to do it:

- Disaster recovery planning will be an outgrowth of the identification of threats in the risk analysis.

- Determine outcomes for each of the threats and the impact on the operations of the practice.

- With regard to the disaster recovery plan, "The final rule calls for covered entities to consider how natural disasters could damage systems that contain electronic protected health information and develop policies and procedures for responding to such situations. We consider this to be a reasonable precautionary step to take since in many cases the risk would be deemed to be low."[33]

---

33. 68 *Federal Register* 8351.

- When preparing a disaster recovery plan, a covered entity should examine worst-case scenarios, even though the probability may be low. Although it is a separate implementation specification, a disaster-recovery plan also would include how operations would be conducted in an emergency.
- Get more information at the Disaster Recovery Institute-International web site at www.dr.org.

The Electronic Healthcare Network Accreditation Commission (EHNAC)[34] has identified several key components to a disaster-recovery plan that mitigate business interruption:

- Procedures for notifying patients of disaster and plan for recovery.
- Procedures for protecting safety of employees and safeguarding facilities when work resumes.
- Annual disaster-recovery training exercises and a written report of results.
- Annual testing of the recovery of mission-critical telecommunications and information systems from simulated failures and a written report of results.
- A plan for resumption of normal business operations.
- Capability of restoring mission-critical telecommunications and information systems and systems processing within a defined recovery period, say 24 to 48 hours, or less.
- Capability of preserving data integrity and security and restoring databases to state and mode of operation immediately preceding the disaster.

3. Emergency Mode Operation Plan (required)

What to do:

Establish (and implement as needed) procedures to enable continuation of critical business processes for protection of the security of electronic protected health information while operating in emergency mode.

How to do it:

- This plan will be part of the disaster recovery plan, discussed immediately above.
- It is important to get input from each workforce member as to duties and workflow in order to establish a workable emergency mode operation plan.

4. Testing and Revision Procedures (addressable)

What to do:

Implement procedures for periodic testing and revision of contingency plans.

How to do it:

- After the disaster-recovery plan is created, it is important to test the plan by creating a disaster scenario and going through the recovery steps in the plan.

---

34. See "Electronic Transactions Criteria for the Healthcare Industry," Version 8.0, March 31, 2003. Visit www.ehnac.org for additional information.

- This drill should be planned in advance and conducted at a time when the practice is not open for business, such as a weekend afternoon.

- Be sure to document the successful provisions in the plan, response times, and, most importantly, any failures that require correction.

- Make corrections to the plan as soon as possible, and make sure all workforce members know the new procedures and why they are being implemented.

- Test the plan at least annually, making sure that any deficiencies from the preceding test are evaluated to ensure that they have been corrected.

5. Applications and Data Criticality Analysis (addressable)

What to do:

Assess the relative criticality of specific applications and data in support of other contingency-plan components.

How to do it:

- Contingencies will be identified as part of the risk analysis.

- Remediation will be part of determining risk-mitigation strategies.

As use of electronic information increases, it is prudent to have in place the three required implementation specifications relating to contingencies. "Contingency planning will be scalable based upon other factors, office configuration, and risk assessment."[35]

CRITICAL POINT

Some scenarios that might invoke a disaster recovery and emergency operation plan for a covered entity would be just a contingency or an inconvenience in other businesses. Remember, for example, because the Security Rule pertains to electronic protected health information, loss of electricity is critical and should be dealt with in a covered entity's risk analysis.

Standard: Evaluation

What It Is

Perform a periodic technical and nontechnical evaluation. It should be based at first on the standards implemented under the Security Rule and, subsequently, in response to any environmental or operational changes affecting the security of electronic protected health information. Evaluation should establish the extent to which an entity's security policies and procedures meet the requirements of Security Standards for the Protection of Electronic Protected Health Information.

---

35. 68 *Federal Register* 8351.

Implementation Specification

The Implementation Specification is reflected in the standard and is required.

What to do:

Design an evaluation format, establish an evaluation committee chaired by the security official and comprised of workforce members, and set up a schedule for evaluating security systems, risk mitigation, and compliance with Security Rule safeguard standards.

How to do it:

While your practice must perform periodic evaluation, you have the option of conducting the evaluation internally using your own workforce or using an external accreditation agency. The preamble to the Security Rule recognizes that cost may be a consideration for an external evaluation, especially for some covered entities such as small physician's practices. Good sources of information and guidance pertaining to evaluation of standards under the Security Rule are the following:

- National Institute of Standards and Technology.
- URAC/American Accreditation HealthCare Commission.
- Electronic Healthcare Network Accreditation Commission.
- Strategic National Implementation Process initiative of the Workgroup for Electronic Data Interchange.[36]

Standard: Business-Associate Contracts and Other Arrangements

What It Is

A covered entity, in accordance with general rules of the security standards, may permit a business associate to create, receive, maintain, or transmit electronic protected health information on the covered entity's behalf. This is permissible only if the covered entity obtains satisfactory assurances that the business associate will appropriately safeguard such information in accordance with the standard for business associate contracts or other arrangements under Organizational Requirements, discussed later in this chapter. Also, see the sample business-associate agreement in Appendix A for contractual requirements that underpin the concept of "satisfactory assurances."

---

36. Information via the Internet on NIST is available at www.niap.nist.gov, on URAC at www.urac.org, on EHNAC at www.ehnac.org, and SNIP at www.wedi.org/snip. WEDI is charged in the HIPAA legislation and regulations as a consultant to the secretary of the Department of Health and Human Services and an advisor to the National Committee on Vital and Health Statistics (NCVHS), respectively, on matters related to HIPAA Administrative Simplification.

CRITICAL POINT

Business associates must provide satisfactory assurances that they will protect electronic protected health information.

This standard has three parts:

■ Satisfactory assurances, mentioned previously, which are outlined in the sample business associate agreement in the Appendix and outlined in the implementation specification for this standard.

■ The standard does not apply in three defined circumstances, one of which is relevant to healthcare providers, including physicians. "Transmission by a covered entity of electronic protected health information to a healthcare provider concerning the treatment of an individual."[37] Simply put, such transmissions do not require a business-associate agreement for protection of electronic protected health information.

■ The third part of the standard relates to a covered entity that is a business associate of another covered entity. An example would be where a healthcare clearinghouse is a business associate of a healthcare provider. This part of the standard says that the covered entity that "violates the satisfactory assurances it provided as a business associate of another covered entity" will not be in compliance with this standard and the similar standard that is part of Organizational Requirements, discussed in the following section, "Implementation Specification."

Implementation Specification

There is one required implementation specification for this standard:

1. Written Contract or Other Arrangement (required)

What to do:

Document the satisfactory assurances required by part one of this standard on the preceding page through a written contract or other arrangement with the business associate that meets the applicable requirements of the similar standard that is part of Organizational Requirements.

How to do it:

There are two issues concerning the relationship between covered entities and business associates under the Security Awareness and Training and Evaluation standards. With regard to the Security Awareness and Training standard, the preamble to the Security Rule states: "Business associates must be made aware of security policies and procedures, whether through contract language or other means. Covered entities are not required to provide training to business associates or anyone else that is not a member of their workforce."[38] With regard to

---

37. 68 *Federal Register* 8378.

38. 68 *Federal Register* 8350.

the Evaluation standard, if a covered entity chooses an external accreditation agency to evaluate its security measures, the agency is considered a business associate of the covered entity and must give satisfactory assurances that it will "appropriately safeguard the [electronic protected health] information."

Business-associate agreements must include provisions that are in a section of the Security Rule known as "Organizational Requirements."[39] In general, these agreements must have the following provisions for business associates, as stated in the preamble:[40]

- "Implement safeguards that reasonably and appropriately protect the confidentiality, integrity, and availability of the electronic protected health information that it creates, receives, maintains, or transmits on behalf of the covered entity.

- Ensure that any agent, including a subcontractor, to whom it provides this information agrees to implement reasonable and appropriate safeguards.

- Report to the covered entity any security incident of which it becomes aware.

- Make its policies and procedures, and documentation required by Security Standards for the Protection of Electronic Protected Health Information relating to such safeguards, available to the Secretary [of HHS] for purposes of determining the covered entity's compliance with [the Security Standards].

- Authorize termination of the contract by the covered entity if the covered entity determines that the business associate has violated a material term of the contract."

PHYSICAL SAFEGUARDS

Physical safeguards are "physical measures, policies, and procedures to protect a covered entity's electronic-information systems and related buildings and equipment from natural and environmental hazards, and unauthorized intrusion."[41]

There are four physical safeguard standards,[42] each of which is discussed in turn in Table 4.3.

---

39. 68 *Federal Register* 8379.

40. 68 *Federal Register* 8358-8359.

41. 68 *Federal Register* 8376.

42. The physical safeguard standards are at 68 *Federal Register* 8378.

TABLE 4.3

Physical Safeguards[43]

Physical Safeguards Security Standards	Implementation Specifications (IS)	Required (R) or Addressable (A)
Facility access controls.	Contingency operations.	A
	Facility security plan.	A
	Access control and validation procedures.	A
	Maintenance records.	A
Workstation use.		R
Workstation security.		R
Device and media controls.	Disposal.	R
	Media re-use.	R
	Accountability.	A
	Data backup and storage.	A

Standard: Facility Access Controls

What It Is

Implement policies and procedures to limit physical access to its electronic information systems and the facility or facilities in which they are housed, while ensuring that properly authorized access is allowed.

Implementation Specifications

This standard has four addressable implementation specifications:

1. Contingency Operations (addressable)

What to do:

Establish (and implement as needed) procedures that allow facility access in support of restoration of lost data under the disaster-recovery plan and emergency-mode operations plan in the event of an emergency.

How to do it:

- Determine in the risk analysis the outcomes of specified disaster scenarios and their impact on access to the practice's operations.

- Outline procedures in the disaster-recovery plan for access to the practice's operations and how to conduct emergency operations.

- Take into consideration in the planning that the facility may be unavailable (for example, fire damage) or that the facility may be available but inoperable (for example, no electricity).

- As part of the disaster-recovery plan, consider alternative sites for restoration of data and conduct of emergency operations.

---

43. 68 *Federal Register* 8380.

2. Facility Security Plan (addressable)

What to do:

Implement policies and procedures to safeguard the facility and the equipment therein from unauthorized physical access, tampering, and theft.

How to do it:

- As part of the risk analysis, develop a threat-management assessment pertaining to unauthorized access to practice's facility.

- Develop access policies and implement procedures to safeguard facility and equipment, using devices such as locks, passcards, and the like, suitable to the business environment.

3. Access Controls and Validation Procedures (addressable)

What to do:

Implement procedures to control and validate a person's access to facilities based on their role or function, including visitors, and to software programs for testing and revision.

How to do it:

- Implement procedures to control access and movement within the facility by persons.

- Establish a visitor sign-in and badge system.

- Escort visitors in areas that would have access to electronic database systems and electronic protected health information if there is a reason for the visitors to be in such areas.

- Ensure that software technicians representing business associates who are working on systems or databases containing electronic protected health information are aware of the practice's security policies and procedures.

4. Maintenance Records (addressable)

What to do:

Implement policies and procedures to document repairs and modifications to the physical components of a facility related to security (for example, hardware, walls, doors, and locks).

How to do it:

- Create a log and description of each such repair and modification and maintain the log as documentation of actions for a period of six years.

The language of the implementation specifications above is straightforward. Specifications will be determined based on a covered entity's risk analysis and other factors. Several clarifications are important: First, this standard applies to a covered entity's "business location or locations," and the facility includes "physical premises and the interior and exterior of a building(s)."[44] Facility is extended to include the premises of workforce members who work at home with EPHI.

Next, a covered entity "retains responsibility for considering facility security even where it shares space with other organizations."[45] This is an important consideration in the risk analysis that physician practices must prepare for their office locations, which are likely to be part of a larger facility. In such circumstances, the physician practices must document in their risk analyses third-party security measures.

Standard: Workstation Use

What It Is
Implement policies and procedures that specify the proper functions to be performed, the manner in which those functions are to be performed, and the physical attributes of the surroundings of a specific workstation or class of workstation that can access EPHI.

Implementation Specification
The Implementation Specification is reflected in the standard and, as such, is required.

What to do:

Write and implement policies and procedures for workstation placement and use in the practice. Workstations include a variety of electronic media, such as desktops, laptops, tablet computers, and personal data assistants (PDAs), to name a few, that transmit, receive, or store electronic protected health information.

How to do it:

- An example of a policy and accompanying procedure pertaining to this standard would be that users log off before leaving a workstation unattended.

- Another example would be an automatic logoff of a workstation without activity for a span of time, for example, two to five minutes. This type of logoff generally can be applied using existing operating systems.

- A final example pertaining to this standard and also to Privacy Rule standards is that workstations in receptionist areas in a practice may not be visible to patients who are signing in with the receptionist. Workstations used throughout the practice should not be readable to passersby, such as unauthorized persons (patients, vendors, etc).

---

44. 68 *Federal Register* 8354.

45. 68 *Federal Register* 8353.

Standard: Workstation Security

What It Is
Implement physical safeguards for all workstations that access electronic protected health information to restrict access to authorized users.

Implementation Specification
The Implementation Specification is reflected in the standard and, as such, is required.

What to do:

The compliance solution for this standard will be "dependent on entity's risk analysis and risk management process."[46]

How to do it:

- An example of a policy and accompanying procedure pertaining to this standard would be that users log off before leaving a workstation unattended.

- Another example would be an automatic logoff of a workstation without activity for a span of time, for example, two to five minutes. This type of logoff generally can be applied using existing operating systems.

- A final example pertaining to this standard and also to Privacy Rule standards is that workstations in receptionist areas in a practice may not be visible to patients who are signing in with the receptionist. Workstations used throughout the practice should not be readable to passersby, such as unauthorized persons (patients, vendors, etc).

Standard: Device and Media Controls

What It Is
Implement policies and procedures that govern the receipt and removal of hardware and electronic media that contain EPHI into and out of a facility, and the movement of these items within the facility.

Implementation Specifications
This standard has four implementation specifications, two of which are required, and two of which are addressable.

1. Disposal (required)

What to do:

Implement policies and procedures to address the final disposition of electronic protected health information and/or the hardware or electronic media on which it is stored.

---

46. 68 *Federal Register* 8354.

2. Media Reuse (required)

What to do:
Implement procedures for removal of electronic protected health information from electronic media before the media are made available for reuse.

3. Accountability (addressable)

What to do:
Maintain a record of the movements of hardware and electronic media and any person responsible for them.

4. Data Backup and Storage (addressable)

What to do:
Create a retrievable, exact copy of electronic protected health information, when needed, before movement of equipment.

With regard to the required implementation specifications for disposal and media reuse of electronic storage media in particular, such as hard disks, it is important to examine carefully the instructions and specifications pertaining to file deletion or erasure. Even though the software may claim to delete files, it may only delete the file name and not erase the underlying data content.

With regard to the addressable accountability implementation specification, it "does not address audit trails within systems and/or software. Rather it requires a record of the actions of a person relative to the receipt and removal of hardware and/or software into and out of a facility that are traceable to that person. The impact of maintaining accountability on system resources and services will depend upon the complexity of the mechanism to establish accountability ... such as receipt and removal restricted to specific persons, with logs kept."[47]

Finally, with regard to the addressable accountability and data backup and storage implementation specifications, "small providers would be unlikely to be involved in large-scale moves of equipment that would require systematic tracking, unlike, for example, large health care providers or health plans."[48]

---

47. *Ibid.*

48. *Ibid.*

TECHNICAL SAFEGUARDS

Technical safeguards consist of "the technology and the policy and procedures for its use that protect electronic protected health information and control access to it."[49] There are five technical safeguard standards,[50] each of which is discussed in turn in Table 4.4.

TABLE 4.4

Technical Safeguards[51]

Technical Safeguards Security Standards	Implementation Specifications (IS)	Required (R) or Addressable (A)
Access control.	Unique user identification.	R
	Emergency access procedure.	R
	Automatic logoff.	A
	Encryption and decryption.	A
Audit controls.		R
Integrity.	Mechanism to authenticate electronic protected health information.	A
Person or entity authentication.		R
Transmission security.	Integrity controls.	A
	Encryption.	A

Standard: Access Control

What It Is
Implement technical policies and procedures for electronic information systems that maintain electronic protected health information to allow access only to those persons or software programs that have been granted access rights as specified in the Administrative Safeguard standard of Information Access Management.

Implementation Specifications
For this standard there are four implementation specifications, two required and two addressable. Each of the implementation specifications requires technical assistance from the practice's systems administrator or by the practice-management system vendor, depending on the size of the practice and configuration of systems.

49. 68 *Federal Register* 8376.

50. The Technical Safeguards are at 68 *Federal Register* 8378-8379.

51. 68 *Federal Register* 8380.

1. Unique User Identification (required)

What to do:
Assign a unique name and/or number for identifying and tracking user identity.

2. Emergency Access Procedure (required)

What to do:
Establish (and implement as needed) procedures for obtaining necessary electronic protected health information during an emergency.

3. Automatic Logoff (addressable)

What to do:
Implement electronic procedures that terminate an electronic session after a predetermined time of inactivity.

4. Encryption and Decryption (addressable)

What to do:
Implement a mechanism to encrypt and decrypt electronic protected health information. The required unique user identification and addressable automatic logoff implementation specifications are procedural. They are easily implemented technically, because current operating and network system software packages have those capabilities.

The emergency access procedure implementation specification would be a consideration in the preparation of the covered entity's risk analysis and contingency plan. "In a situation when normal environmental systems, including electrical power, have been severely damaged or rendered inoperative due to a natural or manmade disaster, procedures should be established beforehand to provide guidance on possible ways to gain access to needed electronic protected health information."[52] For a physician practice, such ways might include an alternative power source such as battery or offsite backup of EPHI.

Standard: Audit Controls

What It Is
Implement hardware, software, and/or procedural mechanisms that record and examine activity in information systems that contain or use electronic protected health information.

---

52. 68 *Federal Register* 8355.

Implementation Specification

The Implementation Specification is reflected in the standard and, as such, is required.

What to do:

According to the preamble to the Security Rule, while the standard is mandatory, "Entities have flexibility to implement the standard in a manner appropriate to their needs as deemed necessary by their own risk analyses."[53] Two NIST publications cited in the preamble provide guidance:

■ NIST Special Publication 800-33, *Underlying Technical Models for Information Technology Security*, December 2001.[54]

■ NIST Special Publication 800-14, *Generally Accepted Principles and Practices for Securing Information Technology Systems*, September 1996.[55]

Standard: Integrity

What It Is

Implement policies and procedures to protect electronic protected health information from improper alteration or destruction.

Implementation Specification

This standard has one addressable implementation specification.

1. Mechanism to authenticate electronic protected health information (addressable)

What to do:

Implement electronic mechanisms to corroborate that electronic protected health information has not been altered or destroyed in an unauthorized manner.

How to do it:

The covered entity's risk analysis will address EPHI that needs to be authenticated. "Error-correcting memory and magnetic disk storage are examples of the built-in data authentication mechanisms that are ubiquitous in hardware and operating systems today."[56]

53. *Ibid.*

54. This document is available via the Internet at www.csrc.nist.gov/publications/nistpubs/800-33/sp800-33.pdf.

55. This document is available via the Internet at www.csrc.nist.gov/publications/nistpubs/800-14/sp800-14.pdf.

56. 68 *Federal Register* 8356.

Standard: Person or Entity Authentication

What It Is
Implement procedures to verify that a person or entity seeking access to electronic protected health information is the one claimed.

Implementation Specification
The Implementation Specification is reflected in the standard and, as such, is required.

How to do it:

This standard is an example of a technologically neutral implementation specification, as there are a number of possible solutions, including biometric identification systems, password systems, personal identification numbers, telephone callback, physical or soft token systems, and digital signatures, among others.

Standard: Transmission Security

What It Is
Implement technical security measures to guard against unauthorized access to electronic protected health information that is being transmitted over an electronic communications network.

Implementation Specifications
This standard has two addressable implementation specifications.

1. Integrity Controls (addressable)

What to do:

Implement security measures to ensure that electronically transmitted electronic protected health information is not improperly modified without detection until disposed of.

2. Encryption (addressable)

What to do:

Implement a mechanism to encrypt electronic protected health information whenever deemed appropriate.

The preamble to the Security Rule states that "when electronic protected health information is transmitted from one point to another, it must be protected in a manner commensurate with the *associated risk* [emphasis added]."[57]

Assessing relative risks of alternative methods would be done as part of the required risk analysis. The preamble indicates that "switched, point-to-point

---

57. *Ibid.*

connections, for example, dial-up lines, have a very small probability of interception."[58] With regard to the Internet, "covered entities are encouraged, however, to consider use of encryption technology for transmitting electronic protected health information."[59] We strongly recommend its use.

It is the covered entity's responsibility to secure its transmissions. Increasingly, physicians as covered entities receive electronic mail from patients, some of which may contain the patient's EPHI and may be delivered in an unsecured manner. The patient is not a covered entity and is not under the same obligation as the covered entity with regard to transmission security. Upon receipt, however, the physician as covered entity is required to secure electronic protected health information that the physician receives and possesses. Many of the newer commercially available operating system software packages include encryption tools. We recommend that any outgoing transmissions of electronic protected health information be encrypted. A patient requesting such information from a covered entity practice should be directed to the practice's secure web site to gain access to such information.

---

58. 68 *Federal Register* 8357.

59. *Ibid.*

Communicating HIPAA: Inquiring Patients Want to Know

In a book about HIPAA, why bother with communications?

Our experience tells us that training and communications go hand in hand. Good communication comes from good training. You can have bad communications from good training, but you cannot deliver good communications from bad training.

This is especially true when it comes to the Privacy and Security Rules that specify what you must do to protect written, oral, and electronic communication. We'll cover that in this chapter, along with a quick reference grid on permitted incidental uses and disclosures (see Table 5.1) and a communications plan that will help you in a crisis.

Some people put communications into that touchy-feely category and shrug it off as fluff. But ask anyone who has been the subject of an Office for Civil Rights investigation or questioned by a nosy reporter about the importance of good communication. When carefully managed, what seems touchy-feely becomes poise and dignity.

What You Will Learn In This Chapter:

- What HIPAA says about oral and written communications.
- How the staff can confidently deal with HIPAA.
- What patients want to know about HIPAA.
- How to customize your internal and external communications plan.
- HIPAA crisis-communication management.

Key Terms

Administrative Safeguards: Administrative actions, and policies and procedures, to manage the selection, development, implementation, and maintenance of security measures to protect electronic protected health information and to manage the conduct of the covered entity's workforce in relation to the protection of that information.

Confidentiality: The property that such information is "not made available or disclosed to unauthorized persons or processors."

Health information: Any information whether oral or recorded in any form or medium that is created or received in any form or medium that is created or received by a healthcare provider, public health authority, employer, life insurer, school or university, or healthcare clearinghouse and relates to the past, present, or future physical or mental health condition of an individual; the provision of health care to an individual; or the past, present, or future payment of provision of health care to an individual.

Physical Safeguards: Physical measures, policies, and procedures to protect a covered entity's electronic information systems and related buildings and equipment from natural and environmental hazards and unauthorized intrusion.

Technical Safeguards: The technology and the policy and procedures for its use that protect electronic protected health information and control access to it.

WHY TALK ABOUT COMMUNICATIONS IN A HIPAA BOOK?

For the first year or two into HIPAA's Privacy Rule, staff and patients are going to say things that may seem scary or embarrassing. That's nervous energy. At some time, each of you will have a HIPAA epiphany—a reality moment when nerves and privacy training decisively conflict. When it happens to you, you'll be deeply grateful for a chapter on strategy, poise, and dignity.

A good oral and written communications plan is the best defense if a patient files a claim against you, if the Office for Civil Rights (OCR) launches an investigation, or if a staff member gets into a jam. Do more than develop the plan. Implement it.

Implementing HIPAA is more about changing culture (behavior, actions) than it is about accepting a law. But general guidelines on how to manage culture and behavioral change have largely been ignored. That's because HIPAA is a law to be interpreted by lawyers. Thank goodness for lawyers—really! We pay significant attorney's fees each year to make sure our content is legally sound and ethical.

Until now, most of us have been rushing to meet the letter of HIPAA's law. But patients think that if our offices are now "HIPAA-compliant," we're culturally and behaviorally reconditioned and we take precautions to protect their confidential health information.

True, but reconditioning takes more than a one- or two-hour seminar. We've gone through the motions to meet the law. Now, we've got to make privacy happen. And that is why it's so critical for us to be straight with patients. Let patients know that health care is in the throes of a major change and privacy and security are central to that process.

Communication starts with the "director of first impressions"—the front-line employee (receptionist, nurse, billing clerk).

The fact is, the first line of defense is the front-line employee who interacts with the patient, creates, accesses, and files his or her information, and passes it along to others in the delivery chain. Members of resistant or inappropriate cultures are the most frequent reason for failure of such organizational initiatives—and, in fact, can undermine and even derail implementation. The culture must be pulling in the same direction as the plan. Only those organizations that focus on the attitudes and behavior of their workforce can hope to achieve HHS's objective for HIPAA privacy and security implementation—a healthcare delivery environment that is conscientious, diligent, and thorough in its protectiveness of privacy rights and the confidentiality of health information.[1]

CRITICAL POINT
Communication begins with the director of first impressions—the first voice or the first person an individual sees or hears.

WHAT HIPAA SAYS ABOUT ORAL AND WRITTEN COMMUNICATION

Most of us believe we can reasonably protect the privacy of written communications on faxes, patient files, handwritten notes, and the like. But some of us have been fairly cavalier about what we say within earshot of others—physicians talking to each other in the hall about a patient, billing clerks making insurance inquiries on a speaker phone, or nurses answering questions about another patient.

Oral Communications in the Medical Office

There's a reason why HIPAA's Privacy Rule includes guidelines on how to protect oral communications. Most people think oral communications begins when someone starts talking.

But oral communication doesn't have a life unless someone is listening—even if that conversation is one person talking to herself.

---

1. Article by D'Arcy Guerin Gue in the March 2002 issue of *HIPAAdvisory*. The full article can be found at http://www.hipaadvisory.com/action/Compliance/culture.htm.

People spend more time listening than any other communication activity. The communication process looks like this:

- 40 percent listening.
- 35 percent talking.
- 16 percent reading.
- 9 percent writing.[2]

The patient-physician process begins by knowing the difference between hearing and listening. Hearing is a passive activity. You're not actively involved. You're simply allowing sound waves to penetrate your ears. When you're listening, you are an active participant determining the meaning of what you hear.

Physicians listen to patients—to the words used to describe a pain or illness, to the sounds of the body, to the heartbeat, and so forth. When patients come into a medical office, they have several incentives to be an active listener. They are likely to feel better if they listen to the nurse or physician's recommendations; and they are likely to feel better quicker if they believe someone listened to them. When patients are in the medical office, their listening quotient is very high. So when a provider is talking in an open area about another patient, that person may as well be talking into a megaphone.

CRITICAL POINT

When patients come into a medical office, they have an incentive to be an active listener.

Written Communications in the Medical Office

In the HIPAA world, except for psychotherapy notes, you are required to give patients access to their medical records unless you believe that doing so will cause harm. In the past, written communication was used to focus on what the medical and office staff wrote in the medical, coding, or billing record. But written communication now covers a much broader scope:

- Notice of Privacy Practices, including written summaries of the NPP.
- HIPAA policies and procedures.
- Test results from HIPAA training.
- Forms, such as confidentiality forms, authorization forms, consent forms.
- Documentation and logs of all types.
- Business-associate agreements.
- E-mail messages or faxes.
- Notes shared with another provider.
- Summaries of patient files.

---

2. Ruth Hermann Siress, Carolyn Riddle, and Deborah Shouse, *Working Woman's Communications Survival Guide,* Prentice Hall, 1993, p. 136.

Ask your attorney to review your written materials for consistency and legal accuracy. For example, you want your Notice of Privacy Practices to be consistent with your policies and procedures. You don't want to tell your patients that they can access their medical records within 30 days and then tell staff in your policies and procedures that they can take up to 60 days to respond to this request. Incidents like this can easily happen if you purchased an NPP from one vendor and a HIPAA policies and procedures manual from another vendor just to meet the HIPAA compliance deadline. If this is the case in your office, consult your attorney on how to modify one or both of the documents.

Incidental Uses and Disclosures

Many providers questioned the use and disclosure section of the law, and in HHS's December 4, 2002, guidance, Standards for Privacy of Individually Identifiable Health Information,[3] the secretary of HHS provided clarity about what can be written and spoken. Table 5.1 gives you an overview of incidental uses and disclosures, but we encourage you to read the guidance in its entirety or talk to your attorney if you have any questions about what you can do or say.

TABLE 5.1

Incidental (Allowable) Oral and Written Uses and Disclosures

Written Incidental Uses and Disclosures	Oral Incidental Uses and Disclosures
You may use sign-in sheets to call out the names of patients in waiting rooms.	Physicians can engage in confidential conversations with other providers, even if there is a possibility that they can be overheard. Use reasonable precautions (lowered voices or talking apart from others). Some examples:
You are permitted to leave medical charts at bedside or outside exam rooms. Implement safeguards to protect the individual's privacy by placing patient charts with identifying information facing the wall.	■ Healthcare staff orally coordinates services at nursing stations.
In a hospital, you may display patients' names next to the door of the hospital room they occupy unless the patient opts out.	■ Nurses or other healthcare professionals may discuss a patient's condition over the phone with the patient, a healthcare provider, or family member.
Covered entities are not required to document incidental uses and disclosures provided to the individual.	■ A healthcare professional may discuss lab test results with a patient or other provider in a joint treatment area.

continued

---

3. This 123-page guidance can be found at http://www.hhs.gov/ocr/hipaa/guide-lines/guidanceallsections.pdf.

T A B L E 5.1 (continued)

Incidental (Allowable) Oral and Written Uses and Disclosures

Written Incidental Uses and Disclosures	Oral Incidental Uses and Disclosures
You are not obligated to prevent any incidental use or disclosure of protected health information. The rule requires that you implement reasonable safeguards to limit incidental uses or disclosures.	■ A physician may discuss a patient's condition or treatment regimen in the patient's semi-private room. ■ Healthcare professionals may discuss a patient's condition during training rounds in an academic or training institution. ■ A pharmacist may discuss a prescription over the pharmacy counter, or with a physician or the patient over the phone. Offices do not need to be retrofitted to provide soundproofed walls to avoid conversations that may be overheard. Physicians' offices may leave brief messages on an answering machine, or with a family member to remind them of appointments. Reasonably safeguard the individual's privacy, and limit the information on the message system. Protected health information in group therapy settings are treatment disclosures and are allowed.

HOW THE STAFF CAN CONFIDENTLY DEAL WITH HIPAA

The first step in confidently dealing with HIPAA is to understand that HIPAA Administrative Simplification is a complex law filled with standards on how to handle patient health information. Talking about patient privacy for a few hours once a year will meet the training requirement, but it won't change anyone's actions unless there is a cohesive training and communications plan.

CRITICAL POINT

Talking about patient privacy for a few hours once a year will meet the training requirement, but it won't change anyone's actions unless there is a cohesive training and communications plan.

Follow this five-step plan to implement an internal process so that no one feels that he or she must carry the HIPAA burden alone. Everyone in the office must work together.

Step 1 Educate the staff, and invite conversations about Privacy breaches and Security incidents.

■ Make HIPAA training a year-round process.

■ Be a team. No one can do HIPAA alone.

■ Help each other with answers.

■ Set aside personal differences in the best interests of the patients and the practice.

■ Build esprit de corps around ensuring privacy and security in the practice. Your patients will notice the pride you take in your accomplishments.

Step 2 Schedule regular training sessions.

■ Use ideas from the training calendar provided for you in Appendix A.

■ Invite staff members to take leadership roles on training topics.

■ Schedule a session on computer security. Explain why the practice can no longer allow computer games or Internet shopping on office equipment.

■ Do impromptu "stand-up" meetings at which staff comes together and stands for a quick briefing. These work if you are suddenly aware of a problem and have to inform the staff.

Step 3 Develop a line of fire.

■ The Privacy Rule and Security Rule require your practice to identify a contact person to receive patient complaints.

■ The rules also require one person to be named the privacy official, and the same or another person the security official. The privacy and security officials are accountable parties and take responsibility for learning many legal and practical HIPAA details.

■ Train a backup privacy and security team in the event the officials are not available should an incident occur. Ultimately, the official is the accountable party, but this situation highlights the need to get each staff member involved with privacy and security in the practice.

Step 4 Conquer the fear of conflict.

■ HIPAA gives patients six new rights, and for a while, patients are likely to press for those rights. You can review those rights in Chapter 3.

■ Use one of the following techniques to ease a trying situation:

(a) Get out of the line of fire. You say, "I understand your position. Let's talk to the privacy official." Avoid saying words like but or however. That puts you back on the firing line and negates the first part of the sentence.

(b) Be an active listener. Repeat what you have heard the patient say so that the patient knows you are listening and ask for a response: "What I'm hearing from you is that you're concerned that the insurance company will see too much information. Is that right?"

(c) Compliment your adversary. You say, "With your ability to analyze facts, I know we'll come to a great solution."

(d) Work together rather than separately. Resolve the concern while the patient is still in the office. It's your best chance to find a resolution.

(e) Establish comfort. Make the other person feel at ease.

(f) Ask for help. If the day's events are too stressful, ask for help from another staff member.

Step 5 People will make mistakes.

■ No practice can be HIPAA-compliant all of the time. People will unintentionally and inadvertently make a mistake, but mistakes can be fixed before they become major incidents. If you discover you've made a mistake, tell your privacy or security official right away so that the practice can begin to look for a solution. Problems that continue unresolved cost time and money, and can damage your credibility, reputation, and business.

> **CRITICAL POINT**
> Mistakes that continue unresolved become incidents. Incidents cost time and money. Incidents can damage your reputation.

■ If someone in your office makes the same mistake several times and doesn't show signs of understanding the privacy or security policy, that employee may need to be retrained or receive disciplinary action, such as time off without pay, depending on how your office addresses sanctions in the policies and procedures manual.

■ Go to the regulations for clarification. The Privacy Rule, enforced by HHS's Office of Civil Rights, can be found at www.hhs.gov/ocr. The Security Rule, enforced by HHS's Centers for Medicare and Medicaid Services Office of HIPAA Standards, can be found at www.cms.hhs.gov.

■ Include legal counsel on your HIPAA team. If there is an error, and you feel you need legal assistance, consult your attorney.

WHAT PATIENTS WANT TO KNOW ABOUT HIPAA

For most office visits, patients just want to know how soon they will feel better. Often, though, patients will want to make sure their health information is kept in strict confidence. For example:

■ A woman is pregnant and she doesn't want her husband or parents to know.

- A teenager is experimenting with drugs and needs help.
- A man tests positive for hepatitis C and is afraid he'll lose his job.

There are thousands more cases like these, and patients will want to know what you're doing to protect privacy. It's doubtful that they'll ask about your security systems or about whether you lock the doors at night. But they will ask who has access to the medical file in addition to the nurse and physician. They will ask to see their medical records, and some will want an accounting of where you've disclosed medical records.

We've been tracking consumer stories about patient privacy, and what we've learned is that "patient rights" rank highest among consumer concerns. The Notice of Privacy Practices has been very well received as a move in the right direction. Table 5.2 lists some of the questions that you might be asked and gives some possible answers.

T A B L E   5.2

Privacy Questions Patients Often Ask

Frequently Asked Questions and Requests	Possible Answers
Why am I receiving so many privacy notices?	Every healthcare provider that is a covered entity is required to send an NPP to individuals who seek treatment.
I appreciate this privacy notice. Why is it coming now?	The compliance date to meet HIPAA's Privacy Rule was April 14, 2003, and our NPP is part of that process. We want you to know how we'll protect your health information.
May I get a copy of the NPP for my records?	Sure. And we've also posted our NPP on our web site in case you want additional copies. (Note: If you have a web site, you must post your NPP on that site.)
I'd like to request access to my medical record.	Please sign this form that you'd like access to your record, and I'll set up an appointment for you to talk to our privacy official.
I don't want the insurance company to know everything in my record.	They'll receive only the minimum necessary for them to make payment decisions.
I want you to send my medical records to another physician.	We'll be happy to do that if you will provide us with the physician's name and the address where you want them sent. (Authorizations are not necessary.)
I don't want this information in my medical record and I want to amend it.	I'll set up an appointment for you to talk to our privacy official about that.
How will I know you amended it?	If we agree to make the amendment, we'll send you a copy of the changes. Where would you like us to send the copy?

continued

T A B L E 5.2 (continued)

Privacy Questions Patients Often Ask

Frequently Asked Questions and Requests	Possible Answers
Don't call me at home anymore. Call me on my cell phone.	I'll acknowledge that in writing in your file, and when you're next in the office, please sign this documentation.
How did you handle my patient records before this rule?	Our office has always treated patient information confidentially. And now HIPAA's Privacy Rule requires that we document our privacy efforts. That's the biggest change.
I'd like an accounting of where your practice has sent my health records.	I'll set up a meeting with our privacy official to talk about that.
Can I still have my (spouse) pick up my prescriptions?	Yes, you may.
Your office referred me to another physician, but that physician's office tells me I need to sign an authorization before they will look at my medical records. What are they talking about?	Referred physicians do not need a signed authorization to receive the patient's PHI. The Privacy Rule includes referred physicians as part of treatment, payment, and healthcare operations.
Who in your office has access to my medical records?	We follow our privacy policies and procedures regarding this question. Would you like to talk to our privacy official about that?
I want to file a complaint.	Thanks for bringing your concerns to us first. You have the right to file a complaint. Would you like to speak with our contact person about that?
What will happen to me if I file a complaint?	Our policy here is that we will not take any action against a patient who files a complaint. Would you like to speak to our privacy official?
I didn't give you authorization for this.	We keep excellent documentation here, but if you have a question about our privacy activities, you may speak to our privacy official.
What are you going to do to discipline the person who breached my confidentiality?	Any action is the decision of our privacy official and our practice's management team based upon the practice's written sanction policy.
How many of these rights apply to my children?	We follow state and federal laws when it comes to unemancipated minors. Would you like to talk to our privacy official about that?
I demand to know why my (son/daughter) was in here.	We follow state and federal laws that dictate when we can release patient information about a minor. Would you like to talk to our privacy official about that?

This list could go on for pages. Note that there's a common response formula used in the majority of the answers:

■ Respect the individual's request.

■ Refer to your policies and procedures or federal and state laws.

■ Ask if the individual wishes to speak to a privacy official.

CRITICAL POINT

Respect the individual's request, refer to your policies and procedures, and ask if the individual wants to speak to the privacy or security official.

CUSTOMIZE YOUR INTERNAL AND EXTERNAL COMMUNICATION PLAN

Like it or not, we are all participants in an internal and external communications program. When our communications are unplanned or undirected, stories about our offices are left to politics, whim, and gossip. But a well-designed communication plan can control strategic messages and put a structure around what you most want others to know about your practice.

Develop an Internal Communication Plan

Ask two or three people to assemble a communication committee to think this through. The most important goal in your internal communication plan is to help staff accept new privacy and security standards. Use humor or cartoons to help make a point.

What to do:

Decide on one or two common communication goals, such as, "Prepare everyone on staff to know what to do and say if there are patient inquiries, complaints, privacy breaches, or security incidents." Create an environment where everyone feels part of the HIPAA solution.

How to do it:

1. Offer an incentive to encourage positive results.

■ Bring in lunch on Friday when the office has had a good week.

■ Give an extra half-day vacation for staff.

■ Acknowledge someone who has helped another staff member through a difficult complaint process.

2. Create a reminder e-mail program.

■ No one has time to read long e-mails, but you can send quick one- or two-line reminders through your e-mail system that may actually be fun to read. Put them as multiple-choice or true/false questions such as:

True or False: You can shop the Internet from your computer without putting medical records at risk.

Multiple Choice: When an individual asks for access to medical records, say:

a. Come back when we're not busy.

b. Your records are in storage and it will take us 60 days to find them.

c. Call in that request between 8:00 and 10:00 tomorrow morning.

d. I'll get the privacy official, and the two of you can talk about this.

3. Develop an internal newsletter.

■ Do feature stories on physicians and staff, and broaden the scope of the newsletter to include subjects like computer tips, seasonal illnesses, prevention, or policies and procedures. Route the newsletter electronically, or print it and put it in employee mailboxes.

4. As a team, analyze potential violations.

■ At the beginning of each monthly meeting, bring up a fictitious scenario and ask the staff to rate the violation.

Use a scale of 1 to 5, with 5 being the highest risk. The first rating is your evaluation of how the Office for Civil Rights would respond. The second rating is how much attention you think this patient will give to the violation.

A sample rating system might look like this:

Office for Civil Rights Rating

1 = OCR is likely to read this complaint and call to check out the details.

2 = OCR is likely to send an official letter.

3 = OCR is likely to send out an investigator and provide technical assistance to improve patient privacy in your office.

4= OCR is likely to send out an investigator, request access to practice's written records pertaining to HIPAA policies and procedures, discover a preventable breach, and assign a penalty.

5 = OCR is likely to launch a major investigation that could result in penalties and fines if you don't do something to mitigate the privacy breach or security incident now. A very serious privacy breach could be referred to the US Department of Justice for criminal investigation.

Patient Rating

1 = The patient will probably leave with a bad feeling about our practice.

2 = The patient will likely talk about this breach to a friend or family member.

3 = The patient will likely file a complaint with your contact person.

4 = The patient will likely call the ACLU to determine if rights have been violated.

5 = The patient will likely file a complaint with the Office for Civil Rights, call an attorney, and the news media may also be contacted.

Develop an External Communication Plan

Your business associates and patients are your two primary external audiences. Keep the practice's management informed of any communication efforts so that they can support you as you implement key messages. Your approach to business associates will be different from the messages you send to patients.

What to do:

Regularly communicate with your business associates about privacy and security issues.

How to do it:

- Your privacy official will talk to each business associate about the privacy and security regulations and also obtain signatures on business-associate agreements. (Business-associate agreements must be in place by April 14, 2003, unless you already have a confidentiality agreement in place. In that case, your business-associate agreement must be signed by April 14, 2004, or on the current agreement's renewal, amendment, or modification date, whichever comes first.)

- Make a list of questions to discuss with vendors, and then determine who should take those questions to the vendor. Get answers in writing.

- The privacy official should also talk to the staff about the privacy and security safeguards you expect from business associates. In most cases, business associates want to do business with medical offices. Your participation in this relationship should be trustful, and you should present yourself with good business ethics.

- Expect business associates to have some questions. HIPAA is a very big law, and you may not know the answer. Don't guess. Unless you have been trained to answer specific content, refer questions to the privacy official.

- Include business associates in some of your internal e-mail reminders. Ask them if they'd like to submit questions or comments that are not promotional to your communications effort.

What to do:

Regularly communicate with your patients.

How to do it:

- Establish a patient advisory board. Ask select patients to participate in your HIPAA implementation efforts by giving you feedback on what you're doing. Request a signed confidentiality statement before they participate, and be cautious about what issues are brought to the patient advisory board.

- Conduct a survey about patient satisfaction. Include a few questions about privacy and security safeguards.

- When presenting the Notice of Privacy Practices, be positive. Expect that there will only be a few questions that relate to the NPP's content, and be prepared with appropriate answers.

■ Develop a cheat sheet of questions and answers from typical patient questions. You can extract some questions and answers from the list in Table 5.2.

■ Post wall charts or hang posters informing patients of their rights. No kidding. This is an excellent preemptive strategy. It says, "We know your rights, do you?"

■ A one-page patient newsletter from the medical practice goes a long way in building patient-physician relationships. If you are sending your newsletter electronically, ask if patients would like to sign up to be on your newsletter list. Postage is costly, but you can place printed copies of your newsletter in the waiting room. When selecting topics, take a poll of the most common questions patients ask, and put those comments into an easy-to-read format. Be sure to include one column on privacy or security topics.

■ If you are communicating with patients via e-mail or you provide content on the Internet, consult Chapter 4 on security requirements, such as whether encryption is addressable or required for your system. With regard to e-mail, remember, if you, as the covered entity, transmit electronic protected health information to a patient, you are responsible for its security. If the patient, who is not a covered entity, transmits electronic protected health information to you, you, as the covered entity, are responsible for its security on receipt.

CRITICAL POINT

As a covered entity, if you communicate via e-mail with patients, you are responsible for security whether you send or the patient sends an e-mail message.

HIPAA gives medical offices an excellent opportunity to promote themselves. More than ever before, physicians should take the lead on privacy issues and retain their position as a trusted resource.

What to do:

When your communications committee has implemented its internal communication plan, ask committee members to excerpt news clips or articles that can also be used for external audiences.

How to do it:

■ Identify the topics of greatest interest. Typically, those topics include the following:

☐ Care or treatment of illnesses or conditions common to your specialty.

☐ Privacy.

☐ Billing questions.

☐ Who's new in the office?

☐ Ask-the-doctor column.

☐ What to do in emergencies.

☐ The security of e-mail communications between patient and physician.

HIPAA CRISIS-COMMUNICATIONS MANAGEMENT

If the Office for Civil Rights calls or if a reporter calls wanting to follow up on a story, most people's immediate reaction is to hang up the phone. There's a better way to handle what appears to be a crisis situation.

In theory, any communications crisis can be managed using the following strategy.

Step 1 Get the facts.

What to do:

Evaluate what is happening and remain calm. Do not assume that anyone is guilty. Establish a level of trust by asking questions, not by making judgments, accusations, or statements of guilt.

How to do it:

- Ask what happened. Ask others if they also know what happened. Disregard answers that include "it wasn't my fault" until later.

- Examine the damage. Did we do something to create an investigation? Has a patient taken a complaint to the state's attorney general? Are we going to be sued (longer response time) or will we be on the five o'clock news (shorter response time)?

- Find out if anyone was hurt—emotionally or physically. Immediately inquire about the person's condition or state of mind.

- Buy time to gather your thoughts. Don't shoot from the hip. If this is a reporter, ask if you can call back in 15 minutes—and then call back! If this is the Department of Justice or the Office for Civil Rights calling, get the facts, ask if you can have a reasonable amount of time to conduct a quick internal review, and schedule an appointment to meet with the caller.

- Ask for the focus of the investigation or story.

- Stay calm. The temperature of most crises escalates within the first three to five hours. People like to draw conclusions about what will likely happen next, and the fear factor can kick in. Depending on how the leadership handles the crisis, one of four things can happen:

1. Employees will start to blame each other, which cripples morale.

2. Management responds with a knee-jerk reaction and loses critical data. This forces employees to run into hiding.

3. Management loses focus on the big picture and focuses on the problem, resulting in lost cash flow and disloyal patients. That compromises the organization's public image.

4. Management keeps it together, stays calm, evaluates this crisis as opposed to other crises, and then calls together a team of advisors to determine next steps. This builds teamwork and trust.

Step 2 Call together your team of advisors.

What to do:

Your advisors' job is to develop a plan.

How to do it:

- The worst thing to do is to do nothing.
- Your advisory team is made up of trusted decision-makers and, in most cases, your corporate or personal attorney. Team members may be a colleague, an office manager, a practice-management consultant, or others in whom you have great confidence.
- Briefly tell the advisors what happened as best you know it without adding any interpretations or conclusions. Those opinions should be left to your advisors.
- Your advisors should give you directions about the following.

   —How should we handle this situation?

   —What are we legally bound to do and what are we ethically bound to do?

   —What are our key messages? "No comment" is not a key message; it is an admission of guilt. This includes what we should tell our employees. Count on information getting out, unless you tell employees to keep it absolutely confidential, and then you can depend on it getting out. It also includes what should we tell the public, and who is our spokesperson. This is one person who is influential with the public and knowledgeable about the situation.

Step 3 Prepare the spokesperson.

What to do:

Show no mercy by grilling the spokesperson.

How to do it:

- Ask the spokesperson three questions that you hope you'll never be asked. At least one of them will come up in the investigation.
- Think about questions the caller is likely to ask. Questions from OCR and the Department of Justice are more likely to be focused on your policies and HIPAA implementation. Questions from a reporter will likely have a consumer angle, such as, "How did this happen?" or "Could you have prevented this?" or "Could this happen somewhere else?"
- Coach the spokesperson by giving feedback on the messages.
- Directly connect the answers to the question. Do not give more information than is asked for.
- Practice allowing silence to happen. Reporters and federal investigators like to use silence to their advantage, hoping you'll fill the void with chatter. Don't do it.

Step 4 Do your homework. Know who you're talking to.

What to do:

Conduct research about the caller before providing any detailed information.

How to do it:

- Find out who the caller is. If you are uncertain, get the caller's office switchboard telephone number, and call back to verify identity. After the call, do some reasearch. Inquire about the journalist's writing style (combative, argumentative, soft news) and whether the journalist gets first-page assignments. A quick search on Nexis Lexis can pull that information up for you. You can ask your attorney to do this if you aren't a subscriber to the Nexis Lexis database. If it's a federal employee of HHS calling, go to the federal government's Office for Personnel Management web site (www.opm.gov) and conduct a search for that person's name. Or, call back at OPM's main telephone number and ask to speak to this person or the supervisor. You may only learn the person's title and region, but it's a start.

- If this caller is a journalist, send an e-mail message to friends inquiring whether or not any of them have had an experience with this person. Journalists are the gatekeepers of information to consumers. Yet few are informed about HIPAA. They usually cover several beats and health-information management is just one of those beats. Most journalists are financially rewarded for writing a good story. Many are parents, attend a church or synagogue, believe in family, and are members of the community. (Consult Table 5.3 as you prepare.)

Step 5 Make the call back.

What to do:

Take the lead in making the call back.

How to do it:

- Keep your promise to call back when you said you would.
- Place a cheat sheet beside you on your desk.
- Speak slowly. Think before you speak. If you're to be quoted, make sure you articulate so that the interviewer understands what you are saying. Don't make jokes. Don't compare yourself to your competition. This gives the interviewer a reason to call your competitors to see if they want to say something about you.
- Respond to the questions while you're on the phone or set up an in-person interview. With reporters, we recommend an in-person interview so that you can size up each other and build a relationship. OCR and Department of Justice will have their own processes, but most government agencies will prefer the phone interview first.
- Be honest. Do not lie. If you do not know, say that you do not know. Nothing causes a six-part investigative-team series faster than a lie.
- Ask if you can tape-record the conversation.
- Ask someone else to sit in and listen to the conversation.

- Answer the questions, but don't be a slave to the questions. Provide the key message several times so that the caller understands what you're trying to say.

- When the interview is done, ask the interviewer if you can provide answers to questions not asked. This usually throws the interviewer off, but it's your turn to say what your advisory team wanted to be said.

- If this is a print interview, ask if you can preview your quotes before it goes to press. Most journalists will let you preview your own quotes.

- When you're done with the interview, hang up. Do not call back with "just one more thing" unless you made an incorrect statement and need to clarify.

CRITICAL POINT
Ask someone else to sit in and listen to the conversation.

Step 6 Prepare differently if this is a TV interview.

What to do:
Prepare for the visual story.

How to do it:
- A television story is 85 percent visual and 15 percent content, just the opposite of a written news story or federal investigation.

- Present your business card to the interviewer and also to the cameraman. Don't forget the camera operator. This is the person responsible for making you look good.

- Television news is a show. It generates the highest advertising dollars. If you think you're providing news, think again. Television news anchors are actors, except on the national television news. Then they are very smart journalists and actors.

- Viewers will determine whether to believe you based on whether they like you. They will believe your body language over what you say.

- Be confident. Smile, even when asked a mean-spirited question. Remember that you're conveying believable body language.

- Don't slouch. Slouching says "victim."

- Pull your jacket down over your posterior, and sit on it so that your jacket doesn't bunch up around your shoulders.

- Speak directly to the interviewer. Do not speak to the camera. Viewers think that you can see them, and that will make you appear to be a voyeur.

- Wear clothes that draw attention to your face. Men usually wear red or blue ties. A woman should wear a scarf or blouse that highlights her face. Don't wear dangling earrings.

- If this is a live story, keep your answers short—15 seconds or less. If this is a taped interview and you stumble, ask if you can present that answer again.

- Do not repeat a negative. Such as, "No, we don't breach a patient's privacy." In the edit room, that could be cut into "We breach patient's privacy."

T A B L E 5.3

On-camera or In-person Interview Performance Techniques

Interview Do's	Interview Don'ts
Use good posture.	Slouch.
Maintain eye contact.	Look away from reporter.
Keep notes and refer to them.	Talk "off the cuff."
Use key messages.	Be a slave to the reporter's questions.
Ask for clarification.	Answer the question, then say what you
Ask to see quotes.	want the audience to know.
Follow up with a thank-you note.	Argue with reporter.
	Ask to preview the article.
	Accuse the reporter.

Step 7 Plan for a communications crisis.

The number of crises that you'll experience is inversely proportional to the amount of time you spend planning for contingencies and training about scenarios. The more time spent planning, the less time you'll spend managing crises.

> **CRITICAL POINT**
> The more time you spend planning for contingencies and training about scenarios, the less time you'll spend managing crises.

What to do:

Develop a plan so that you can use it if you need it. All the better if you never need it. But communication plans are usually three times as expensive when you need them and don't have one.

How to do it:

- Develop a high-level, trusted, strategic team, including a lawyer and spokesperson.
- If you think you may be featured in a television news spot, get media trained before you go on camera. It's not at all the same as speaking to a live audience.
- Establish a spokesperson policy and stick to it. In doing a story, TV media will talk to anyone on the street, capture the story, and then put it on the evening news. Your policy should be that no one speaks to the media except for the designated spokesperson.
- Practice, practice, practice.
- Remember that crises happen all the time. It's how you manage them that determines whether it's a crisis or not.
- Ask for help if you need it.

HIPAA Compliance Costs and Return on Investment

In the earlier chapters, we presented considerable information on how to comply with HIPAA Administrative Simplification standards on transactions, code sets, privacy, and security. Sprinkled throughout the text have been references to costs of compliance, but we really haven't focused on how to calculate those costs. We did note at the end of Chapter 4 that cost is a factor in achieving compliance with transactions, although cost cannot be the reason for noncompliance with the HIPAA standards.

What You Will Learn in This Chapter:

■ Questions to ask as you build a budget and begin to determine your return on investment.

■ How to assemble teams that help you get the answers you need.

■ Determining how much you will save by adopting electronic transaction standards.

■ How HIPAA will affect patient-physician relationships.

■ Whether you should invest internally or outsource.

■ Costs of technology versus costs of policies and procedures.

■ How to assemble the workforce to reinvent the future.

■ How to raise the bridge and lower the river.

■ Other healthcare paradigm shifts besides HIPAA Administrative Simplification that will affect your practice in the years ahead.

QUESTIONS TO ASK AS YOU BUILD A BUDGET AND DETERMINE YOUR RETURN ON INVESTMENT

Each of the HIPAA Administrative Simplification rules includes a section on regulatory impact, including costs. But calculations are based on assumptions and averages that are not of much use in calculating an individual practice's costs and return on investment. In fact, each practice must tailor its calculations to its own practice, because what works in one may not work in another. One practice may have systems and procedures that are nearly compliant, while another is just getting started.

As you prepare your practice's HIPAA compliance efforts, you probably have these questions in mind:

- How much is compliance going to cost?
- How do we figure out the cost of transactions systems?
- How much will we save by conducting more of our business activities using electronic business methods?
- Are there alternatives to having our own transaction system?
- What are the benefits of HIPAA compliance?
- Will I receive a return on my investment in HIPAA compliance?
- How do I measure that return on investment?

PUTTING YOUR TEAM TOGETHER

The previous questions are all good ones, but there are no easy answers to them. Each person in your practice will have to participate in developing answers to those questions, you may need the help of outside experts, and you definitely will need help from your accountant and attorney.

A good team to put together not only for cost analyses, but also for developing policies and procedures, would include key managers in the practice, the privacy official, security official, information-technology (IT) officer, human-resources officer, a representative from a systems vendor, your attorney, and your accountant. Identify the best writer in the group, or hire an outsider to put your findings down on paper. If your practice is small, you may combine the functions above or hire a consultant to do the work. Remember, if you hire a consultant, you know your practice better than any outsider, so you must participate in the analytical process and provide guidance to the consultant.

Your practice likely prepares an annual budget, in which you estimate revenues for the year and calculate costs, such as office rent, payroll, benefits, office expenses like telephone and paper, equipment maintenance, staff training, and so on. Your practice also budgets what it spends on new equipment, such as medical diagnostic equipment, computers, copiers, software, and the like.[1] As a result of these budgeting activities, your practice has the tools in place to begin to measure what HIPAA compliance is going to cost and what your return on investment will be. Some of your answers will be exact, while others will be rough estimates. In fact, each practice will come up with different answers, based on how it transacts business today, how big it is, what type of policies and procedures it has already in place, what it does internally, what it outsources to vendors, and so on.

HOW MUCH WILL YOU SAVE?

The HIPAA cost-comparison tool is a worksheet that you can download from the web. This worksheet, developed by the Utah Health Information Network, www.uhin.com, can help you determine how much your practice may save by switching to an electronically based administrative system.

The worksheet calculates your yearly administrative costs based on the five HIPAA transactions that you are most likely to use:

- eligibility,
- referral/prior authorization,
- claim/encounter submission,
- claim status, and
- claim payment.

To download either the Microsoft Word or Microsoft Excel version of the spreadsheet to your computer, follow this process.

Step 1   Go to www.uhin.com.

Step 2   Click "Education."

Step 3   Go to the "Tools" section.

Step 4   Download the easier file for you to use. Excel version is a little easier to use.

Step 5   Use the "File-Save As" buttons to save the worksheet to your computer.

Step 6   Open the worksheet and follow the instructions.

---

1. You probably know how you would deploy these types of equipment in your practice and the objectives of such deployments. However, analyses of the costs of these types of equipment in relation to return on investment are not easy, and you may need to ask your accountant for help. "Calculations of the IT business case are particularly problematic, given the rapidly changing capabilities and costs of both hardware and software." See Rushika Fernandopulle, et al., "A Research Agenda for Bridging the 'Quality Chasm,'" *Health Affairs,* v. 22, n. 2, March/April 2003, fn. 20, p. 190.

CRITICAL POINT

However you do your cost analysis, approach HIPAA compliance as an investment in the future of the practice. Compare the benefits of HIPAA transaction standards to paper-based technology to determine if the investment in electronic transactions is right for you.

It is very important that you analyze HIPAA compliance as an investment in the future of your practice rather than just as an expense to be borne to conduct business today. Remember, as a healthcare provider, you can choose to embrace HIPAA transaction standards or continue to use paper-based technology to mail claims to health plans and telephone technology to determine patient eligibility and claim status. Only your practice can make these determinations, taking into consideration how other practices conduct business, how your patients communicate with you, how payers are communicating with and making payments to you, and how the country is embracing new technologies, such as the Internet.

Other industries that have embraced electronic transactions in their business operations realized significant returns on investment over time. Think about how electronic business processes like the ATM, credit-card transactions, airline-ticket and boarding-pass kiosks, and Internet shopping, to name a few, have changed your life. Think about how electronic claims processing and electronic funds transfer will change your practice in the years ahead. As you think about implementing HIPAA Administrative Simplification standards, also think about reinventing your business processes, making them more efficient, more customer centric, and the like.

WILL E-COMMUNICATIONS ENHANCE OR DETRACT FROM PATIENT RELATIONSHIPS?

Stanford University Professor Laurence Baker recently conducted a study of how physicians and patients communicated. "Professor Baker's research found that using online messaging technology, including e-mail, dropped the total cost per patient by $1 per month. What's more, 78 percent of patients and 63 percent of physicians were satisfied with the technology. The approval rating for telemedicine jumped to 87 percent among doctors younger than forty-five."[2] The questions you need to answer are: Is a one dollar-per-month drop in cost per patient a meaningful change in your practice? Are patients going to embrace new ways of communicating? Will change increase productivity in the practice? Will the practice attract new patients?

---

2 "The Doctor Is Online," in *IQ Magazine,* March/April 2003, p. 15.

What to do:

Measure the potential increase or decrease in productivity.

How to do it:

■ For a month, keep a log of patient contacts that includes patient contact in the office (including contact by other providers treating your patients); patient contact outside of the office by telephone or mail; the reason for the contact, such as follow-up on patient visit, inquiry about laboratory results, and so on; and the amount of time required for completing the purpose of the contact

■ As you build that log contact by contact, also ask your patients how they would respond to alternative ways of communicating. Remember, it may be more convenient for the patient to receive a secure e-mail message or download a message from your practice's secure web site than wait for a telephone call that could be delayed if the practice was otherwise engaged in treating patients or telephone appointment time was overlooked or delayed.

■ At the end of the month, tally the results. For each type of contact, what is the average amount of time spent? How is that time valued, based on who handles the contact? What is the cost of the telephone or letter preparation time and mailing expense to complete the purpose of the contact? Is there a better way of handling contacts, such as using encrypted e-mail response from the physician to the patient? How much would that cost compared to the way your practice handles contacts today? Would you need to invest in new hardware or software to make the change, or could you adapt existing technology, for example, by just making sure e-mail messages going out to patients are encrypted? Is the return in dollars and qualitative terms worth the investment in changing the process?

INTERNAL INVESTMENT VERSUS OUTSOURCING

The foregoing is an example of the areas in which to analyze your practice's costs for complying with HIPAA Administrative Simplification standards. As you go through the exercise of calculating your costs, you will find that some areas may need a complete overhaul to meet the standards, while other areas already are compliant or can be made so with little effort or cost.

This point is acknowledged in the final Security Rule published in the *Federal Register* on February 20, 2003:

Virtually all providers, health plans, and clearinghouses that transmit or store data electronically have already implemented some security measures and will need to assess existing security, identify areas of risk, and implement additional measures in order to come into compliance with the standards adopted in this rule. We cannot estimate the per-entity cost of implementation because there is no information available regarding the extent to which providers', plans', and clearinghouses' current security practices are deficient. Moreover, some security solutions are almost cost-free to implement (for example, reminding employees not to post passwords on their monitors), while others are not.[3]

If your practice has not implemented electronic transmission and storage capabilities, your costs likely will be higher than one that has. Manage those costs just as you would an investment that will yield a return over time. Discuss this with your accountant.

You will need outside assistance in determining whether to implement a system internally or to outsource and use a healthcare clearinghouse as a business associate that would handle standard transactions on your behalf.[4] To make a choice, you would compare the cost of using clearinghouse services over, say, a three-year period, for example, with the cost of the investment in equipment, the cost of personnel to maintain the system, and maintenance costs.[5]

The Workgroup for Electronic Data Interchange (WEDI) has directories of physician management system vendors and of clearinghouses that will give you guidance, and the Electronic Healthcare Network Accreditation Commission (EHNAC) [6] identifies accredited healthcare clearinghouses on its web site. Also, check with colleagues to find out what practice-management and transaction systems have worked for them and with your local and state medical-society offices to see what information they may have.

COSTS OF TECHNOLOGY VERSUS COSTS OF POLICIES AND PROCEDURES

You may be surprised to learn that your largest overhead expenditure will be conducting internal activities, including carrying out your risk analysis, developing policies and procedures, creating forms and notices, imple-

---

3. 68 *Federal Register* 8373.

4. Clearinghouses have several methods of charging for their services, including subscription fee, per-transaction fee, fee for special services, and combinations of such fees.

5. In contrast to using a clearinghouse as a business associate to handle your practice's transactions, you may need to use a clearinghouse as a covered entity, which would accept your standard transaction and forward it on to a payer. This would be akin to a network switch, just as you would find in an ATM transaction that was executed at an ATM terminal of a bank that was different from the customer's bank. There could be a fee to the provider for such networked transactions.

6. The Electronic Healthcare Network Accreditation Commission (EHNAC) accredits healthcare clearinghouses. The standards of measurement relate to privacy and confidentiality, technical performance, business practices, and resource criteria that have been developed by industry. Candidates prepare a self-assessment that measures its performance against the criteria, and EHNAC conducts a site visit to verify the information provided in the self-assessment.

menting compliance training, and performing ongoing monitoring of HIPAA compliance efforts. These are nontechnical activities, and the risk analysis and policies and procedures that you develop have to have certain characteristics, including:

■ Explanation of policy goals.

■ Explanation of procedures for attaining goals.

■ Nonspecific description of technologies to use.

■ Descriptions of measures to determine compliance success.

■ How to alter your compliance plan in the event that technology changes, you retain existing technology, or you change vendors.[7]

In contrast, installing or beefing up an electronic billing system may mean getting claims to payers faster, receiving payments faster, reducing claims errors, and so on. The cost has revenue offsets and other quantitative, measurable benefits. [8] Unlike an electronic billing system that is used to ease revenue collection, the described activities have no revenue offset and have benefits that are hard to measure, given the expenditure. For example, you may find that workflow processes

■ enhance productivity,

■ increase patient (customer) satisfaction,

■ mitigate risk of a privacy breach or security incident,

■ strengthen corporate culture,

■ enhance reputation in the community, and so forth.

Each of these is difficult to measure, yet each offers benefits that must be taken into consideration when looking at costs of HIPAA compliance and return on investment.

A recent study identified 10 key areas of "potential value" that you should consider when doing your cost analysis.[9] They are, with examples of questions to ask in applying them to your analysis:

■ Better, Faster Product Designs

　□ Will HIPAA transaction standards speed up your practice's claims process, determination of eligibility, and inquiries about claim status?

---

7. For a discussion of these points, see Al Berg, "6 Myths About Security Policies: Leave Your Preconceptions Behind and Write Policies That Work in the Real World," *Information Security*, October 2002, pp. 48-53.

8. There is a concept of "revenue distance," which is the gap between investment and the revenue mechanism that the investment supports. The closer a company is to its customers, the smaller the revenue distance. An electronic billing system that linked the practice with the payer would be an example of an investment that would lower the revenue distance. This concept is explored in more depth in "Expanding the ROI Toolbox," *Lines 56,* November 2001, p. 51.

9. Eric J. Adams, "Eye on Results," *IQ Magazine,* November/December 2002, pp. 74-78.

- Better Products
  - ☐ Will e-mail communications with patients increase treatment options?
  - ☐ Will electronic prescriptions reduce or eliminate prescription errors or contraindications?
- New Revenue Streams
  - ☐ Will better communications with patients lead to new business referrals from existing patients?
  - ☐ Will better electronic communications with payers lower accounts receivable, enhance cash flow, and mitigate the need for factoring of receivables?
- Improved Service to Patients
  - ☐ Will the Notice of Privacy Practice lead to a greater degree of patient satisfaction with practice's medical-record confidentiality procedures?
  - ☐ Will improved communications with patients enhance their satisfaction?
  - ☐ What impact will a patient's right to review medical records have on the practice?
- Greater Employee Effectiveness
  - ☐ Will assembling a team to conduct cost and risk analyses foster greater communication within the staff and strengthen the practice's corporate culture?
  - ☐ Will risk assessment and mitigation activities lead to opportunities to change workflows that enhance productivity in the practice?
- Greater Process Effectiveness
  - ☐ Will new safeguard standards that are required and addressable lead to a more secure working environment?
  - ☐ Will implementation of privacy and security policies and procedures eliminate weaknesses in how the practice processes its business today?
- Increased Brand Value
  - ☐ Will changes that you make to achieve HIPAA compliance lead to greater recognition in the community?
  - ☐ Will changes that you make to achieve HIPAA compliance enhance your practice's reputation with existing and prospective patients?

- Creation of Intellectual Capital
  - ☐ Will your policy-and-procedure-development efforts to achieve HIPAA compliance result in enhancing the value of your most important asset, your staff?[10]
- Better Connectivity with Partners and Vendors
  - ☐ Will implementation of electronic business processes facilitate transactions with business associates and allow cost-effective communication with a wider orbit of business associates?
  - ☐ Will implementation of electronic business processes with business associates and other covered entities lead to improved risk mitigation?
- More Effective Use of Assets
  - ☐ Will implementation of HIPAA transactions standards enhance the value of existing systems?[11]
  - ☐ Will implementation of HIPAA transaction standards lead to a more efficient deployment of the practice's workforce?

HOW TO USE YOUR WORKFORCE TO REINVENT THE FUTURE

The questions in each of the key areas above are meant to be illustrative and suggestive. They make up a framework with which to begin compiling content for your cost and risk analyses. Again, your practice is unique, so your questions and answers will be unique, too.

What to do:
Develop questions that are germane to your practice.

How to do it:
- Get the practice staff together for a defined period of time, for example, one hour.
- Get an easel with a writing pad, and assign one person to take notes, and another to lead the session.
- Then, allowing five minutes for each of the key areas above, the lead person asks the staff to identify as many questions as it can think of in the time allotted.

---

10. EHNAC-accredited parties have informed EHNAC that the self-assessment exercise that is part of the accreditation process has resulted in material improvement in intellectual capital. Based on knowledge of co-author Ed Jones, a founding commissioner of EHNAC.

11. In contrast to handling additional paper-based transactions, which are labor intensive, adding more electronic transactions is not labor intensive, and the marginal cost of such transactions is not only less at a given level of output but tends toward zero.

At the end of the session, ask the best writer in the group to compile the questions, circulate for further comment, revise, and then use the revised questions as a starting point in developing cost and risk analyses. The cost and risk analyses are not about expenses for conducting business today, but about investments for being in business tomorrow.

What to do:

Convene another session that has a defined objective: figuring out what the practice will be like two years in the future.

How to do it:

- This session should be short, for example, one hour, which forces participants to think fast, off the top of their heads, and without a lot of deliberation. This is an effective way to elicit thoughts based on a combination of intuition and experience.
- At the end of the session, ask the best writer in the group to compile the answers to the questions, circulate for further comment, revise, and then use the revised answers as further input in developing cost and risk analyses.

There are six questions to be answered. They are:

- What is the core purpose of the practice? Whatever you suggest as the core purpose should be visionary, focused on the patient, of indefinite duration, and able to withstand market or regulatory changes. The core purpose should be one sentence only, beginning with: The core purpose of *your practice* is....

- What is the mission statement of the practice? Whatever you suggest as the mission statement should support the core purpose, be focused on the patients of the practice, and be evaluated periodically as market or regulatory changes happen. No more than two sentences comprise the mission statement. The first is: The mission of *your practice* is to....The second is: The practice will accomplish its mission by....

- In order of importance, list the three most important things that the practice has done and that it does to bring value to its patients. The description of these things should be brief, no longer than a phrase or sentence.

- Again, think two years into the future. Implementing HIPAA Administrative Simplification transaction, privacy, and security standards has been an opportunity for the practice to help establish a sustainable competitive advantage among healthcare providers, enhance value for existing patients, and attract new patients. As a result, the practice is likely to prosper well into the future. How will the practice do it? To realize this opportunity, the practice had to accomplish three critical business objectives, which were new or involved change. The description of these three objectives should be brief, no longer than a phrase or sentence.

■ Put yourselves in the shoes of your patients. They may or may not know much about HIPAA Administrative Simplification other than through Notices of Privacy Practices from healthcare providers and health plans, but you do. Each of you also is a patient of this or another practice. From the patient's perspective two years hence, what are three threats that likely would have the greatest impact should the practice experience a privacy breach or security incident? The description of these three threats should be brief, no longer than a phrase or sentence.

■ The answers to this final question are dependent upon the answers you gave in the preceding question. The answers to this question are critical, should be in priority order, and will focus your attention on risk mitigation and threat management. The answers to the preceding question were from the patient's perspective. The two answers to this question are from the practice's perspective: What two things, in priority order, can the practice do to minimize or eliminate those threats in the preceding question? The description of these two risk-mitigation and threat-management procedures should be brief, no longer than a phrase or sentence.

The answers to these six questions provide the foundation for building the practice's cost and risk analyses.

> **CRITICAL POINT**
> Build a team that will help you reinvent your future and develop a sustainable and durable competitive advantage.

To realize the value and return from the types of exercises suggested in this chapter, you do not have to get out a spreadsheet, put on an eyeshade, and calculate a number. Rather, you should assemble your workforce, consider as a team how the questions here can help you answer questions that will lead you, working together, to reinvent your future and develop sustainable competitive advantages. Working to comply with HIPAA Administrative Simplification standards serves as a catalyst in this regard.

RAISING THE BRIDGE AND LOWERING THE RIVER

Complying with HIPAA Administrative Simplification Transaction, Privacy, and Security standards is going to cost time and money and produce benefits over time. We have a friend in Chicago who is a third-party administrator (TPA) for employer self-funded healthcare benefit plans. Over the past several years, he has converted paper-based and telephone-response systems to Internet-based and electronic data interchange based computer systems. He did this in anticipation of HIPAA and because it made good business sense. He already has realized a return on investment and has attracted a significant number of new health-plan customers. Providers can inquire about eligibility and claim status via the Internet, and they can send claims using HIPAA EDI standards. This TPA has been able to redeploy its workforce from answering telephone inquiries to more effective and productive business activities.

Our friend has a favorite expression in his business that is germane to our discussion, "You have two choices: you can raise the bridge, or you can lower the river." Of course, you may end up doing both. *Raising the bridge* means generating more revenue per unit of service. *Lowering the river* means lowering costs per unit of service. Either, controlling for the other, will increase net revenue. Both will increase it even more. As we have tried to illustrate in this chapter, we believe that successful implementation of HIPAA Administrative Simplification standards will help your practice raise the bridge and lower the river.

YOUR ACCOUNTABILITY WITH OTHER HEALTHCARE PARADIGM SHIFTS

In this book, we have attempted to provide guidance on implementing the HIPAA standards and identifying resources that you can draw upon to help you do so. As we write in early 2003, we see several critical guidelines on the horizon and covered entities striving to be compliant by the deadlines. There is little systematic evidence at this point to provide definitive cost and return-on-investment figures. That evidence will come over the next several years as studies focus on the challenges and successes associated with HIPAA compliance efforts.

HIPAA Administrative Simplification compliance is not happening in a vacuum. Other events are happening in the healthcare sphere that will have an impact on the medical practice. Like HIPAA Administrative Simplification, some are paradigm shifts, when business rules change appreciably and businesses must adjust to survive as viable entities. These include, but are not limited to:

- Demographic Factors
  - □ An increasingly older population demands more healthcare resources.
  - □ Medicare beneficiaries are expected to nearly double by 2030, and there will be relatively fewer workers to finance healthcare delivery.
- Shift in and Management of Risk
  - □ We are undergoing a shift from defined-benefit to defined-contribution plans such as flexible spending accounts and healthcare reimbursement arrangements.
  - □ Individuals will have more choice in managing healthcare risk and choosing healthcare providers but at a higher cost.

- Financing of Healthcare
  - ☐ Worldwide, the political issue heating up pertains to who pays (government versus private sector).
  - ☐ Domestically, political and economic issues increasingly pertain to who pays for what such as pharmaceutical coverage under Medicare.
- Population Coverage
  - ☐ Who is covered and by whom?
  - ☐ The uninsured population is growing, which is more a problem of financing than delivery.
  - ☐ Employers are reducing medical-benefits packages, and providers have to adjust.
- Medical Practitioner Availability
  - ☐ The shortage of nurses, who are overworked, underpaid, and saddled with burdensome administration, continues.
  - ☐ There is a shortage of physicians, who are overworked, undercompensated (Medicare), uncompensated (uninsured population), and must deal with burdensome administration.

These shifts must be taken into consideration when preparing the cost and risk analyses. They will have material impacts on practices in years ahead.

GOING FORWARD

There are certain things that you can do to increase the value of your efforts tactically and strategically.

- Visit periodically the web sites that we have mentioned in the book. HIPAA Administrative Simplification is an ongoing effort.
- Ask your vendors to keep you informed in writing about how their systems help you to achieve HIPAA compliance. Remember, only covered entities can be HIPAA compliant, but you will rely on others to help you get there and stay there.
- After you have developed your policies and procedures, periodically review them with your staff. These are living documents, helping your business to thrive.
- Make sure that your privacy and security officials are in place and that they have the resources to make your practice HIPAA compliant.
- Training is not a one-shot deal. Initially, you will focus on HIPAA awareness, but training, including role playing and testing scenarios, has to be an ongoing activity.

- Finally, treat resource requirements for attaining HIPAA compliance as an investment in a more efficient healthcare transaction future rather than as an expense only to be borne today.[12]

---

12. These suggestions, along with a detailed discussion on how the resources of the Workgroup for Electronic Data Interchange (WEDI) can help you achieve HIPAA compliance, are in Edward D. Jones III, "WEDI, HIPAA, and U," *American Society of Anesthesiologists (ASA) Newsletter*, v. 66, n. 2, December 2002.

Contents

Documents included in this appendix are meant to be helpful to the reader. They are samples and must be customized by the practice before being used. Consult an attorney before releasing legal documents to patients.

NOTICE OF PRIVACY PRACTICES REQUIRED LANGUAGE

An individual has a right to receive a Notice of Privacy Practices from the practice that describes the following:

■ Uses and disclosures of protected health information (PHI) that may be made by the practice.

■ Individual's rights with respect to PHI.

■ Practice's legal duties with respect to PHI.

The Notice of Privacy Practices must be written in plain language and contain the following required information:

■ The **header** to the notice must be in all capital letters and read as follows: THIS NOTICE DESCRIBES HOW MEDICAL INFORMATION ABOUT YOU MAY BE USED AND DISCLOSED AND HOW YOU CAN GET ACCESS TO THIS INFORMATION. PLEASE REVIEW IT CAREFULLY.

■ Uses and Disclosures

  ☐ Description, with at least one example, of the types of uses the practice is permitted to make for treatment, payment, and health-care operations.

  ☐ Description of each of other purposes for which practice is permitted or required to use or disclose PHI without individual's written authorization.

  ☐ Description of any use or disclosure that may be prohibited or materially limited by other applicable law and how more stringent law affects use or disclosure.

  ☐ The practice must put sufficient detail in its descriptions and must include sufficient detail on uses and disclosures that are permitted or required by the Privacy Rule and other applicable law to put the individual on notice.

  ☐ The practice must include a statement that other uses and disclosures will be made only upon written authorization by the individual and that the individual may revoke such authorization, in writing, as long as the practice has not taken action that was authorized.

  ☐ The practice must include a separate statement if it intends to contact the individual to provide appointment reminders, information about treatment alternatives, or other health-related benefits and services that may be of interest to the individual, or to raise funds for the practice.

■ **Individual Rights**

  ☐ Statement of individual's rights regarding PHI and a brief description of how the individual may exercise those rights. The individual has a right to:

- Request restrictions on certain uses and disclosures of the individual's PHI, including a statement that the practice is not required to agree to a requested restriction.
- Receive confidential communications about the individual's PHI.
- Inspect and copy the individual's PHI.
- Amend the individual's PHI.
- Receive an accounting of disclosures of the individual's PHI.
- Receive a paper copy of the Notice of Privacy Practices from the practice upon request, even if the individual has agreed previously to receive the notice electronically.

■ **Duties of the Practice**

☐ Statement that the practice is required by law to maintain the privacy of PHI and to provide individuals with notice of its legal duties and privacy practices regarding PHI.

☐ Statement that the practice is required to abide by the terms of the notice that is in effect.

☐ Statement that the practice reserves the right to change the terms of its notice and to make the new notice provisions effective for all PHI that it maintains. The statement must include a description of how the practice will provide the revised notice to individuals.

■ How the Practice Handles Complaints

☐ Statement that an individual may complain to the practice and to the Secretary of the US Department of Health and Human Services if the individual believes that his or her privacy rights have been violated.

☐ Description how the individual may file a complaint with the practice.

☐ Statement that the individual will not be retaliated against for filing a complaint.

■ Contact Person in the Practice

☐ Name or title and telephone number of a person or office in the practice that an individual may contact for further information.

■ Effective Date of the Notice of Privacy Practices

☐ The notice must contain the date on which the notice is first in effect, which may not be earlier than the date on which the notice is printed or otherwise published.

■ Revisions to the Notice of Privacy Practices

☐ The practice must promptly revise and distribute its notice whenever there is a material change to uses and disclosures, individual's rights, the practice's legal duties, or other privacy practices stated in the notice.

- ☐ Except when required by law, a material change may not be implemented before the effective date in the notice in which the material change is published.
- ■ Provision of Notice
  - ☐ The practice must make the notice available upon request to any person and to individuals with a direct treatment relationship in the following ways:
    - No later than the date of the first service delivery, including service delivered electronically.
    - In an emergency treatment situation, as soon as reasonably practicable after the emergency treatment situation.
  - ☐ Except in an emergency treatment situation, the practice must make a good-faith effort to obtain a written acknowledgment of receipt of the notice, and, if not obtained, document its efforts to obtain such acknowledgment and the reason why it was not obtained.
  - ☐ The practice must have copies of the notice available for individuals to take upon request and post the notice in a clear and prominent location where it is reasonable that individuals may be able to read notice.
  - ☐ Revised notices must be provided according to the aforementioned requirements.
- ■ Electronic Notice
  - ☐ A practice that maintains a web site that provides information about the practice's services must prominently post its notice on the web site and make the notice available electronically through the web site.
  - ☐ A practice may provide the notice to an individual by e-mail if the individual agrees to electronic notice and such agreement has not been withdrawn.
  - ☐ If the practice provides the first service delivery electronically, it must provide electronically the notice automatically and contemporaneously in response to the individual's first request for service.
  - ☐ An individual who receives an electronic notice retains the right to request a paper copy of the notice.
- ■ Documentation
  - ☐ The practice must retain copies of initial and any revised notices, acknowledgments of receipt, and a log of good-faith efforts to obtain such acknowledgments.

Name of practice:

Address:

Privacy official:

Contact person:

Telephone:

Notice of Privacy Practices Receipt

I acknowledge that the medical practice named at the top of this page provided me with the Notice of Privacy Practices.

Patient's name: _____
       (print)

Patient's signaure: _____
          (signature)

Today's date: _____

Patient's date of birth: _____

Patient's ID/chart number: _____

If signed by a personal representative:

Name of personal representative: _____
                  (print)

Signature of personal representative:_____
                     (signature)

Relationship to patient: _____

Today's date: _____

For practice use only:

Signature of employee: _____ Date: _____

Name of practice: _____

Address: _____

Privacy official: _____

Contact person: _____

Telephone: _____

Request to Access Records

Patient's name: _____
(print)

Describe records requested and approximate dates of records you wish to review:

_____

_____

What would you like for us to do for you?

☐   I wish to inspect the requested records.

☐   I wish to obtain a copy of the requested records.

☐   I wish to inspect and copy the requested records.

Fees:

Our practice charges a reasonable fee to copy the records and also for postage to mail your requested records.

Questions?

Please contact our privacy official listed at the top of this page if you have any questions about your request to inspect or copy records.

Patient information:

Patient signature: _____ Date: _____

Date of birth: _____

For the personal representative of the patient:

Print the name of the personal representative: _____

Relationship to the patient: _____ Date: _____

I certify that I have the legal authority under applicable law to make this request on behalf of the patient identified above.

Signature of personal representative: _____

Sample Authorization

Note to patients: This document is for review only. Consult your lawyer to modify the content of this form to your particular needs and purposes.

[Your medical practice]
[Your address]

Authorization for Use or Disclosure of Health Information

Patient name: _____
               (print or type)

I hereby authorize the use and disclosure of individually identifiable health information relating to me, which is also called "protected health information" under HIPAA's Privacy Rule to be used as described below.

Specific description of the information to be used or disclosed:

Dates of service: _____

Begin date: _____

End date: _____

Person or job title(s) of persons authorized to make the use or disclosure:

_____

Person or job title(s) of persons authorized to receive the use or disclosure:

_____

The protected health information will be used and/or disclosed for the following purposes:

_____

_____

The person making the request is (check one):

☐   The individual

☐   Someone else representing the individual

Authorization Agreement

I understand that if the person or entity receiving this information is not a health plan or health care provider covered by federal privacy regulations, the information may be re-disclosed by the recipient and may no longer be protected by federal or state law.

I understand that I may revoke this authorization at any time by notifying (YOUR MEDICAL PRACTICE) in writing and that if I choose to do so, my request to revoke will not affect any actions taken by (YOUR MEDICAL PRACTICE) before receiving my revocation.

I understand that I may refuse to sign this authorization. My refusal does not affect my treatment, payment, or eligibility for benefits.

(FOR MARKETING AUTHORIZATIONS ONLY—I understand that the person I am authorizing to use and/or disclose information for marketing purposes will receive compensation for doing so.)

This authorization expires on _____ (date)

Name of patient: _____

Signature of patient: _____

Date: _____

Patient's date of birth: _____

Patient's Social Security number: __ __ __ __ __ __ __ __ __

If a personal representative is making the request on behalf of the patient:

Name of personal representative: _____

Describe personal representative's relationship (parent, guardian, person acting in loco parentis, executor) : _____

Signature of personal representative: _____

Date: _____

Name of practice: _____

Address: _____

Privacy official: _____

Contact person: _____

Telephone: _____

Request to Amend Records

Note to patients: Please use this form to make a request that our practice amend or make corrections to information maintained about you.

Patient information:

Name of patient: _____

Signature of patient: _____

Date: _____

Patient's date of birth: _____

For personal representatives of the patient:

Your name: _____

Your relationship to patient: _____

Please complete this form in its entirety and return it to the front desk. If mailing, please return it to the attention of the privacy official.

Patient name: _____

Requested Amendment:

Please describe in detail how you want your records amended.

Reason for Requested Amendment:

Contact Person:

Please contact our practice's privacy official if you have any questions relating to your request to amend records.

Signatures:

Patient: _____

Date: _____

I hereby certify that I have legal authority under applicable law to make this request on behalf of the patient identified above.

Signature of personal representative: _____

Date: _____

Name of practice: _____

Address: _____

Privacy official: _____

Contact person: _____

Telephone: _____

Request to Restrict Uses and Disclosures of Protected Health Information

Note to patients: You may use this form to request that we agree to restrict certain uses and disclosures of protected health information about you for treatment, payment and healthcare operations.

The HIPAA Privacy Rule permits you to make a request, but it does not require us to agree with your request. However, if we agreed, we will do what we agree upon.

Patient name: _____
    (print)

Requested restriction: (Please describe how you would like our practice to restrict the use and disclosure of your protected health information.)

_____

_____

_____

. Reason for further restriction request: (Please specify your reason(s) for this request.)

_____

_____

_____

Contact Person:
Please contact our privacy official listed above if you have any questions about this request.

Patient Information:
Signature of patient: _____ Date: _____
Date of birth: _____

For personal representatives of the patient:

Your name: _____ Relationship: _____

I hereby certify that I have the legal authority under applicable law to make this request on behalf of the patient identified above.

Signature of personal representative: _____

Date: _____

Name of practice: _____

Address: _____

Privacy official: _____

Contact person: _____

Telephone: _____

Request for Alternative Communications

Note to patients: Use this form to request that our practice communicate with you by alternative means or at alternative locations. Fill out this request in its entirety.

Patient name: _____
         (print)

Alternative communication request: (Please describe your request to be contacted at an alternative location or by alternative means.)

_____

_____

_____

Payment Information:

Your request to be contacted at an alternative location may affect our normal billing and payment procedure. Please specify your alternative method for handling payment.

_____

_____

_____

Alternative Address or Alternative Means of Contact:

_____

_____

Contact Person:

If you have any questions about this request, you may contact our privacy official provided at the top of this page.

Patient Information:

Signature of patient: _____ Date: _____

Date of birth: _____

For personal representatives of the patient:

Print name of personal representative: _____

Relationship to the patient: _____

I hereby certify that I have the legal authority under applicable law to make this request on behalf of the patient identified above.

Signature: _____Date: _____

Name of practice: _____

Address: _____

Privacy official: _____

Contact person: _____

Telephone: _____

Sample Complaint Form

Note to patients: We will follow up on your complaints, whether they are submitted to us in oral or written form. You are not required to complete a written report, but your comments are helpful to us as we continue to provide excellent service to our patients.

Date: _____

Name of complainant: _____

Address: _____

_____

Phone: _____

Description of Complaint:

Signature of complainant: _____

What would you like to happen?

_____ I want someone from the office to contact me by ____phone ____ mail.

_____ I don't want to be contacted.

Other: _____

_____

Name of practice: _____

Address: _____

Privacy official: _____

Contact person: _____

Telephone: _____

(For internal use only)

Follow-Up on Privacy Complaint

Use this form if you believe the information contained in the complaint will be used in a civil, criminal, or administrative action or legal proceeding.

Date: _____

Name of complainant: _____

Address: _____

_____

Phone: _____

Patient ID number: _____

Description of complaint:

Person completing this form: _____ Date: _____

Medical Privacy—National Standards to Protect the Privacy of Personal Health Information

Sample Business Associate Contract Provisions

(Published in *Federal Register* 67 No.157 pp. 53182, 53264 [(August 14, 2002)])

Statement of Intent

The department provides these sample business-associate contract provisions in response to numerous requests for guidance. This is only sample language. These provisions are designed to help covered entities more easily comply with the business-associate contract requirements of the Privacy Rule. However, use of these sample provisions is not required for compliance with the Privacy Rule. The language may be amended to more accurately reflect business arrangements between the covered entity and the business associate.

These or similar provisions may be incorporated into an agreement for the provision of services between the entities, or they may be incorporated into a separate business-associate agreement. These provisions only address concepts and requirements set forth in the Privacy Rule and alone are not sufficient to result in a binding contract under state law. They do not include many formalities and substantive provisions that are required or typically included in a valid contract. Reliance on this sample is not sufficient for compliance with state law and does not replace consultation with a lawyer or negotiations between the parties to the contract.

Furthermore, a covered entity may want to include other provisions that are related to the Privacy Rule but that are not required by the Privacy Rule. For example, a covered entity may want to add provisions in a business associate contract in order for the covered entity to be able to rely on the business associate to help the covered entity meet its obligations under the Privacy Rule. In addition, there may be permissible uses or disclosures by a business associate that are not specifically addressed in these sample provisions, for example, having a business associate create a limited data set. These and other types of issues will need to be worked out between the parties.

SAMPLE BUSINESS ASSOCIATE CONTRACT PROVISIONS[1]

Definitions (alternative approaches)

Catch-all definition:
Terms used, but not otherwise defined, in this Agreement shall have the same meaning as those terms in the Privacy Rule.

Examples of specific definitions:

a. *Business Associate.* "Business Associate" shall mean [Insert Name of Business Associate].

b. *Covered Entity.* "Covered Entity" shall mean [Insert Name of Covered Entity].

c. *Individual.* "Individual" shall have the same meaning as the term "individual" in 45 CFR § 164.501 and shall include a person who qualifies as a personal representative in accordance with 45 CFR § 164.502(g).

d. *Privacy Rule.* "Privacy Rule" shall mean the Standards for Privacy of Individually Identifiable Health Information at 45 CFR Part 160 and Part 164, Subparts A and E.

e. *Protected Health Information.* "Protected Health Information" shall have the same meaning as the term "protected health information" in 45 CFR § 164.501, limited to the information created or received by Business Associate from or on behalf of Covered Entity.

f. *Required By Law.* "Required By Law" shall have the same meaning as the term "required by law" in 45 CFR § 164.501.

g. *Secretary.* "Secretary" shall mean the secretary of the Department of Health and Human Services or his designee.

Obligations and Activities of Business Associate

a. Business Associate agrees to not use or disclose Protected Health Information other than as permitted or required by the Agreement or as Required By Law.

b. Business Associate agrees to use appropriate safeguards to prevent use or disclosure of the Protected Health Information other than as provided for by this Agreement.

c. Business Associate agrees to mitigate, to the extent practicable, any harmful effect that is known to Business Associate of a use or disclosure of Protected Health Information by Business Associate in violation

---

1. Words or phrases contained in brackets are intended as either optional language or as instructions to the users of these sample provisions and are not intended to be included in the contractual provisions.

of the requirements of this Agreement. [This provision may be included if it is appropriate for the Covered Entity to pass on its duty to mitigate damages to a Business Associate.] Business Associate agrees to report to Covered Entity any use or disclosure of the Protected Health Information not provided for by this Agreement of which it becomes aware.

d. Business Associate agrees to ensure that any agent, including a subcontractor, to whom it provides Protected Health Information received from or created or received by Business Associate on behalf of Covered Entity agrees to the same restrictions and conditions that apply through this Agreement to Business Associate with respect to such information.

e. Business Associate agrees to provide access, at the request of Covered Entity, and in the time and manner [Insert negotiated terms], to Protected Health Information in a Designated Record Set, to Covered Entity or, as directed by Covered Entity, to an Individual in order to meet the requirements under 45 CFR § 164.524. [Not necessary if business associate does not have protected health information in a designated record set.]

f. Business Associate agrees to make any amendment(s) to Protected Health Information in a Designated Record Set that the Covered Entity directs or agrees to pursuant to 45 CFR § 164.526 at the request of Covered Entity or an Individual, and in the time and manner [insert negotiated terms]. [Not necessary if business associate does not have protected health information in a designated record set.]

g. Business Associate agrees to make internal practices, books, and records, including policies and procedures and Protected Health Information, relating to the use and disclosure of Protected Health Information received from, or created or received by Business Associate on behalf of, Covered Entity available [to the Covered Entity, or] to the Secretary, in a time and manner [insert negotiated terms] or designated by the Secretary, for purposes of the Secretary determining Covered Entity's compliance with the Privacy Rule.

h. Business Associate agrees to document such disclosures of Protected Health Information and information related to such disclosures as would be required for Covered Entity to respond to a request by an Individual for an accounting of disclosures of Protected Health Information in accordance with 45 CFR § 164.528.

i. Business Associate agrees to provide to Covered Entity or an Individual, in time and manner [insert negotiated terms], information collected in accordance with Section [insert section number in contract where provision (i) appears] of this Agreement, to permit Covered Entity to respond to a request by an Individual for an accounting of disclosures of Protected Health Information in accordance with 45 CFR § 164.528.

Permitted Uses and Disclosures by Business Associate

General Use and Disclosure Provisions [(a) and (b) are alternative approaches]

a. *Specify purposes:*

Except as otherwise limited in this Agreement, Business Associate may use or disclose Protected Health Information on behalf of, or to provide services to, Covered Entity for the following purposes, if such use or disclosure of Protected Health Information would not violate the Privacy Rule if done by Covered Entity or the minimum necessary policies and procedures of the Covered Entity:

[list purposes].

b. *Refer to underlying services agreement:*

Except as otherwise limited in this Agreement, Business Associate may use or disclose Protected Health Information to perform functions, activities, or services for, or on behalf of, Covered Entity as specified in [insert name of services agreement], provided that such use or disclosure would not violate the Privacy Rule if done by Covered Entity or the minimum necessary policies and procedures of the Covered Entity.

Specific Use and Disclosure Provisions [only necessary if parties wish to allow Business Associate to engage in such activities]

a. Except as otherwise limited in this Agreement, Business Associate may use Protected Health Information for the proper management and administration of the Business Associate or to carry out the legal responsibilities of the Business Associate.

b. Except as otherwise limited in this Agreement, Business Associate may disclose Protected Health Information for the proper management and administration of the Business Associate, provided that disclosures are Required By Law, or Business Associate obtains reasonable assurances from the person to whom the information is disclosed that it will remain confidential and be used or further disclosed only as Required By Law or for the purpose for which it was disclosed to the person, and the person notifies the Business Associate of any instances of which it is aware in which the confidentiality of the information has been breached.

c. Except as otherwise limited in this Agreement, Business Associate may use Protected Health Information to provide Data Aggregation services to Covered Entity as permitted by 42 CFR § 164.504(e)(2)(i)(B).

d. Business Associate may use Protected Health Information to report violations of law to appropriate Federal and State authorities, consistent with 42 CFR § 164.502(j)(1).

Obligations of Covered Entity

Provisions for Covered Entity to Inform Business Associate of Privacy Practices and Restrictions [provisions dependent on business arrangement]

a. Covered Entity shall notify Business Associate of any limitation(s) in its notice of privacy practices of Covered Entity in accordance with 45 CFR § 164.520, to the extent that such limitation may affect Business Associate's use or disclosure of Protected Health Information.

b. Covered Entity shall notify Business Associate of any changes in, or revocation of, permission by Individual to use or disclose Protected Health Information to the extent that such changes may affect Business Associate's use or disclosure of Protected Health Information.

c. Covered Entity shall notify Business Associate of any restriction to the use or disclosure of Protected Health Information that Covered Entity has agreed to in accordance with 45 CFR § 164.522 to the extent that such restriction may affect Business Associate's use or disclosure of Protected Health Information.

Permissible Requests by Covered Entity

Covered Entity shall not request Business Associate to use or disclose Protected Health Information in any manner that would not be permissible under the Privacy Rule if done by Covered Entity. [Include an exception if the Business Associate will use or disclose protected health information for, and the contract includes provisions for, data aggregation or management and administrative activities of Business Associate.]

Term and Termination

a. *Term.* The Term of this Agreement shall be effective as of [insert effective date], and shall terminate when all of the Protected Health Information provided by Covered Entity to Business Associate, or created or received by Business Associate on behalf of Covered Entity, is destroyed or returned to Covered Entity, or if it is infeasible to return or destroy Protected Health Information, protections are extended to such information, in accordance with the termination provisions in this Section. [Term may differ.]

b. Termination for Cause. Upon Covered Entity's knowledge of a material breach by Business Associate, Covered Entity shall either:

   1. Provide an opportunity for Business Associate to cure the breach or end the violation and terminate this Agreement [and the _____ Agreement/ sections _____ of the _____ Agreement] if Business Associate does not cure the breach or end the violation within the time specified by Covered Entity;

2. Immediately terminate this Agreement [and the _____ Agreement/ sections ____ of the _____ Agreement] if Business Associate has breached a material term of this Agreement and cure is not possible; or

3. If neither termination nor cure is feasible, Covered Entity shall report the violation to the Secretary.

[Bracketed language in this provision may be necessary if there is an underlying services agreement. Also, opportunity to cure is permitted, but not required by the Privacy Rule.]

c. Effect of Termination.

1. Except as provided in paragraph 2 of this section, upon termination of this Agreement, for any reason, Business Associate shall return or destroy all Protected Health Information received from Covered Entity or created or received by Business Associate on behalf of Covered Entity. This provision shall apply to Protected Health Information that is in the possession of subcontractors or agents of Business Associate. Business Associate shall retain no copies of the Protected Health Information.

2. In the event that Business Associate determines that returning or destroying the Protected Health Information is infeasible, Business Associate shall provide to Covered Entity notification of the conditions that make return or destruction infeasible. Upon [insert negotiated terms] that return or destruction of Protected Health Information is infeasible, Business Associate shall extend the protections of this Agreement to such Protected Health Information and limit further uses and disclosures of such Protected Health Information to those purposes that make the return or destruction infeasible, for so long as Business Associate maintains such Protected Health Information.

Miscellaneous

a. *Regulatory References.* A reference in this Agreement to a section in the Privacy Rule means the section as in effect or as amended.

b. *Amendment.* The Parties agree to take such action as is necessary to amend this Agreement from time to time as is necessary for Covered Entity to comply with the requirements of the Privacy Rule and the Health Insurance Portability and Accountability Act of 1996, Pub. L. No. 104-191.

c. *Survival.* The respective rights and obligations of Business Associate under Section [insert section number related to "Effect of Termination"] of this Agreement shall survive the termination of this Agreement.

d. *Interpretation.* Any ambiguity in this Agreement shall be resolved to permit Covered Entity to comply with the Privacy Rule.

PRIVACY OFFICIAL JOB RESPONSIBILITIES

General duties: Coordinate all activities of the practice that relate to maintaining the privacy of individually identifiable health information consistent with federal and state laws. Report periodically to practice management.

Specific duties: The Privacy Official has the following specific duties:

Management

Work with the management team and lawyers to comply with federal and state laws governing the privacy and security of individually identifiable health information. Stay abreast of privacy laws and regulations, changes in accreditation standards, and updates in privacy technology. Cooperate with outside organizations in compliance investigation or review. Develop a year-round training program to keep staff abreast of laws and regulations and how to implement those regulations.

Human Resources

Take a leadership role in developing and implementing the practice's HIPAA policies and procedures and integrate those policies and procedures into the practice's operations. Oversee the practice's efforts to maintain compliance with applicable laws and with policies and procedures. Coordinate policies and procedures with legal counsel. Oversee sanctions as appropriate for individuals who fail to comply with privacy and security requirements.

Risk Management

Coordinate assessments of information privacy and security risks and compliance, and determine where the practice's privacy initiatives are integrated with other compliance efforts and administrative functions. Lead the practice in creating, executing, and overseeing contracts with business associates and other contracts as appropriate to ensure that the practice is managing privacy activities.

Patient Rights

Oversee patient requests to the practice and help the practice's employees to understand how to address patient questions about the practice's privacy initiatives. Develop an effective internal and external communications effort to help patients and staff understand what the practice will do to protect patient rights.

Complaint Management

Implement and manage complaints regarding the practice's standards and protocols, including documenting and investigating and, if necessary, mitigating those complaints. Educate the practice's lawyer when necessary on complaints. Educate employees on prohibited retaliatory actions against persons who exercise their patient rights.

Qualifications

Excellent problem solver and researcher. In conflicts, considers several points of view before making a decision. Familiar with clinical and administrative functions of the medical office. Has an interest in laws and regulations relating to privacy of health information. High integrity, very detail-oriented. Strong organizational and communications abilities. Works well with practice management and staff.

SECURITY OFFICIAL JOB DESCRIPTION

Standard: Assigned security responsibility.

The Security Rule requires, as an Administrative safeguard to:

IDENTIFY THE SECURITY OFFICIAL WHO IS RESPONSIBLE FOR THE DEVELOPMENT AND IMPLEMENTATION OF THE POLICIES AND PROCEDURES REQUIRED.

The security official will be responsible for administrative, physical, and technical security safeguard initiatives, strategies, and actions, as outlined in Chapter 4 of this book. Below we outline *responsibilities and duties* and *qualifications* for a security official in a medical practice. This is the responsible individual who is accountable for ensuring that the practice is in compliance with the HIPAA Security Rule. The security official and privacy official may be the same person if it is reasonable and appropriate.

Responsibilities and Duties

Conduct assessment of the practice's security safeguards and vulnerabilities

- Identifies the practice's strategic objectives with respect to protection of individually identifiable health information that are consistent with the practice's vision and mission.
- Identifies the practice's existing security safeguards for electronic transmission and storage of individually identifiable health information and prepares an assessment of vulnerabilities and security risks.
- Analyzes current security practices and assesses the degree of compliance with standards and implementation specifications of the HIPAA Security Rule, with particular attention given to identification of vulnerabilities.
- Prepares a security-risk assessment, a plan for remediation of risks and compliance with HIPAA Security Rule standards and implementation specifications, discusses the plan with practice management and staff, and incorporates suggestions for mitigating risks.
- Completes the security plan for the practice and initiates implementation according to a schedule agreed upon with practice's management.

Implement and monitor security safeguards

- Working with vendors, as appropriate, recommends to practice's management appropriate security safeguards systems to protect individually identifiable health information that comply with the HIPAA Security Rule.

- Working with vendors, human resources, and legal counsel, as appropriate, exercises responsibility for implementation of security safeguards plan, including a disaster-recovery plan.

- Prepares and distributes to appropriate practice staff security policies and procedures, forms, notices, and reminders.

- Initiates training curriculum that meets requirements of the HIPAA Security Rule and ensures that practice management and staff are current on and periodically reminded of security policies and procedures and that new employees receive security-awareness training.

- Is the accountable official for security in practice, and implements and administers policies and procedures for handling complaints regarding the practice's security safeguards. Such policies shall include procedures for documenting, tracking, and adjudicating complaints.

- Is the accountable official for security in practice, and implements and administers policies and procedures for mitigating security incidents in the practice. Such policies shall include procedures for documenting, tracking, and adjudicating complaints, and definition of sanctions for practice employees who fail to comply with the practice's security policies and procedures.

- Implements a schedule for periodic review of the security plan and performance of staff in complying with security policies and procedures, security enhancements recommended by organizations such as the National Institute of Standards and Technology (NIST), and modifications in the HIPAA Security Rule standards and implementation specifications.

Regulatory compliance

- Maintains a current knowledge of federal and state security and privacy laws and regulations that pertain to practice.

- Serves as a liaison to individuals, external organizations such as business associates, and governmental entities on issues or complaints pertaining to the practice's security policies and procedures.

Qualifications

- Experience working in an information technology systems environment, with knowledge of electronic data interchange, Internet, and networking capabilities; data storage safeguard capabilities; and security matters.

- Experience with risk analysis, testing and auditing procedures, disaster recovery planning, contingency (business risk) planning, evaluating information technology systems, and negotiating contracts with vendors.

- Ability to understand and translate regulatory language into business operations, systems, activities, and policies and procedures.
- Ability to provide leadership to the practice team, with the objective of accomplishing security assessment and implementing goals that are consistent with HIPAA Security Rule standards and implementation specifications.
- Ability to understand and communicate technical and security-related concepts and terms to the practice's management and staff and business associates in oral and written forms.

TWELVE-MONTH TRAINING CALENDAR

First Month (45 minutes)	Second Month (30 minutes)	Third Month (30 minutes)	Fourth Month (10-15 minutes)
Topic: HIPAA reminders	**Topic:** Administrative requirements	**Topic:** Managing patient rights	**Topic:** Managing patient complainst
■ Ask everyone in the office to bring in a photo or description of PHI and identify where it was found in the office. No two people can bring the same sample. ■ This exercise will help staff recognize how many places PHI can be found. ■ Discuss the NPP distribution process and patient acknowl-edgments. Update staff on patient responses. ■ Remind staff of the short- and long-term benefits of HIPAA.	■ Discuss admin requirements: NPP, privacy official, policies, and procedures and how they support privacy issues. ■ Discuss the six patient rights (Chapter 3, Step 3). ■ Discuss the two required documentations. ■ Permissions for use and disclosure (Chapter 3, Step 4).	■ Discuss how your office is doing managing patient inquiries and office responses (Chapter 3, Step 3). ■ Evaluate your documentation process. ■ What is working? What needs to be adjusted? Do the adjustments affect the policies and procedures?	■ Have you had any complaints? To the extent you can without breahing privacy, discuss what happened and how has the complaint changed or reinforced you procedures? (Chapter 3, Step 3).

Fifth Month (10-15 minutes)	Sixth Month (10 minutes)	Seventh Month (20 minutes)	Eighth Month (10 minutes)
Topic: Permissions for use and disclosure	**Topic:** Managing crises (Chapter 6)	**Topic:** Password management and computer security (Chapter 4)	**Topic:** Personal representatives and verification Chapter 3, Step 6)
■ There are 11 permissions and 9 special requirements. Assign a permission or special requirement to each staff person to explain how it has been (or will be) used in your office. ■ Remind staff of policies and procedures and where they can be located.	■ Discuss three crises that invloved staff at multiple layers. Items for discussion: • How could this have been prevented? • What did we do right? • What should we do differently next time? • Do we need help or can we manage this internally?	■ Discuss the importance of keeping passwords to yourself. Other items: What is and is not allowed on office computers? Steps to follow if there is a system problem. What can and cannot be sent via e-mail?	■ Present policies and procedures on how to verify a caller or person requesting information. ■ Identify five or six scenarios in which you deal with personal representatives. ■ Discuss procedures if personal repre-sentatives are confrontational.

continued

Ninth Month (15 minutes)	Tenth Month (15-20 minutes)	Eleventh Month (10 minutes)	Twelfth Month (1 hour)
Topic: Public good (Chapter 3, Step 4)	**Topic:** Business Associates (Chapters 2, 3, and 4)	**Topic:** Marketing and documentation	**Topic:** Year-end evaluation
■ Discuss procedures to follow when a public official requests information about a patient. ■ Discuss confidentiality and patient rights for use and disclosure and accounting of disclosures if patient requests these rights (Chapter 3, Step 3).	■ Discuss the following: • PHI as it relates to business associates. • Business associates and office staff must work together to protect PHI. • Policies and procedures if you suspect a breach at the business-associate level. • How to make the most of the business-associate relationship.	■ Discuss the definition of marketing and authorization forms. ■ Reevaluate your documentation process. • How are we doing on documentation? ■ Schedule an audit of documentation processes. ■ Assign teams to review the NPP, business-associate agreement, and policies and procedures. ■ Assign another team to evaluate forms and logs.	■ Report findings of the internal audit. ■ Report findings of NPP, business-associate, and policy-and-procedure team's research. ■ Report findings of forms and logs team. ■ Discuss how HIPAA may or may not be providing better cash flow than previous year. ■ Evaluate training needs, particularly of new staff members or staff with new responsibilities.

Check for Understanding Self Test

Check for understanding by taking the following self test. Use this as a pretest to measure your current knowledge, and then take it again after you've read *HIPAA Plain and Simple* to see what you have learned. Or, take this test when you have finished the book. Answers can be found at the end of this appendix.

1) **What do the initials HIPAA stand for?**
   a) Health Information Protection and Administrative Act
   b) Health Insurance Portability and Accountability Act
   c) Healthcare Indemnity and Payment Administration Authority
   d) Housing Information and Protected Assistance Administration

2) **What is the primary objective of Administrative Simplification?**
   a) To improve efficiency and effectiveness of the healthcare system via electronic exchange of information and reduce high transaction costs
   b) To disrupt your office and complicate your life
   c) To clearly define fraud and abuse regulations
   d) To combine the Medicare and Medicaid systems under one agency

3) **Which three of the following are included in Administrative Simplification?**
   a) The Golden Rule, the Principle of Reciprocity, and Tort Reform Act
   b) Family Medical Leave Act, Equal Employment Opportunity Act, and Access to Health Care Act
   c) Transactions and Code Sets Rule, Privacy Rule, and Security Rule
   d) Privacy Rule, funding mandates, and Occupational Safety and Health Act

4) **Protected health information refers to**
   a) Health information combined with individual information that can be used to identify a patient
   b) Information used to determine which software to implement
   c) Information the federal government uses to complete census reports
   d) Bioterrorism intelligence gathered by the Center for Disease Control

227

5) **In healthcare, an electronic transaction refers to:**
   a) Computers determining how much money a patient has in a bank account
   b) Information managed by the Department of Health and Human Services
   c) A physician conducting a medical procedure via telemedicine
   d) Computers talking to each other to exchange information

6) **If someone in your office conducts an eligibility inquiry, what are they looking for?**
   a) Whether or not a patient is married
   b) Insurance coverage for a particular medical treatment or visit
   c) Whether or not the patient has confirmed an appointment
   d) Whether or not the patient's ICD-9 and CPT codes match

7) **The primary reason for the Privacy Rule is:**
   a) To give the Office of the Inspector General something to do
   b) To prevent insurance companies from sending health information to your employer
   c) To challenge your knowledge of privacy
   d) To protect privacy of transmitted and stored administrative and financial information about the patient

8) **A document that informs patients on how your office intends to use and disclose information about the patient, and also informs patients of their rights is called the:**
   a) Private Right of Action
   b) Notice of Privacy Practices
   c) Freedom of Information Act
   d) UAD of Patient Information

9) **You are required to keep a patient's privacy information for how long:**
   a) six years
   b) sixteen years
   c) six months
   d) As long as you are in practice

10) **The primary reason for the Security Rule is:**
   a) To establish a foundation for integrity, confidentiality and availability of electronic protected health information
   b) To give you technology guidelines when purchasing software
   c) To give you regulations when contracting with your building manager
   d) To provide funding for implementation of electronic security protection

11) **If a state law and HIPAA's federal law disagree agree, which law should you follow?**
   a) The state law, if it is stricter
   b) HIPAA's federal mandates, regardless of which is more stringent
   c) Neither. If they are in conflict, it's up to the courts to decide
   d) HHS' Office of Inspector General will decide

12) **The Privacy Rule protects PHI in what form?**
   a) Electronic
   b) Written
   c) Oral
   d) All of the above

13) **Which of the following is not a patient right included in the Privacy Rule?**
   a) Right to look at and copy medical information
   b) Right to ask you to withhold specific information from a particular individual or organization
   c) Right to ask you to hire and fire specific individuals
   d) Right to ask to be contacted only at home

14) **If a patient requests you amend a medical record, you are required to do so.**
   a) True. The Privacy Rule gives patients the final word.
   b) False. But if the request is reasonable, and you agree to the amendment, you must follow through and make the amendment.

15) **A woman calls to inquire about the results of her husband's blood tests last week in your office. She did not accompany her husband for that test, and says he's too scared to call and find out for himself. What should you do?**
   a) Give her the results of the blood test. As the wife, she's entitled to know.
   b) Ask the doctor if it's okay to speak with the wife.
   c) Give her a hint and tell her to get her husband on the phone.
   d) Refer the question to the privacy official.

16) **If a patient requests that you provide an accounting of disclosures, you do not have to account for disclosures for treatment, payment, and health care operations.**
   a) True
   b) False

17) A *business associate* is:
    a)   A person, group, or organization that has a reason to see protected health information on your behalf, and is not an employee of the practice
    b)   An association of golfers
    c)   The pharmaceutical representatives who call on your physician practice
    d)   Members of the Chamber of Commerce

18) Which of the following are the privacy official's responsibilities?
    a)   Researching the Privacy Rule
    b)   Developing documentation, such as the Notice of Privacy Practices, Policies and Procedures, business associate agreements, and forms
    c)   Training staff on privacy policies and procedures
    d)   All of the above

19) Who is responsible for establishing a plan to manage a computer disaster?
    a)   The managing partner
    b)   The Security official
    c)   The building manager
    d)   All of the above

20) Which of the following are security official responsibilities?
    a)   Evaluate, manage, and report on the security of your electronic data
    b)   Provide training and send out security reminders
    c)   Develop policies and procedures
    d)   All of the above

21) Media device controls refer to:
    a)   Remote controls on your TV
    b)   Switches used by electronic repair servicemen
    c)   Policies that control the use, disclosure, and transfer of data on your electronic devices
    d)   Biometrics used to authenticate who you are when you sign in

22) You could expose content on your personal computer or system network by doing which of the following?
    a)   Shopping on the Internet while you're at work
    b)   Downloading games onto your computer
    c)   Sending and receiving unsecured emails from friends
    d)   All of the above

23) You should feel comfortable sharing your password with others in the office, especially if the physician gives you his password.
a) True
b) False

24) If a patient feels that your office has breached his privacy, what should you ask that he do?
a) Call a lawyer
b) Speak to your contact person so that you can handle it in your office
c) File a complaint with the Office for Civil Rights
d) Take it up with someone else

25) Which agency enforces HIPAA's Privacy Rule?
a) Office for Civil Rights
b) Center for Disease Control
c) Department of Commerce
d) Federal Trade Commission

Answers to the Check for Understanding Self Test

1)	b	10)	a	18)	d
2)	a	11)	a	19)	b
3)	c	12)	d	20)	d
4)	a	13)	c	21)	c
5)	d	14)	b	22)	d
6)	b	15)	d	23)	b
7)	d	16)	a	24)	b
8)	b	17)	a	25)	a
9)	a				

Glossary

Note: Some definitions in this glossary have been altered from the original HHS authorized definitions to help physician offices better understand the term. These definitions do not represent legal advice and can not be used for legal interpretations. To read or use the complete legal definition, consult www.hhs.gov, or consult an attorney.

Access: The ability or allowing the means necessary to read, write, modify, or communicate data/information or otherwise use any system resource. In the Privacy Rule, access includes reading, writing, modifying, or communicating individually identifiable health information or authorizing permitted uses or disclosures of protected health information for any reason. In the Security Rule, access means having the capacity to approach and enter computer workstations, laptops, personal digital assistants (PDAs), information systems, servers, telecommunications, and networking equipment. *See also* role-based access.

Access Controls: The ability to read, write, modify, or communicate individually identifiable health information or to authorize permitted uses or disclosures of protected health information for any reason.

Administrative Simplification: Title II, Subtitle F, of HIPAA, which gives HHS the authority to mandate the use of standards for the electronic exchange of healthcare data; to specify what medical and administrative code sets should be used within those standards; to require the use of national identification systems for healthcare patients, providers, payers (or plans), and employers (or sponsors); and to specify the types of measures required to protect the security and privacy of personally identifiable healthcare information.

Administrative Safeguards: Administrative actions, and policies and procedures, to manage the selection, development, implementation, and maintenance of security measures to protect electronic protected health information and to manage the conduct of the covered entity's workforce in relation to the protection of that information.

Amendments and Corrections: In the final Privacy Rule, an *amendment* to a record would indicate that the data is in dispute while retaining the original information, while a *correction* to a record would alter or replace the original record.

Authentication: The corroboration that a person is the one claimed.

Automatic Logoff: An effective way to prevent unauthorized users from viewing electronic protected health information (EPHI) on computer monitor screens when inactivity has lasted beyond the timeout period.

Availability: The property that data or information is accessible and useable upon demand by an authorized person.

Business Associate: A person, group, or organization that is not a member of the covered entity's workforce that acts on behalf of a covered entity or of an organized healthcare arrangement to assist in the performance of a function or activity involving the use or disclosure of individually identifiable health information, including claims processing or administration, data analysis, processing or administration, utilization review, quality assurance, billing, benefit management, practice management, and repricing; or provides legal actuarial, accounting, consulting, data aggregation, management, administrative, accreditation, or financial services to or for such a covered entity. A covered entity may be a business associate of another covered entity.

Clearinghouse: *See* healthcare clearinghouse.

Code Set: Any set of codes used to encode data elements, such as tables of terms, medical concepts, medical diagnostic codes, or medical procedure codes. A code set includes the codes and the descriptors of the codes.

Common Control: Exists if an entity has the power, directly or indirectly, significantly to influence or direct the actions or policies of another entity.

Common Ownership: Exists if an entity or entities possess an ownership or equity interest of 5 percent or more in another entity.

Compliance Date: Under HIPAA, this is the date when a covered entity must comply with a standard, an implementation specification, or a modification. This date usually falls 24 months after the effective date of the final rule. For future changes, compliance date will be at least 180 days after the effective date, but can be longer for complex changes.

Complaint Submission Forms: To complain about a covered entity that is not compliant with HIPAA electronic transactions and code sets standards, a form is available online at www.cms.gov. Consumers who wish to file a privacy complaint online can find a submission form at www.ocr.gov.

Confidentiality: The property that data or information is not made available or disclosed to unauthorized persons or processes.

Covered Entity: A health plan, a healthcare clearinghouse, or a healthcare provider who transmits any health information in electronic form in connection with a HIPAA transaction.

Covered Functions: Those functions of a covered entity the performance of which makes the entity a health plan, healthcare provider, or healthcare clearinghouse.

Covered Transaction: An electronic exchange of information between two covered entity business partners using the HIPAA electronic data interchange (EDI) for the exchange.

Designated Record Set: Refers to:

(1) A group of records maintained by or for a covered entity that is:

　　(i)　the medical records and billing records about individuals maintained by or for a covered healthcare provider;

　　(ii)　the enrollment, payment, claims adjudication, and case or medical management record systems maintained by or for a health plan; or

　　(iii) used, in whole or in part, by or for the covered entity to make decisions about individuals.

(2) For purposes of this paragraph, the term *record* means any items, collection, or grouping of information that includes protected health information and is maintained, collected, used, or disseminated by or for a covered entity.

Direct Treatment Relationship: Refers to a treatment relationship between an individual and a healthcare provider that is not an indirect treatment relationship.

Disclosure: Release, transfer, provision of, access to, or divulgence of information by an entity to persons or organizations outside of that entity.

Electronic Data Interchange (EDI): Intercompany, computer-to-computer transmission of business information in a standard format.

Electronic Media: (1) Electronic storage media including memory devices in computers (hard drives) and any removable/transportable digital memory medium, such as magnetic tape or disk, optical disk, or digital memory card; or (2) Transmission media used to exchange information already in electronic storage media. Transmission media include, for example, the Internet (wide-open), extranet (using Internet technology to link a business with information accessible only to collaborating parties), leased lines, dial-up lines, private networks, and the physical movement of removable/transportable electronic storage media. Certain transmissions, including of paper, via facsimile, and of voice, via telephone, are not considered to be transmissions via electronic media, because the information being exchanged did not exist in electronic form before the transmission.

Electronic Protected Health Information: Information that comes within paragraphs (1)(i) or (1)(ii) of the definition of *protected health information* as specified in this section.

Encryption: The use of an algorithmic process to transform data into a form in which there is a low probability of assigning meaning without use of a confidential process or key.

Enforcement Agencies: The Office for Civil Rights is the enforcement agency for the Privacy Rule (www.ocr.gov) and the Centers for Medicaid and Medicare is the enforcement agency for the Security Rule, Transactions and Code Sets, and National Identifier Standards (www.cms.gov).

Facility: The physical premises and the interior and exterior of a building(s).

Healthcare: Refers to the care, services, or supplies related to the health of an individual. Includes, but is not limited to, the following:

(1) preventive, diagnostic, therapeutic, rehabilitative, maintenance, or palliative care, and counseling, service, assessment, or procedure with respect to the physical or mental condition, or functional status, of an individual or that affects the structure or function of the body; and

(2) the sale or dispensing of a drug, device, equipment, or other item in accordance with a prescription.

Health Care Component: A component or combination of components of a hybrid entity designated by the hybrid entity in accordance with 164.105(a)(2)(iii)(C).

Healthcare Clearinghouse: Refers to a public or private entity, including a billing service, repricing company, community health management information system, or community health information system, and "value-added" networks and switches, that does either of the following functions:

(1) processes or facilitates the processing of health information received from another entity in a nonstandard format or containing nonstandard data content into standard data elements or a standard transaction; or

(2) receives a standard transaction from another entity and processes or facilitates the processing of health information into nonstandard format or nonstandard data content for the receiving entity.

Healthcare Operations: Refers to any of the following activities of the covered entity to the extent that the activities are related to covered functions, and any of the following activities of an organized health car arrangement in which the covered entity participates:

(1) Conducting quality assessment and improvement activities, including outcomes evaluation and development of clinical guidelines, provided that the obtaining of generalizable knowledge is not the primary purpose of any studies resulting from such activities; population-based

activities relating to improving health or reducing healthcare costs, protocol development, case management and care coordination, contacting of healthcare providers and patients with information about treatment alternatives, and related functions that do not include treatment.

(2) Reviewing the competence or qualifications of healthcare professionals; evaluating practitioner and provider performance; conducting training programs in which students, trainees, or practitioners in areas of health care learn under supervision to practice or improve their skills as healthcare providers; training of nonhealthcare professionals, accreditation, certification, licensing, or credentialing activities.

(3) Underwriting, premium rating, and other activities relating to the creation, renewal or replacement of a contract of health insurance or health benefits, and ceding, securing, or placing a contract for reinsurance of risk relating to claims for health care (including stop-loss insurance and excess of loss insurance), provided that the requirements of (164.514(g)) are met, if applicable.

(4) Conducting or arranging for medical review, legal services, and auditing functions, including fraud and abuse detection and compliance programs.

(5) Business planning and development, such as conducting cost-management and planning-related analyses related to managing and operating the entity, including formulary development and administration, development or improvement of methods of payment or coverage policies.

(6) Business management and general administrative activities of the entity, including, but not limited to:

  (i) management activities relating to implementation of and compliance with the requirements of this subchapter;

  (ii) customer service, including the provision of data analyses for policy holders, plan sponsor, or other customers, provided that protected health information is not disclosed to such policy holder, plan sponsor, or customer;

  (iii) resolution of internal grievances;

  (iv) due diligence in connection with the sale or transfer of assets to a potential successor in interest, if the potential successor in interest is a covered entity, or, following completion of the sale or transfer, will become a covered entity; and

  (v) consistent with the applicable requirement of (164.514), creating de-identified health information, fundraising authorization is not required as described in 164.514(e)(2).

Healthcare Provider: Refers to a provider of services (as defined in section 1861(u) of the Act, 42 U.S.C. 1395x(u)), a provider of medical or health services (as defined in section 1861(s) of the Act, 42 U.S.C. 1395(s)), and any other person or organization who furnishes, bills, or is paid for health care in the normal course of business.

Health Information: Refers to any information, whether oral or recorded in any form or medium, that:

(1) is created or received by a healthcare provider, health plan, public health authority, employer, life insurer, school or university, or healthcare clearinghouse; and

(2) relates to the past, present, or future physical or mental health or condition of an individual; the provision of health care to an individual; or the past, present, or future payment for the provision of health care to an individual.

HIPAA Transaction: An electronic exchange of data between computers in a specified format that includes protected health information.

HHS: Refers to the Department of Health and Human Services.

Hybrid Entity: A single legal entity (1) that is a covered entity; (2) whose business activities include both covered and non-covered functions; and (3) that designates healthcare components in accordance with paragraph 164.105(a)(2)(iii)(C).

Implementation Specification: Specific instructions for implementing a standard.

Indirect Treatment Relationship: Refers to a relationship between an individual and a healthcare provider in which:

(1) the healthcare provider delivers health care to the individual based on the orders of another healthcare provider; and

(2) the healthcare provider typically provides services or products, or reports the diagnosis or results associated with the health care, directly to another healthcare provider, who provides the services or products or reports to the individual.

Individual: The person who is the subject of protected health information.

Individually Identifiable Information: Refers to the information that is a subset of health information, including demographic information collected from an individual; and:

(1) is created or received by a healthcare provider, health plan, employer, or healthcare clearinghouse; and

(2) relates to the past, present, or future physical or mental health or condition of an individual; the provision of health care to an individual; or the past, present, or future payment for the provision of health care to an individual; and

(i) that identifies the individual; or

(ii) with respect to which there is a reasonable basis to believe the information can be used to identify the individual.

Information System: An interconnected set of information resources under the same direct management control that shares common functionality. A system normally includes hardware, software, information, data, applications, communications, and people.

Integrity: The property that data or information have not been altered or destroyed in an unauthorized manner.

Law Enforcement Official: Refers to an officer or employee of any agency or authority of the United States, a state, a territory, a political subdivision of a state or territory, or an Indian tribe, who is empowered by law to:

(1) investigate or conduct an official inquiry into a potential violation of law; or

(2) prosecute or otherwise conduct a criminal, civil, or administrative proceeding arising from an alleged violation of law.

Marketing: Refers to making a communication about a product or service, a purpose of which is to encourage recipients of the communication to purchase or use the product or service.

(1) Does not include communications that meet the requirement of paragraph 2 of this definition and that are made by a covered entity:

   (i) for the purpose of describing the entities participating in a healthcare provider network or health plan network, or for the purpose of describing if and the extent to which a product or service (or payment for such product or service) is provided by a covered entity or included in a plan of benefits; or

   (ii) that are tailored to the circumstances of a particular individual and the communications are:

     (A) made by a healthcare provider to an individual as part of the treatment of the individual, and for the purpose of furthering the treatment of that individual; or

     (B) made by a healthcare provider of health plan to an individual in the course of managing the treatment of that individual, or for the purpose of directing or recommending to that individual alternative treatments, therapies, healthcare providers, or settings of care.

(2) A communication described in paragraph (1) of this definition is not included in marketing if:

   (i) the communication is made orally; or

   (ii) the communication is in writing and the covered entity does not receive direct or indirect remuneration from a third party for making the communication.

Malicious Software: Software, for example, a virus, designed to damage or disrupt a system.

Minimum Necessary: Describes the amount of protected health information that is needed to perform a particular task or function. The Privacy Rule does not specify what the minimum amount of information is; instead, the Privacy Rule requires the Practice to specify what is the Minimum Necessary for routine types of protected health information uses, disclosures, and requests, and develop criteria for determining Minimum Necessary for non-routine uses, disclosures, and requests.

National Drug Code (NDC): A medical code set that identifies prescription drugs and some over the counter products. NDC has been selected for use in the HIPAA transactions.

Organized Health Care Arrangement:

(1) A clinically integrated care setting in which individuals typically receive health care from more than one healthcare provider.

(2) An organized system of health care in which more than one covered entity participates and in which the participating covered entities:

    i. hold themselves out to the public as participating in a joint arrangement; and

    ii. participate in joint activities that include at least one of the following:

        A. utilization review, in which healthcare decisions by participating covered entities are reviewed by other participating covered entities or by a third party on their behalf;

        B. quality assessment and improvement activities, in which treatment provided by participating covered entities is assessed by other participating covered entities or by a third party on their behalf; or

        C. payment activities, if the financial risk for delivering health care is shared, in part or in whole, by participating covered entities through the joint arrangement and if protected health information created or received by a covered entity is reviewed by other participating covered entities or by a third party on their behalf for the purpose of administering the sharing of financial risk.

(3) A group health plan and a health insurance issuer or HMO with respect to such group health plan, but only with respect to protected health information created or received by such health insurance issuer or HMO that relates to individuals who are or who have been participants or beneficiaries in such group health plan;

(4) A group health plan and one or more other group health plans each of which are maintained by the same plan sponsor; or

(5) The group health plans described in paragraph (4) of this definition and health insurance issuers or HMOs with respect to such group health plans, but only with respect to protected health information

created or received by such health insurance issuers or HMOs that relates to individuals who are or have been participants or beneficiaries in any of such group health plans.

Password: Confidential authentication information composed of a string of characters.

Payer: Refers to a health plan: an individual, group, or government health plan that provides or pays the cost of medical care.

Physical Safeguards: Physical measures, policies, and procedures to protect a covered entity's electronic information systems and related buildings and equipment, from natural and environmental hazards, and unauthorized intrusion.

Plan Sponsor: Defined as defined at section 3(16)(B) of ERISA, 29 U.S.C. 1002(16)(B).

Provider: A provider of services defined in section 1861(u) of the Social Security Act, 42 U.S.C. 1395x(u), a provider of medical or other health services as defined in section 1861(s) of the Social Security Act, 42 U.S.C. 1395x(s), and any other person or organization who furnishes, bills, or is paid for health care in the normal course of business.

Protected Health Information: Individually identifiable health information:

(1) Except as provided in paragraph (2) of this definition, that is:
- i.   transmitted by electronic media;
- ii. maintained in electronic media; or
- iii. transmitted or maintained in any other form or medium.

(2) Excludes individually identifiable health information in:
- i.   education records covered by the Family Educational Rights and Privacy Act, as amended, 20 U.S.C. 1232g;
- ii. records described at 20 U.S.C. 1232g(a)(4)(B)(iv); and
- iii. employment records held by a covered entity in its role as employer.

Public Health Authority: Refers to an agency or authority of the United States, a state, a territory, a political subdivision of a State or territory, or an Indian tribe, or a person or entity acting under a grant of authority from or contract with such agency, including the employees or agents of such public agency or its contractors or persons or entities to whom it has granted authority, that is responsible for public health matters as a part of its official mandate.

Required by Law: A mandate contained in law that compels an entity to make a use or disclosure of protected health information and that is enforceable in a court of law. *Required by law* includes, but is not limited to, court orders and court-ordered warrants; subpoenas or summons issued by a court, grand jury, a governmental or tribal inspector general, or an administrative body authorized to require the production of information; a civil or an authorized investigative demand; Medicare conditions of participation with respect to healthcare providers participating in the program; and statutes or regulations that require the production of information, including statutes or regulations that require such information if payment is sought under a government program providing public benefits.

Role-Based Access: Establishing specific guidelines that define how much data or information is available to an employee to create, read, write, modify, or delete data, based on the user's job function or role in the organization. Security and privacy officials should determine the appropriate access based on the user's need to know. For new user accounts, the security official or IT professional can use this pre-approved matrix to establish the new user's access.

Security or Security Measures: Encompasses all of the administrative, physical, and technical safeguards in an information system.

Security Incident: The attempted or successful unauthorized access, use, disclosure, modification, or destruction of information or interference with system operations in an information system.

Security Standards: Administrative, physical, and technical safeguards that protect electronic protected health information.

Staff: Refers to paid full-time and part-time employees who are under the direct control of a covered entity. Staff members are a subset of the workforce.

Standard: Refers to a rule, condition, or requirement, including the privacy and security of individually identifiable health information.

Technical Safeguards: The technology and the policy and procedures for its use that protect electronic protected health information and control access to it.

Transaction: Refers to the transmission of information between two parties to carry out financial or administrative activities related to health care. It includes the following types of information transmission:

(1)   healthcare claims or equivalent encounter information;

(2)   healthcare payment and remittance advice;

(3)   coordination of benefits;

(4)   healthcare claim status;

(5)   enrollment and disenrollment in a health plan;

(6)   eligibility for a health plan;

(7)   health plan premium payments;

(8)   referral certification and authorization;

(9)   first report of injury;

(10) health claims attachments; and

(11) other transactions that the Secretary of HHS may prescribe by regulation.

Unique User Identification (UserID): An alphanumeric combination that uniquely identifies the individual wishing to gain access to electronic data.

Use: With respect to individually identifiable health information, the sharing, employment, application, utilization, examination, or analysis of such information within an entity that maintains such information.

User: A person or entity with authorized access.

Workforce: Refers to employees, volunteers, trainees, and other persons whose conduct, in the performance of work for a covered entity, is under the direct control of such entity whether or not they are paid by the covered entity.

Workstation: An electronic computing device, for example, a laptop or desktop computer, or any other device that performs similar functions, and electronic media stored in its immediate environment.

X12: A group accredited by the American National Standards Institute that defines electronic data interchange (EDI) standards for many American industries, including healthcare insurance. Most electronic transactions standards are X12 standards.